STILL DANCING

To Kevin,

With Warmest Regards.
and appreciation

Yours ever,

Lew.

Grade of Elstree

STILL DANCING

My Story

LEW GRADE

HarperCollins*Publishers*

HarperCollins*Publishers*,
77–85 Fulham Palace Road,
Hammersmith, London W6 8JB

First published by Collins 1987

Reprinted by HarperCollins*Publishers* 1991
9 8 7 6 5 4 3

A catalogue record for this book is
available from the British Library

ISBN 0 00 217780 3

Set in Linotron Imprint

Printed in Great Britain by
Hartnolls Limited, Bodmin, Cornwall

To Kathie

CONTENTS

PART III

ACKNOWLEDGEMENTS

I am extremely grateful to Clive Hirschhorn,
Marcia Stanton and, of course,
my dear wife Kathie
for all their help in the writing of this book.

ILLUSTRATIONS

Prologue

While I was writing this book, I was reminded of how many events in my life have happened by coincidence, and how I used to think of every achievement as a highlight. I was always looking for the ultimate highlight, and, as the years went by, each event seemed to me to be the one.

But one of the most important things in my life is my relationship with people – all people, regardless of race, colour or creed or their position in society – and one of the themes of this book is how these relationships have affected my life.

Other important aspects of my life are caring about my family, always telling the truth, never breaking my word, and never going back on a deal. As far as I am concerned, a verbal agreement has always been better than a contract.

Before I go on to chronicle my story, allow me to give you an example of what I mean when I talk about the importance of relationships.

When I was still an agent, and was booking stars from all over the world to appear all over the world, I felt it would be a tremendous achievement if I could get Bob Hope to appear in London. For over a year I pursued his agent Louis Shurr relentlessly. He was very courteous, took me out to lunches and dinners, and told me that Bob Hope had no desire to work on the stage in London because he was fully committed to films, radio and television.

Meanwhile, I had formed a very close relationship with Myrt Blum, who not only managed some of America's greatest stars, but also happened to be married to Mary Livingstone's sister, making him Jack Benny's brother-in-law. Mary Livingstone was the stage name of Jack's wife and she appeared with him in all his shows.

When Jack Benny came to London for his first appearance at the London Palladium, Myrt and his wife came too, and he was so overwhelmed with his stay in London that he said the next time I was in America I must make a point of seeing him, which I did, at the beginning of 1949.

'I enjoyed London so much,' he said, when we met at his office in Rodeo Drive, Beverly Hills, 'and you were such a great host, that I'll do anything for you. You name it – you've got it.'

'Myrt,' I said, 'I've been trying unsuccessfully for over a year now to get to see Bob Hope and to persuade him to appear in London. But I'm getting nowhere. Can you help?'

Myrt immediately got up, and I should mention at this stage that he was 6 ft 4 ins tall and a well-built man. 'Come with me,' he said, and we went along to Louis Shurr's office, which also happened to be in Rodeo Drive.

He marched straight into Louis's private inner sanctum, ignoring everybody else. 'Louis,' Myrt said, 'I want to see you alone.' Louis then apologized to the client who happened to be with him at the time, and asked to be excused for a few minutes. Myrt then said, 'Louis, this office you're in belongs to Claudette Colbert. Your apartment round the corner belongs to Claudette Colbert, and, as you know, I handle all Claudette Colbert's business affairs. Lew *has* to see Bob today. Do you get the message?'

Louis got the message and immediately called Paramount Studios where Bob was making a film, and arranged for a car to take me there. My name had been left at the gate, and I was directed to an enormous sound stage on the lot.

In the corner, sitting quietly, was a small gentleman in clerical dress. Just at that moment, Bob Hope came off the set, looked at me, and said, 'Hello, Lew.' Evidently he had been warned to expect me. 'Do you know the Reverend Butterworth?' he asked, indicating the priest. I said, 'No.' He then introduced us and we shook hands. 'I've got a few moments to spare,' he continued, 'so let's go to my dressing room.'

We entered his dressing room and he said, 'What can I do for you?' I said, 'I'd like you to appear in London for two weeks.' 'When?' he asked. I told him the dates. He said, 'How much money?' 'The highest we've ever paid – $15,000 per week.'

'Fine,' he said, 'and we'll give all the money to the Reverend Butterworth for the Boys' Club that he runs in London.'

And that's exactly how long it took me to do the deal with Bob Hope.

No piece of paper was signed: Bob Hope came to London as per our verbal commitment. He brought with him a full contingent of people; he personally paid all their transportation costs, hotel expenses and I presume salaries, and gave the full amount of his fee for the engagement to the Reverend Butterworth for the Boys' Club that he was running in the East End of London.

That's relationship!

PART I

1

Planting Roots

I WAS BORN on 25 December 1906 in a little village called Tokmak, near the city of Odessa, close to the Black Sea in the Crimea. My parents were Isaac and Golda Winogradsky, though my mother, whose maiden name was Eisenstadt, changed her first name to Olga when she emigrated to England. I was called Louis, and two and a half years later my brother Boris (now Bernard) was born.

I wish I could remember more about my childhood in Russia, but apart from a clear memory of our house, which stood in its own ground and overlooked an orchard, I was far too young to take away anything other than vague impressions. For example, I remember there were apples everywhere. Along the pebbled path leading up to our house were little huts filled with apples. And, on top of our house, there was a loft – also filled with apples. I remember, too, that attached to our property was a smallish store which, I assume, my father owned, and in which he must have sold some of these apples. But, as I say, I cannot be sure. It has been said that my father owned two small theatres in Tokmak, but this has never been verified, and, as far as I know, isn't the case. I do know, however, that both he and my mother had excellent singing voices and both appeared on the stage either as amateurs or as semi-professionals. In fact, I believe they met while they were both touring round the Ukraine. But again, I cannot be sure. How I wish, today, that I had been more interested in my roots and in my historical background, but by the time I was old enough to ask all the right questions, we were living such a completely new life in London that Tokmak couldn't have been further from my thoughts. Still, I do remember that in Russia we were always well fed and well clothed and

17

could even afford a maid. I particularly remember the maid, because, one night, while my parents were out performing with a local operatic group, I woke up after a bad dream and started calling for her. There was no answer. I got out of bed and called my brother Bernie, who was fast asleep. Then I called for the maid again, and when she still didn't answer, I started banging on the windows until I broke one. Eventually the maid arrived, but by then the damage was done. She was very upset, of course, and had to explain to my parents why she hadn't been in the house looking after us while they were out.

At the age of five and a half I was completely unaware of the political situation in Russia and wasn't even aware of the pogroms or the anti-Jewish attacks happening around the country. As a family, we were certainly never physically attacked. If my parents suffered any mental anguish at what was going on – and I'm sure they must have – they never let it show. All I knew was that suddenly my father was packing his bags in order to go on a long journey across the sea. Just how long he'd be away, nobody knew. The country he was going to was called England and the year was 1912.

Three years earlier my mother's three brothers had decided there was no future for the Jews in the Ukraine, and had emigrated to London. They were all cabinet-makers, two of whom did very well indeed. The youngest, Uncle Morris, was a lovely man, but he was not in a position to help us either. The third and oldest, whose name was Herschell, was the least successful, but, as it turned out, the most supportive. He was adamant that we should leave Russia before it was too late, and it was his letters that persuaded my father to come to England and begin a new life there.

My father was away for three months before he finally sent for us. I later found out that he had insisted that my mother learnt to speak Yiddish while he was away, because without any English we'd be lost in the East End of London. At home, you see, we only spoke Russian.

I have no memory of our upheaval at all. But on the few occasions I heard my mother talk about the journey from Tokmak to London, she spoke about the hazards involved and how unpleasant it had all been. It certainly couldn't have been easy for a young woman, aged twenty four, to have to undergo such a traumatic move with two young children aged nearly six and three and a half to care for. But my mother, I have to say, was always an extraordinarily determined woman. Her family came above everything else in life, and there were no hardships or deprivations she wouldn't suffer for their well-being. She was also a strong woman physically – much more so than my father, whom I never remember as being entirely healthy. He was tall, and aristocratic-looking, but not all that strong. There is no question that my mother was the more dominant personality – and remained so until the day she died. No matter what obstacles she was faced with, she always saw to it that her children – or her 'kinder', as she called us – had clothes on our backs and food in our stomachs. Even after the arduous journey to England, via Berlin and Hamburg, she managed to arrive in London looking much smarter than most of the other women on the boat. She didn't want to look like a 'greener' – someone from the 'outback' – and I'm sure she didn't.

We were met at the docks by my father, who, in three months, had somehow managed to spend most of the capital he'd brought out with him. He was always keen on gambling, and I'm sure he lost a lot of money on horses, card games or whatever else he decided to gamble on. At any rate, our first lodgings were in Brick Lane, in the East End. We were just one of the many Jewish immigrant families living in that area, and my initial impressions of the place were not good. After Tokmak, with our large house and orchard, London looked extremely depressing. I'd never seen so many people in one place, and that took some getting used to. Brick Lane was bleak and rather dark, and so were the two rooms we lived in. There were two other families living in the same building, and I remember that, although we had a toilet, there was no bath. As for the furniture, to call it basic is an understatement. For the first time in our lives we were really poor, and, on top of this, I could barely make myself understood because all I could speak was Russian. Years later, my mother, who – she'll pardon me if I say so – liked to exaggerate a bit, used to claim that she had to borrow money from relatives and friends to pay the rent, and that she and my father often used to go without food themselves to see that her 'kinder' had sufficient. She claimed that there were times when all we had in the house was an apple or a couple of slices of bread, and that she'd lost so much weight she weighed only six stone. All this may be true, of course. But my own memory is that, while there was no money for luxuries, we never went hungry. I know we were helped by our 'poor' relative, Herschell. My mother's other two brothers, who were in a far better position to help because they both had their own business, weren't nearly as generous. They lived in Dalston, which at the time was a very posh area. I remember on the rare occasions that we were invited to visit them, it was a real event. A big deal.

The main problem with my father was that he never had a good business brain. He was capable of doing a great many things, and doing them well, but as my mother used to say, 'he went nowhere with his cleverness'. He was a well-intentioned man, but from the time he arrived in England he was what you'd call a loser. He was really more of a philosopher, and was just not cut out for the business world.

The first job he got in England was with a man called Jack Isowitsky, better known many years later simply as Isow the restaurateur. Today, of course, Isow's, which used to be situated in Brewer Street, doesn't exist anymore. It's now Raymond's Revue Bar. But for many years it was one of the most famous showbiz restaurants in London, catering, especially at lunchtimes, to the Wardour Street film-types. At any rate, in 1912 Jack Isow ran a small cinema, or nickleodeon as I think they were then called, as well as a billiard or snooker club in the East End, and my father – who claims to have been distantly related to him – was offered work as a manager there, which he took. From what I could make out, it was a general dogsbody kind of job. He ran errands, fixed things that needed fixing, and generally made himself useful.

During the two years we were in Brick Lane, from 1912 to 1914, my father had several other jobs – none of them particularly well paid. Like many other Jewish immigrants at the time, he gravitated into the rag trade. He started as a presser for about 8 shillings a week and then became a mechanic. There was a particularly sophisticated sewing machine in the trade, called the Reece buttonhole machine, which required special skills to operate. My father quickly learned all about the machine, and how to service it, and for a while that's what he did: he went round the East End repairing the Reece buttonhole machines. The money wasn't great, but it was more than he was getting at Jack Isow's, and if he wasn't such a gambler I'm sure we'd have managed quite well.

If Herschell Eisenstadt helped us regularly with money, he was also responsible for us moving out of Brick Lane to a new tenement block in which he himself lived called Henley Buildings in Shoreditch, Bethnal Green. Although it was only a mile or so away, our new home was a definite improvement on the last. We still didn't have our own bathroom, but there were two bedrooms, a small sitting room and a kitchen. The building itself, which was built to accommodate over three hundred tenants, was enormous, and consisted of two large blocks separated by a quadrangle. There was an extraordinary sense of community about the place, and because I met a number of families and their children, my English began to improve enormously. At Brick Lane I'd spoken mainly Russian and a bit of Yiddish, but now, as an eight-year-old anxious to make new friends, English – I quickly realized – was priority number one.

About a block away from Henley Buildings was the Rochelle Street School – the first school I ever attended. I remember being somewhat humiliated when my parents first enrolled me because, although I was eight years old, I was put into a class with boys of four to six. My English still wasn't good enough for me to attend classes with children of my own age. It was something I just had to live with, and, believe me, it wasn't easy. Children can be very cruel and the boys at Rochelle Street were no different from anywhere else. There was the usual school bully, who, whenever he saw me, used to punch me in the stomach. I never understood why he did this, and I tried to avoid him as much as possible.

One of the things I've been blessed with is a photographic memory, and within six months I'd memorized enough English to move out of the primary school and into the main boys' school. I also developed a supreme talent for figures. Arithmetic was my favourite subject and there wasn't a kid in the whole school who could touch me at it.

I was at Rochelle Street School when war was declared in 1914, and remained there until it was over four years later. The war made little impression on me as a schoolboy until, in June 1917, a couple of German monoplanes dropped several bombs, in broad daylight, on the Whitechapel and Spitalfields area. The reverberations were felt at Henley Buildings and Rochelle Street, and although neither the school nor our flats suffered any damage on that occasion, my parents decided it was time to 'evacuate' their family – including the latest addition to the Winogradsky clan, a newcomer called Leslie, who was born on 3 June 1916. They chose Reigate, which was then a lovely country town, and enrolled us at the local school. My father remained in London, and visited us every weekend.

Unlike the school in Rochelle Street, the school in Reigate only had one other Jewish boy apart from my brother Bernie (who was in a junior class) and me. I can't remember the other boy's name anymore, but I do remember he had a particular following in the school, and so did I. Being the only two Jews, we should, of course, have become immediate friends. But for some reason a rivalry developed between us, which inevitably led to a showdown. Until this point in my life, I had never hit anyone, and had certainly never been in a fight. In this instance, however, there was no avoiding the situation. I didn't want my new friends in Reigate to think me a coward, so, even though I hate violence, and always have, I arranged to fight my rival in Reigate Park.

I dreaded what was about to happen, but had to go through with it. To my surprise, however, I discovered I had an extremely powerful right-hand punch, and was able to give as good as I got. The fight lasted for about an hour, during which time we both took a lot of punishment – though there was no clear winner. Needless to say, we both gained a certain respect for each other, and even became quite good friends. The best thing about the whole incident is that it gave me a certain physical confidence in myself that I'd never had before, and when, a few months later, we returned to Henley Buildings and Rochelle Street, instead of avoiding the bully at the school who'd previously been the bane of my existence, I actually went looking for him.

True to form, he tried to punch me in the stomach – but this time I was ready for him. With my new-found confidence, I grabbed him, pinioned his arms around his back, and squeezed him until he almost cried. He never came looking for me again.

By the time I was twelve and a half, I found myself in the highest class in the school. It was called X7th and the subject I still excelled in most was arithmetic. Because of my photographic memory and an ability to read very fast – and to absorb everything I read – I wasn't too bad at English either. In fact by now I could speak English better than my parents, particularly my father, who was never able to lose his accent or absorb the 'subtleties' of the language. He took everything literally, which often led to rows, as he never realized that many of the things Bernie and I said to him were said as a joke.

One of the things I was able to do was to read a poem or a large chunk of a book and memorize every word of it. I'd usually take the book to bed with me, read the section I wanted to memorize, then put the book under my pillow. The next morning I'd wake up word perfect. At one of our school concerts I remember reciting by heart pages and pages from a book on King Arthur. It impressed the headmaster – a Mr Baldwin – so much that he gave me a prize: a copy of Sir Walter Scott's *The Antiquary*. It was the most boring book I'd ever read, and I gave up half way through.

I learned my Bar Mitzvah by rote as well. Although we were very much a Jewish family, we weren't particularly religious, and of all the Jewish holy days, we observed only the Jewish New Year – Rosh Hashanah – and the Day of Atonement – Yom Kippur. We had the Passover Seder, and all the food that went with it, and my mother lit candles on Friday night. But that was it. After my Bar Mitzvah, I rarely went to the synagogue on a Saturday morning. Instead, Saturday mornings were usually spent at the local cinema. Moving pictures were extremely popular by 1917 and, as new stars kept coming along, more and more people went to the pictures. My first memory of the movies was seeing a serial with Pearl White called *The Perils of Pauline*. It was most exciting, and I used to go back week after week to see how she managed to survive the terrible things that kept happening to her. I adored Westerns too, but couldn't stand romantic love stories.

23

Occasionally I'd also go to the theatre. I'd sit in the gallery, watching people like Fred and Adele Astaire, and enjoyed every second of it without ever thinking that one day I'd be part of the same business. At that period in my life, my interest in films and music hall was confined to being a spectator. At fourteen I had no interest whatsoever in the entertainment world. There was nothing at all in my personality to suggest that one day I'd be making a good living out of it, and would become a part of it.

But to return to arithmetic. Because I was so good at figures, my teacher Mr Barnett in X7th took a great interest in me and recommended to Baldwin that I should be entered for a scholarship to Parmeters College in London. Baldwin had no objection, and the next thing I knew was that I was sitting in this large hall, with about sixty other boys, waiting to take the exam. There were other subjects apart from maths – like history and geography, which I wasn't particularly good at. But fortunately the first exam was arithmetic. Before we started, the teacher in charge told us that if we needed to leave the room for any reason, we were to clasp our hands behind our heads before approaching him.

We started at 9 a.m. Out of the twenty sums that were set, we were only required to answer fifteen. But as soon as I looked at the paper, I realized I could answer all twenty questions without too much trouble. And I did, in about one hour. I then clasped my hands behind my head, and the teacher beckoned me to come forward. He asked me if I wanted to go to the lavatory, and I said no, I've finished the exam. He said: 'You mean you've done fifteen sums in an hour?' And I said, 'No, sir. I've completed all twenty.' He asked me to bring him my papers, checked over what I'd done, then gave me permission to leave.

I went straight back to Rochelle Street, saw Mr Barnett, and told him about the exam. I was able to go through each question, because my memory is so good, and based on the answers I gave him he told me that I'd got them all correct. Three days later, at about 8.30 a.m., and shortly after my father had already left for work, Mr Barnett arrived at our house and told my mother that the results of the exam were so remarkable that Parmeters had not only offered me a scholarship but had also said that there'd be no need to go through the rest of the examinations in the subjects I wasn't so good at.

Nothing like this had ever happened in our humble household, and for the next few days my parents were so excited they were walking on air. Then came the bad news. The London County Council, which was the authority that approved scholarships, refused permission for me to accept it on the grounds that my father had never been naturalized and that none of the family was British. It was a great disappointment, of course, but it didn't stop Rochelle Street School from putting my name up on their board of honour, and giving everyone a half-day holiday. Shortly after this Mr Baldwin left, and Mr Barnett became the new headmaster. He entered me for three more scholarships – knowing that I wouldn't be eligible to accept them, but feeling that the prestige it brought the school was worth the effort. And every time I won, the school had another half-day holiday. As you can imagine, this did wonders for my popularity. It also brought a certain pride into the Winogradsky home and gave my mother something to boast about to the neighbours for months!

When I was 13½ Mr Barnett decided that, as I could go no higher in the school, it would be a good idea for me to sit outside in the hall with a small desk and act as a kind of assistant to him. This meant I had to be responsible for dishing out punishment in his absence to anybody who deserved it. One day, to my surprise, my little brother Bernie was sent out for a caning. Of course, I couldn't do that, but I did give him a strong ticking off.

Just before I was due to leave school – at the tender age of fourteen and a half – Mr Barnett entered me for one final scholarship. It was really for people aged fifteen and over, and was called the Trade Scholarship. Whoever won it could go to any college, and take up any trade of his choice. As I still hadn't been naturalized, I knew that even if I was successful nothing could come of it. But Mr Barnett felt that not only would it be good for the school, but also helpful to my future career – whatever that turned out to be. It was an occasion I'll never forget.

There were about four hundred entrants, and the exam took place in a large hall called People's Palace in the Mile End Road in the East End. Again I was fortunate, because the first subject was arithmetic. The questions were far more difficult than some of the previous scholarships I'd sat for. As usual, there were twenty sums, of which fifteen had to be completed, including one that was compulsory.

By this time my prowess in maths and arithmetic had been well proven and I was fairly confident I'd come up with the right answers. The fact that I couldn't benefit from the scholarship, and that it was therefore just a game, helped me to feel very relaxed about it all.

As usual, I turned the paper over, and completed nineteen sums in just under an hour. The twentieth sum was the compulsory one, and took me a full two hours to complete it. Even then I wasn't sure whether I'd answered it correctly. I went back to Mr Barnett after the exam was over and told him I was pretty confident about most of the sums, but had my doubts about the compulsory one. He told me he'd take the paper home with him, and would let me know the following morning whether my answers were correct. He saw me the next day and said he needed a bit more time. Two days went by and finally he told me he *thought* I'd got it right but still couldn't be sure. I wasn't really concerned because, whatever happened, I'd be leaving school and would be looking for work.

Moreover, at this point, I had other things on my mind. For the third time in eight years the family were on the move again – this time to No. 10 Grafton Street off the Mile End Road, right in the heart of Stepney. Though there were a great many Jewish immigrants in the area, it was altogether a nicer part of the world, and a definite improvement on 11 Henley Buildings. Our apartment, which had its own entrance, was over twice the size of our previous one, and even had a basement. The house was big enough for us to let off some rooms, which my mother did to make some extra money. And we even had our own bathroom. What luxury!

Three months later – long after I'd forgotten about the Trade Scholarship – Mr Barnett paid us a call in Grafton Street. He said that I was the only candidate out of all the entrants who had got the compulsory sum right, and, in view of this achievement, the LCC had decided to waive their rule about British citizenship and were offering me the scholarship.

Well, you can imagine the excitement in the Winogradsky household! This was the kind of 'acceptance' most immigrant families longed for – and, finally, after eight years, it had happened. Many Jewish mothers want their sons to become either doctors or lawyers, and my mother was no exception. Ideally, of course, she'd wanted me to become a doctor, but as there was no way this was going to happen she was happy to accept me as an accountant, which, to all intents and purposes, I seemed destined to become.

But nothing, as I have discovered in this life, ever works out as planned. We hadn't been in Grafton Street for more than six months or so when the family became friendly with a man called Alfred Goldstein, who lived in a house opposite us. Goldstein, I later discovered, worked for the Eric Wollheim Agency, who were exclusive booking agents for the cabaret room at the Savoy Hotel – then the prime cabaret engagement in London. Goldstein was the kind of man you went to for advice because he gave it so willingly and so sensibly. He seemed to take a liking to me, and one day suggested to my parents that if I really wanted to make a business career for myself – which, of course, I did – the best thing for me would be to get a job as soon as possible rather than return to school or college. He felt that practical experience was far more valuable than learning from text books, and my father absolutely agreed with him. Goldstein said he knew of an opening with a firm call Tew and Raymond in Little Argyll Street in the West End. They were known as the British Model House, and manufactured women's quality clothing.

Call it an omen or a coincidence that the man who got me my first job was in the entertainment industry himself. But then my life is full of little coincidences, as you will see. The fact that Little Argyll Street was the address of my first job is also, in a sense, a coincidence, because, not only is it seconds away from the London Palladium – which has played such a great part in my life – but it is also less than a hundred yards from 241 Regent Street, which is where Lew and Leslie Grade eventually had their headquarters.

Anyhow, Goldstein, it turned out, was a good friend of both Tew and Raymond and arranged things so that I'd spend a bit of time in every department of the company, 'learning the ropes'.

I was about fifteen and a half when I joined Tew and Raymond, and the first department I went into was the costing department, where I immediately memorized all the prices of the various materials, the buttons, and the numerous accessories that go into the manufacture of women's clothes. Within a couple of weeks I was able to look at a finished garment, and I'd know exactly how many yards of material went into it, the cost per yard, the number of buttons used, and so on. In less than a minute I was able to work out the total cost, adding 50 per cent for overheads, as well as a 50 per cent mark-up. My memory was so good that all I had to do was look at the style number of any item we manufactured to know exactly what the garment cost us, and how much profit we would make on it.

That particular department was run by a Mrs Burgess, who was pretty good with figures herself, but she was so astonished at my own abilities that she made me her assistant. I was slim at the time, and very personable, and because I always knew my place, and didn't get big-headed, I wasn't resented by the rest of the staff – all of whom were older than me. My starting salary was 15 shillings a week, which, for a youngster in those days, wasn't too bad. But the money wasn't all that important – particularly as I handed most of it over to my mother anyway. What mattered was my progress in the firm, and, after six months in the costing department, there was nothing more for me to learn, and nowhere further for me to go – other than becoming head of the department. But at the age of sixteen however, that was out of the question. So I moved into silks, and after about a month or so I knew everything there was to know about that particular fabric. Next came the embroidery department, and I quickly learned all about the finer points of embroidery. The year was 1922, and the country had gone embroidery-mad. Embroidery, everyone had discovered, was a way of making the simplest fabric more interesting, and nearly every item of women's clothing in those days had some embroidery on it.

Now at this point I'd been with Tew and Raymond for eighteen months. Raymond I liked. But Tew irritated me. It was a strange partnership. Raymond was brilliant with designs; Tew was the businessman. Money was everything to him and he was as mean as hell. One gloomy day he walked into my office, and he switched off all the lights. 'We don't need lights on in the middle of the day,' he said. 'This isn't a philanthropic organization.'

LEFT: Lew's father, Isaac Winogradsky. 'An excellent singer, but not a good business man…'

CENTRE: Lew (back row, second left) at Rochelle Street School.

BELOW: A typical East End Jewish workshop in the early 1920s, similar to Lew and his father's embroidery factory.

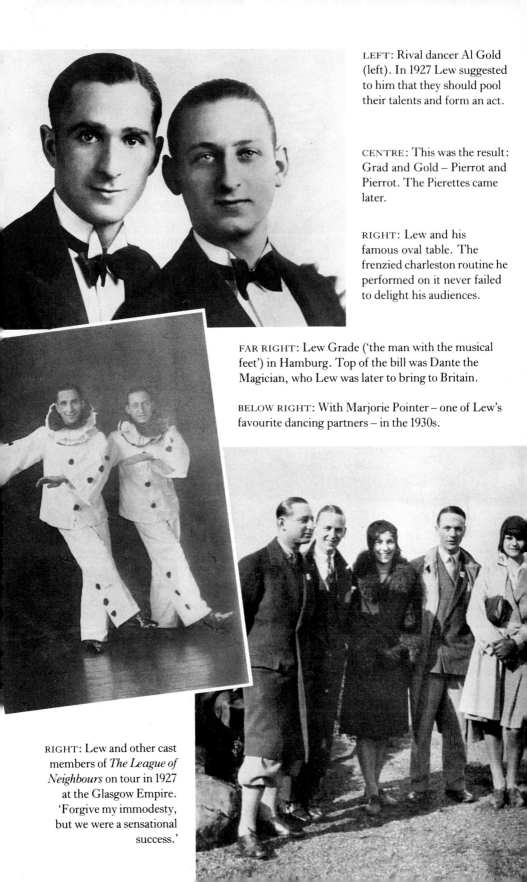

LEFT: Rival dancer Al Gold (left). In 1927 Lew suggested to him that they should pool their talents and form an act.

CENTRE: This was the result: Grad and Gold – Pierrot and Pierrot. The Pierettes came later.

RIGHT: Lew and his famous oval table. The frenzied charleston routine he performed on it never failed to delight his audiences.

FAR RIGHT: Lew Grade ('the man with the musical feet') in Hamburg. Top of the bill was Dante the Magician, who Lew was later to bring to Britain.

BELOW RIGHT: With Marjorie Pointer – one of Lew's favourite dancing partners – in the 1930s.

RIGHT: Lew and other cast members of *The League of Neighbours* on tour in 1927 at the Glasgow Empire. 'Forgive my immodesty, but we were a sensational success.'

CIVA
DAS RIESEN-VARIÉTÉ AM MILLERNTOR
im vollständig umgebauten CIRCUS BUSCH
Vom 1. — 15. Januar 1930. täglich
Internationales Variété

DANTE
Der berühmte amerikanische
MAGIER UND JLLUSIONIST
EINE STUNDE
WUNDER ÜBER WUNDER

Prof. Hans I. und Frau
mit ihren menschlichen Hunder

LEW GRADE   Der Mann mit den
musikalischen Füssen

Brothers Dewers
and Miss Passy
Die Wunder der Körperbeherrschung

THE SOUNDY'S
LUSTIGES MUSIKALISCHES POTPOURRI

DAS MONDÄNE   DOLLY & GERT
TANZ...

FE...
UN...
NA...

ABOVE: Kathleen Moody.
'The first time I saw her I felt
very protective towards her.'

'The best deal I ever made.' Lew and Kathie were married on 23 June 1942.

Lew and Kathie, with Kathie's mother (centre) and sisters Nell, Phyllis and (front) Nora.

Kathie. 'She had
a sensational voice: a
wonderful, pure,
coloratura.'

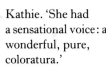

Lew in the 1940s. Only one
thing missing: the cigar.

LEFT: Lew and
Kathie's son Paul.

RIGHT:
Olga Winogradsky,
Lew's mother.
'An extremely
determined woman.
In the early days no
matter what hardships
she was faced with,
she always saw to it
that we had clothes
on our backs and food
in our stomachs.'

ABOVE: Lew's nephew
Philip, with his
mother – Kathie's
sister Nora – and his
father, Solly Black –
Lew's best friend.

LEFT: Lew and Kathie
on their way to a Royal
Garden Party in 1958.

ABOVE: A rare photograph indeed! Lew and his family on vacation. 'I have always been a workaholic and rarely go on holiday…'

ABOVE: The 'baby' of the family: Lew's sister Rita.

RIGHT: A show-business dynasty: Lew, Bernard and Leslie Grade in top hat and tails celebrating the wedding of Leslie's son, Michael Grade.

Kathie and son Paul accompany Lew to his investiture on 1 January 1969.
'An important-looking letter had arrived from Downing Street. It was marked
"Private and confidential" and "Urgent"…'

The great moment arrives as Her Majesty the Queen bestows a knighthood on Lew
Grade. 'The Queen usually speaks to each of the people she honours for about thirty
seconds; but when it came to me, she spoke for much longer. It seemed like an
eternity, but it was probably only about two minutes.'

Well, that sort of thing really annoyed me. He didn't have a sense of humour either, and that to me, even at the age of seventeen, was a drawback.

No doubt if I'd wanted to stay on for several more years I might have been offered a junior partnership. But that was well into the future, and I was keen to do something more ambitious with my life than hang around earning what was, by now, about a pound a week.

So, one day after work, I went home, sat my father down and discussed with him the possibilities of opening up an embroidery factory of our own. My father was still working for the Reece Buttonhole Company – on a salary, of course – and I think the idea of being involved in his own business really appealed to him. Also, he'd seen how well I'd been doing at Tew and Raymond and I'm sure he felt that, with his particular skills and my business brain, we could really make a go of it. He didn't know anything about embroidery – except that it was popular in the women's clothing industry – but I did, and that was good enough for him. My mother also gave us her blessing, which was most important in the Winogradsky family. She was under no delusions about my father as a businessman, but she had complete confidence in me – after all, I'd won all those scholarships – and she felt it was a risk that was definitely worth taking.

The first thing I did was to give in my notice to Tew and Raymond, who were sorry to see me go. I then persuaded one of the women who worked with me in the embroidery department there – as well as her twenty-year-old son – to join me in this new business venture. Like me, they knew everything there was to know about embroidery, and were keen to do something more profitable with their lives, even though it meant, initially, taking something of a risk.

The next priority was to find premises – which we did at Aldgate East Chambers in the East End, for two pounds a week. After that I negotiated my first-ever business deal: I bought a couple of extremely cheap secondhand embroidery machines – which my father financed. We had them installed and, with a staff of two, Winogradsky and Son went into business. And a really thriving little business it turned out to be. The embroidery boom was in full swing, and, within a matter of just two or three

29

months, we installed six more machines and several additional workers. I had never worked so hard in my young life, often staying on at the factory (as we called it) to make sure all the orders were ready for delivery first thing in the morning. I'd also spend days walking across London, going from one clothing manufacturer to another, showing them designs I'd copied from other embroiderers and generally giving them a fantastic sales-pitch. By the time I left their offices, I'd convinced most of them that they needed us more than we needed them! And it paid off. All that leg work resulted in more business than we could handle. Six months after we opened, we had eight machines working well into the night. There were some days I didn't get home until two or two thirty in the morning, and was back at work at six thirty a.m. to prepare the accounts and invoices. Arriving early at the office has always been a practice of mine and continues to be so to this day. Those extra few hours have often proved extremely valuable to me in the past, because by ten o'clock I'd already done a full day's work when most of my competitors were just starting.

Anyway, business was terrific and, for the first time since our arrival in Great Britain, the Winogradskys were actually making quite a good living. I'm not sure exactly *how* much we brought home every week, because money, believe it or not, has never been that important to me. During my lifetime I've given away much more of the stuff than I've kept. As far as I'm concerned, it's the *deal* that counts. For me, the fun of business is making the deal, not counting up the profits. Of course, no one likes to lose money, and I'm no exception. But it has never been a motivating force for me. And it wasn't way back in 1923. All I wanted was to be comfortable and to have enough to keep decently clothed, fed and, occasionally, entertained – usually in the cinema or the music halls.

Unfortunately, as I have mentioned, my father liked to gamble – and a great deal of the money we were making went to pay off his gambling debts. If it hadn't been for this we would, I believe, have been quite well-off. But there was nothing any of us, including my mother, could do about his gambling. After all, he was still the head of the household. The main thing was that we never starved. If money *had* meant a great deal to me, I'd have made quite sure that we split the profits. As it was, all I took home each week was a couple of pounds for myself. What I *did* do, though, was make quite sure that all the bills at home were paid. As well as handling the salaries and rent at work, I was the family accountant, and while there wasn't a great deal left over for luxuries after my father had slipped out to play the horses or have a quick game of cards, the necessities were always taken care of. As far as I can remember, my mother was more concerned about the fact that weeks would go by when she'd hardly ever see us. My father was a very caring person and a hard worker, and, like me, he'd often arrive home after midnight, and be back at the factory at six a.m. Little wonder that my mother and my brother Leslie, who was seven years old at the time, became so close. She saw more of him than the rest of us put together, and, until our sister Rita was born a couple of years later, he was still the baby of the family.

Apart from the cinema and the music halls, one of the things I enjoyed most was dancing. Working near us in Aldgate East Chambers at the time was a fellow by the name of Sid Starr. Sid's father was a tailor in a factory next to ours, and Sid worked for him. Sid's passion in life was ballroom dancing, and one evening, after we'd both packed up for the day, he invited me to go with him to the East Ham Palais de Dance. I'd never gone to such a place before, but I had nothing better to do that night, so I thought why not? It might be fun, and it was a chance to meet some girls.

How could I possibly have known that this one casual outing was about to change my life?

31

2

The Crossover

THE FIRST THING to be said about me and ballroom dancing is that I was never very good at it. And, certainly, the evening I accompanied Sid Starr to the East Ham Palais I was a 'greener', as my mother would say. I didn't know a waltz from a foxtrot, a quickstep from a tango. But, as I have already made clear, I was a quick learner, and, just by watching the various steps and committing them to my photographic memory, I managed to get by. I was only passable, mind you, and was far better in the faster dances, such as the quickstep, than I was in a waltz. The fact that both my parents had been performers may have had something to do with how readily I picked up dance steps. It didn't help me, however, in picking up girls. On the dance floor, that is. Sid, who was a far better ballroom dancer than I ever was, had no difficulty dancing with the best-looking girls in the hall. In fact, like so many youngsters at the time, he went to the Palais with the expressed purpose of meeting girls. These places were the discos of their day, and that's where you went to meet members of the opposite sex.

Until this point in my life, I hadn't had a great deal of experience with girls. For a start, where sex was concerned, I was rather shy and reserved – not like my brother Bernie, who, by the time he had turned seventeen, was much more confident with women than I was. Also, I didn't have the time for casual relationships as I was too busy working my head off at the factory for fifteen hours a day. It wasn't until I started going to the Palais on a regular basis – like two or sometimes three nights a week – that girls played any part in my life. It was at the Palais that I met the first girl I ever slept with. I was about eighteen and she was a couple of years older. She didn't hide the fact that she fancied me and I remember hiring a punt from Kingston and taking it up the Thames. After that, I developed a little more confidence where women were concerned, but I was no lady-killer and never pretended to be.

I met several other girls at the Palais, but most of them were little more than dancing partners – and, as I wasn't very good, the girls were hardly queuing up for me, as they were for Sid Starr. Then all that changed too.

A new dance craze arrived from America called the charleston. Unlike most of the other ballroom dances, the beauty of the charleston was that it could be done as a solo. So you didn't have to rely on finding a partner, as you did for the foxtrot or the waltz. It was new, it was fresh, it was exciting, and it was showy. Added to all this was the fact that dance halls began to hold charleston competitions, offering cash prizes (or silver cups or plates) to the winners. These prizes weren't so much a motivation to enter as an added inducement. Having the extra cash was pleasant – but it was the *winning* that provided the real pleasure.

My father, apart from having an excellent singing voice, was also a good dancer, who, even as a middle-aged man, had never forgotten how to do the *kaztatzke* and other acrobatic Russian-style dances. Over the years he'd taught me a few Cossack steps, so, when the charleston arrived, I was pretty nimble on my feet and found that I took to this new dance craze from America very easily. So did my brother Bernie. But, aged fifteen, he wasn't yet in a position to do much about it.

As charleston fever swept the country, I found myself becoming more and more popular at the East Ham Palais. The girls were now fighting to charleston with me, and I have to admit that this new-found success with the opposite sex definitely went to my head. The discovery that I could actually do something better than anyone else on the dance floor gave me the kind of confidence I really admired in someone like Sid Starr.

At home I spent a lot of time in front of the mirror, trying out new steps and improvising whole routines for myself. I was getting better and better and faster and faster. It finally reached a point when as soon as I stepped on to a dance floor, the other dancers would move back, watch me and applaud. I had added another string to my bow.

One of the first charleston competitions I can remember was held at the Ilford Hippodrome. Sid Starr, and another friend of ours, Harry Tasker (who worked in his father's barber shop in Brady Street, off Whitechapel Road), persuaded me to enter, and, as I was more than confident that I could win, I put my name down for the qualifying heats – which I passed without any difficulty at all. The first performance on the following Friday night was to be the semi-finals, and the second performance, that same night, the finals. At this point I'd been charlestoning for several months, and had worked out an entire three-minute routine for myself – complete with straw hat and cane. I wore a natty brown suit, and, though I say so myself, I looked pretty good.

Ilford Hippodrome was offering a prize of £25 to the winner – a lot of money in those days – and the atmosphere in the hall was electric. When my turn at the semi-finals arrived, I walked on to the stage and, because I'd already made a small reputation for myself, I received tremendous applause. The band struck up, I danced for three whirlwind minutes, and when I came off Sid assured me that I had it in the bag. Based on the reception I'd received, I, too, felt quite sure the first prize of £25 was going to be mine.

In my dressing room, however, I suddenly heard a burst of thunderous clapping for someone who'd gone on after me, and I rushed out to see who it was. There were two of them, a brother-and-sister team called The Rubens, who, I learned, had just come in from Paris where they'd won the European Charleston Championship. Because of this, they were allowed to enter the semi-finals without having to compete in the preliminary heats, which is why I hadn't seen them before. Well, after hearing the ovation they both received, I knew I'd have to make do with second prize. And, for me, coming second was the same as coming last. To me, second best is nothing, and always has been.

Naturally, I was rather depressed about this turn of events, and because I was so keyed up I suddenly lost heart. But Sid and several of my other friends, who'd gathered in the dressing room to give me moral support, told me not to worry, and persuaded me to go with them to a pub across the road and to relax. I'm not a drinker, but I agreed to go with them for a glass of lemonade.

The Crossover

Walking into the pub I noticed a large mirror. For no reason at all I thought I'd try a new step which suddenly came into my mind, and which I later called the 'crossover'. It was entirely my own invention, and, to my knowledge, had never been done before. There and then I practised it for Sid and the others in front of the mirror, and they were all so enthusiastic they convinced me to include it in the routine I'd planned for the finals. I did some more work on it, examined it in the mirror, and thought it interesting.

Back at the Hippodrome, the Rubens team went on before me, and received tremendous applause all over again. They were clearly the favourites, and I knew I was up against some real competition for the first time. I was the next to go on and I must admit I felt slightly downhearted.

My appearance on the stage also met with applause – but nothing as great as the Rubens had received. For the first minute of my routine, I did my usual stuff, then suddenly went into the crossover step I'd invented less than an hour ago in the pub.

Well, the place suddenly erupted. The audience went wild, and they continued to applaud and cheer for the last two minutes right until the end of my dance. Nothing like this had ever happened to me, and it was the most exciting night of my young life. To have a thousand people or more roaring their approval at me was music to my ears, and, as I walked off that stage floor, I felt that life could never quite be the same for me again. The show-business blood I'd inherited from my parents suddenly came to the boil and I knew that, whatever happened, and in whatever capacity, the world of entertainment was the world for me.

It hardly seemed to matter that I was awarded the first prize and given the title of Charleston Champion of London – not to mention the £25, which pleased my mother enormously. I was doing something I really enjoyed. And excelled in. It was a great feeling and I still haven't forgotten it.

After winning this competition I was filled with my own importance. I have since been told it was not a very attractive quality, and one of my partners, a girl called Fay Zack, has gone on record as saying I was 'ruthless and bombastic'. I was certainly arrogant and full of myself, but, all I can say in my defence is that I was a young, immature and unworldly 18-year-old – and still had a great deal of growing up to do.

At any rate, after winning the Charleston Championship of Great Britain, I started entering competitions all over London. Many of the competitions held in a Palais de Dance required girl partners – and they weren't always easy to find. The above-mentioned Fay was one of them, and, despite what she may have thought about me personally, she was very good indeed. She was an assistant on the shoe counter at the Houndsditch Warehouse, and we first met at the East Ham Palais Sunday Club. She had come dancing with her sister, and, as soon as I saw her, I asked her to dance with me. As I've said, I wasn't basically a very good ballroom dancer; so we weren't all that great together doing the foxtrot. But the moment we started to charleston, something gelled between us, and we entered several competitions together – and won.

I also entered competitions which were held on a stage in a cinema, and for these I would do a solo.

I must say that, despite the success I was having with the charleston, dancing was still just a hobby for me. I had no intention of becoming a professional, or of giving up my work in Aldgate Chambers. I was on to a fairly lucrative and enjoyable sideline, and that, as 1924 drew to a close, was the extent of it. I may have been bigheaded and full of confidence on the dance floor, but at home I was still Louis Winogradsky – the would-be businessman.

Not very long after I won the Championship at Ilford, another first-rate charleston dancer appeared on the scene. His name was Al Gold, and there was a lot of talk in dancing circles as to which of us was the better dancer. I thought I was. After all, hadn't I won a major championship to prove it, as well as almost every other competition I'd entered?

One Sunday evening, Sid and I and several of our friends decided to go to a school dance near Bow. As soon as we arrived we heard there was to be a charleston competition. Among the competitors was this Al Gold, whom I'd never met, and his regular dancing partner. Naturally, I was asked to enter as well, but I wasn't keen. I didn't have my partner with me, and all I really wanted to do was relax.

Well, my friends wouldn't hear of it. They said if I refused to enter, people would say I was scared to compete against Gold and that it would do my reputation no good at all. When I pointed out that I had no one to dance with, they told me to select a girl from the crowd.

They continued to put such pressure on me that I eventually said okay. I knew if I danced·the way I usually did with Fay Zack I wouldn't stand a chance. The only way to survive the situation was by making sure that the judge never saw a great deal of my partner.

So what I did was to keep the girl I chose moving around. For example, when the judge moved around the floor, I moved in the same direction, so that all he saw was the back of me and the movements of my flying feet!

Need I mention it, but I won the competition, and Al Gold came second.

After that there was no stopping me. As the undisputed best charleston dancer in town, I entered more and more competitions, competing in as many as three or four in a single night. I'd find out where they were all being held, and if, say, two of the bigger competitions clashed with each other, I'd telephone the dance halls in advance and ask them to adjust the times to suit me. And, because I had become quite an attraction by now, they usually agreed. On some nights I'd win as much as £20 or more – to say nothing of all the silver cups or cutlery, or whatever else they happened to be dishing out as prizes.

At this point in my youthful dance career, I realized that I couldn't go through the rest of my life entering competitions as Louis Winogradsky. It was too much of a mouthful, so I simply took the centre part of my name and became Louis Grad. The first part of my name would never do. I couldn't go through life as Louis Wino!

By the time I was nineteen, I'd become so well known in dance circles that I wasn't all that surprised when Jack Hulbert approached me to choreograph a dance routine for his wife, Cicely Courtneidge, who was appearing in a new show at the Winter Garden Theatre. I was delighted to do something a bit different, and, although I had no ambitions as far as choreography was concerned, I worked with her on the routine I'd

37

devised, and she seemed very happy with it. But this was an isolated event. At that stage of my life I wasn't part of the 'showbiz' world at all. I didn't mix with a theatrical crowd, and barely went to the theatre. I was too busy entering competitions for that. I didn't even know a great deal about the professional dancers of the time – though, of course, I had heard of Fred Astaire, and had even seen him dance. The only other dancer I can remember enjoying was an American called Hal Sherman. He was what was known as an eccentric dancer, and I can remember filching some of his steps. Sherman was a regular in the music halls, and whenever he was on, I'd make a point of going. But otherwise there were not that many great dancers around. We're talking about 1924 or 1925 – long before the time of the Hollywood musical film, and all the dancers the talkies introduced to the world.

By 1926, the charleston craze was reaching its peak, and in December of that year the World Charleston Championship was being held at the Albert Hall. There were various sections in competition, such as doubles, singles and formations. As you can imagine, the event generated a great deal of excitement. Several thousand people filled the hall and the atmosphere was electric. I had never seen so many great dancers assembled under one roof and the tension backstage was almost too much to bear. The section I was competing in was the World Solo Charleston Championship, and the winner's prize was a four-week cabaret appearance, one performance nightly, at the Piccadilly Hotel in London. The salary was £50 a week, a fantastic sum of money to a 20-year-old.

It is only recently that I discovered that the judges for the competition were Charles B. Cochran, the impresario and English equivalent to Florenz Ziegfeld, and the great Fred Astaire himself! Had I known this at the time, I'd have been so nervous I doubt whether I could have gone through with it. But I didn't know it – and I did go through with it. And furthermore, I won! The sound of thousands of people cheering at me was even more thrilling than the crowd at the Ilford Hippodrome – and that, too, was a night I shall never forget. Louis Winogradsky, a.k.a. Louis Grad, was named Charleston Champion of the World. Who would have believed it? My mother, of course,

claimed that she had always known I had it in me. But then she
was always tremendously supportive of her 'kinder' and never,
for an instant, doubted that we would all succeed, no matter
what we decided to do.

The four weeks at the Piccadilly that followed the competition
were among the most important of my life. Although my 'act' –
such as it was – was a mere four minutes long, those four minutes
were the most exciting part of my day. Maybe I'd been suppres-
sing it for the last four years or so, but finally I realized that show
business was more than just a hobby for me. It was something I
wanted to be a part of every waking minute of the day. I loved
performing, and I loved the approval of the crowds. And to be
paid £50 a week on top of it! Well, that was *really* living. So I
made another major decision. I was going to become a professional dancer. The problem was how to tell my parents.

As it turned out, it was not a problem at all. Because of their
own interest in the stage, they understood completely. Had I
been less good at what I was doing, they may have tried to
discourage me. But, as they couldn't argue with the kind of
success I was having, they gave me their blessing. Apart from
appearing for four weeks as amateurs at the Scala Theatre when
they first arrived in Britain, fourteen years earlier, they had more
or less given up their own show-business aspirations, and I think
they saw in me – and later in Bernie – a chance to live the kind of
life which, in the end, they had never had the courage to pursue.

As far as our business, Winogradsky and Son, was concerned,
for the time being my father decided to run it on his own – with a
little help from Bernie and me.

Even before I'd decided to become a professional dancer, the
business wasn't doing all that well anymore. By 1926 the
embroidery craze was over and the combination of my father's
gambling and the lack of clients made it difficult for all concerned. And although Bernie, who had left school in 1924, and
who at this stage was working for a crockery company, helped
out whenever he could, his heart wasn't in the rag trade either.
At the time of the Albert Hall Championship, Bernie was seventeen and a half – and quite a keen dancer himself. In fact, unlike
me, he also had a good singing voice, and whereas I entered
dance competitions, Bernie was more interested in talent shows

and he usually won. So, as soon as it became obvious that neither of Isaac Winogradsky's sons had any intention of carrying on the family business (Leslie was still a child of ten), my father decided, sometime in 1927, to sell up. The job he had fourteen years earlier with Jack Isow was still available to him if he wanted it, and he did.

By this time, my parents had had another child – a daughter called Rita who was born on 23 January 1925 – so, although Bernie and I were making our own way in the world, my father still had three other people to support, and it wasn't easy. Had he managed to save some of the money we made in the good years of the embroidery business, life would have been a lot more pleasant for him. But he hadn't, and it was up to Bernie and I to contribute as much of the money we were making on our own to the upkeep of the family which we both did, without question. For example, out of the £200 I earned for my four-week engagement at the Piccadilly Hotel, I kept just enough to buy myself a dinner jacket, silk alpaca trousers and a sash. (Later I bought my first jockstrap because, when you dance the way I did, if you didn't have any protection there you'd kill yourself!) My abiding memory of the time, financially speaking, was always handing over money to my mother, and only keeping enough for the necessities of my life. So, in a sense, from about 1927 onwards, it can honestly be said that Bernie and I supported the family. The money my father earned didn't amount to much more than pocket money.

With my parents relying so heavily on my financial help, I was under a great deal of pressure to keep working. And that, I was soon to discover, was easier said than done.

The first thing I did was to go on the usual round of agents' offices. What, in fact, I was selling them was my Charleston Championship title and about three and a half to four minutes of a so-called dance routine – hardly enough to stop Astaire in his tracks. I also had confidence, and that, of course, helped me get through the day without wondering whether or not I'd made the right decision by turning professional. It didn't help get me an agent though, and it was in a theatrical newspaper called *The Stage* (which still exists today) that I read that Murray Pilcer, the dance-band leader, was preparing a show to tour the country, and needed a dancer who would sit in the orchestra, holding an instrument, then suddenly come forward and dance.

I auditioned for Pilcer – in fact, my audition was my whole act! – and he was delighted with it. He gave me a contract, and my first week's engagement was at the Brighton Hippodrome.

I realized, of course, that just doing the charleston was not going to be enough. I needed more than three and a half minutes and had to come up with something quickly. That's how my famous gimmick with the table was born. In case there are still some people unaware of the fact that Louis Grad and his table were inseparable, allow me to explain.

The table, which was oval in shape, was about three and a half feet high and two feet wide, and travelled with me wherever I went, causing headaches and problems galore. But it provided me with the climax to my act and was a guaranteed applause-getter – my *pièce de resistance*, you could say. The table would be brought on to the centre of the stage, whereupon I'd jump on to it in a quite spectacular fashion. The trick was for me to jump on to the very centre of the table, otherwise there was every chance it would topple over with me on it.

Once securely on the table, I'd then go into the most frenzied charleston routine ever seen, and it usually brought the house down. I even managed to bowl over the critics. 'His dexterity and speed were wondrous to behold . . .' wrote one of them. It was an invaluable gimmick, that table, and never failed to thrill the crowds.

Pilcer was duly impressed, and when, during my second week with him, we played the Holborn Empire in London, I really felt I'd arrived. For, next to the London Palladium, the old Holborn Empire was the second most prestigious music hall in London.

There must be something in the maxim which says you should always leave audiences asking for more, for, although I only did about four or five minutes a show – the full extent of my repertoire – I was a sensation. Pilcer couldn't have been happier, and for the next four weeks, at a salary of £20 a week, I really wowed them in the provinces.

Then suddenly Pilcer decided he was tired of touring, and gave it up. So, it was back to the drawing board, and another out-of-work period. I was still living at home, and whenever I was out of work it meant more mouths to feed and less money with which to feed them.

I soon realized that, although I got exceptionally good notices wherever I appeared, if I was going to make it as anything other than part of a dance band, I'd have to have a better, and longer, act. A four-minute spot was too short for music hall, and I just had to face this fact of life. To be a success in the halls, I needed at least twelve minutes. And I knew that, given the energetic nature of my dancing, and the fact that I couldn't sing or play a musical instrument, I was never going to manage twelve minutes on my own.

So I decided to contact my old rival Al Gold – or Abraham Goldmaker, as he was born. Like me, Al had changed his name, and had also come from the Ukraine to the East End. He was six years old when he arrived and couldn't speak a word of English. And just as my parents had landed without birth certificates or the proper documents, so had his too. In fact, our backgrounds couldn't have been more similar. His father was a barrel-maker, and, for a short time after leaving school, Al worked with him. But he hated being a cooper, and as soon as he realized he had a talent for something else – dancing – he quit the family business.

By 1927 Al and I had become quite good friends and when I suggested to him that we should pool our talents and form an act together, he didn't need convincing.

The first thing we did was to cobble together some kind of an act. As I recall, it consisted of a soft-shoe shuffle which we both did, followed by an eccentric comedy routine from Al. Then I'd do my charleston on the oval table, and we'd finish up by doing the charleston together – at breakneck speed. That way we eked out about ten to twelve minutes.

The main problem, though, was getting work, which we found heartbreakingly difficult to do. In retrospect, we probably went about it the wrong way. In the late 1920s the public loved seeing big bands on stage, with featured vocalists or dancers, so what we did was to find out which of the orchestras were planning stage tours. For the first three months of our partnership we auditioned for innumerable bands – but to no avail. It may have had something to do with our act, of course, but somehow we just didn't click.

The Crossover

My daily routine while looking for work was always the same. The family was still living in Grafton Street, and, before leaving the house each morning, my mother gave me an allowance of sixpence. The fact that I was a grown-up man of twenty cut no ice. Sixpence was all that I was allowed while I was out of work. It would cost me a penny to ride up to Aldgate East station. Then, to save money, I'd walk the rest of the way to meet Al Gold somewhere in the West End. Together we'd do the usual round of all the agencies, trying to arrange auditions wherever we could. We were called 'Grad and Gold – the XN Trick Dancers', but nobody wanted to know. We couldn't *give* ourselves away! Out of my remaining five pennies, I'd spend fourpence on tea and buns. In the evening I'd walk the four and a half miles back to Aldgate, and, with my remaining penny, take a bus ride from there to Grafton Street. As I say, this dreary routine went on for nearly three months. Eventually, we auditioned for a band in the presence of a producer called George Shirley. Shirley was looking for talent for a new show of his called Shirley's Follies, and although he didn't like the band we were auditioning with, he signed us up.

Our first engagement was at the Newcastle Empire. We travelled up by train with the rest of the company, and, as soon as we arrived in Newcastle, headed towards the theatre. To our astonishment, we caught sight of the posters advertising the show. There we were, billed in huge letters of fire, headlining as Grad and Gold – The Charleston Champions. Sharing the bill with us were the famous Houston Sisters, who were as big in their day as the Andrews Sisters were in theirs. Being on the same bill with them was a tremendous thrill, and I could hardly believe it. We were so excited. We really thought this was it. We were in show business!

Our act went down even better than we'd hoped, and for the next six weeks we toured several other towns before returning to Newcastle for a second engagement. This time, though, we were not booked into the Empire but the Hippodrome, where, as good luck would have it, we were seen by a man called Thomas Convery, the producer of several touring revues.

Convery offered us a year's contract to appear in a revue of his called *The League of Neighbours*, whose principal star was a great

43

northern comedian called Albert Burden. We joined the show
and – you'll forgive my immodesty – were a sensational success.
The company also consisted of six male chorus boys, plus a
chorus line of sixteen gorgeous girl dancers. I don't remember all
that much about the show itself, except for one long scene which
was a kind of show-within-a-show, in which we were all dressed
in Pierrot costumes. I remember one of the actors in the company stepping forward, and boastfully saying in an American
accent something to the effect that 'in America everything we've
got is bigger and better than you've got in England. For example,
in America we have the best charleston dancers.' Then Albert
Burden would get up and disagree. 'England has the best
charleston dancers,' he'd say. Then the American said, 'We'll see
about that. I've got some dancers from America with me right
here.' At which point two of the chorus boys would come on and
do a fairly good routine, to some fairly good applause. Then
Albert Burden would say: 'That's nothing. Wait until you see
what we've got in Newcastle' (or whatever town we happened to
be in!). This was the cue for Al Gold and me to jump down from
the Pierrot stage and go into our charleston routine – which, of
course, got a riotous response. It was a corny routine, but it
worked every time. Then, in different spots in the show, Al and
I would do our own solos: mine was always the charleston on the
oval table.

We had a really great time with *The League of Neighbours*.
There was a terrific team spirit among the cast and several of us
stayed together in digs. We paid 30 shillings a week for board
and lodging, and in between shows managed to have a lot of fun
together. Because Albert Burden was such a hit in Newcastle, we
kept playing quick return engagements, and we always stayed at
the same lodgings. The landlady was a nice woman who adored
show-people and who specialized in telling fortunes. One night,
after coming home from the theatre, she told my fortune by
looking at my hand and reading cards. The news was good. I'd
be a star, she said, go overseas, and see my name in lights. We all
considered it to be a huge joke, of course, and laughed about it.
What she didn't tell me was that recently my brother Bernie had
formed an act with a young man called Albert Sutan – and
together they were known as the Delfont Boys. That particular

piece of information I had to glean from *The Stage*.

Ever since he left the crockery company, Bernie had made up his mind that he, too, wanted a show-business career. I had no idea, however, that he'd formed a partnership and was doing an act very similar, as it turned out, to mine and Al's. The reason he called himself Delfont was because his agent, Sidney Burns, felt that to have two Grad brothers appearing with two separate partners in two different acts would be confusing. The story goes that Burns had a poster in his office of a popular American dance team called the Dufor Boys, and suggested that Bernie and Sutan called themselves the Delfont Boys. They did, and to this day Bernie has kept the name. I saw their act – and, I have to tell you, it was pretty good.

But back to Newcastle. We had a really great time for about six months, particularly as both Al and I had got to know lots of girls, and really had the time of our young lives.

In June 1928 we had two weeks' holiday and I suggested to Al that we both go to Paris for a week and see what it was like. The idea was that when our contract with Convery came to an end, we might consider making a career for ourselves in Europe.

We scraped together £20 each, and booked our passage for Paris well in advance. I then discovered that I needed a passport if I wanted to travel to Europe. But being a Russian-born immigrant and a 'stateless' person, I didn't have one. For a stateless person to travel abroad, you had to have a Nansen document, which was the equivalent of a passport. So, my father and I went to the department where Nansen documents were issued. The authorities, however, insisted on seeing an identity card (which I didn't have), and then suggested I tried my local police station. The sergeant in charge there asked me my age, and when I told him I was twenty-one he said that every stateless person over the age of sixteen had to have an identity card. My father, quite truthfully, said he hadn't known this.

The sergeant looked at him and said, 'Can you see any green in my eyes?', meaning, of course, 'Do you take me for a fool?'

My father, whose English was never particularly good, looked into the man's eyes, and, in all innocence, said: 'No, I see no green in your eyes.'

The sergeant almost went crazy, but I managed to calm him

down, apologizing for the misunderstanding, and explaining to him that I was a professional dancer who was going to Paris to try to advance my career.

Finally, the sergeant relented, but my father was, by now, so flustered that when he gave the man the details of my birth, he gave him my sister Rita's birthdate by mistake. So, to this day, my passport gives the date as 23 January instead of 25 December.

Paris was everything I expected it to be – and more. Nothing had prepared me for the beauty of the city and its wonderful, carefree atmosphere. Everyone seemed so jolly and happy, and I loved the idea of all the sidewalk cafés. I particularly enjoyed drinking coffee at the Café de la Paix near the Paris Opera, and 'watching the world go by' was one of the highlights of the trip for me. There was a delightful bonhomie about the place. Unfortunately, though, I didn't have a great deal of time to spend sightseeing. The purpose of our visit was to meet some agents who might put some work our way.

And one of the most important Parisian agents at the time was a man called Rottenberg of the Rottenberg and Goldin Agency. After he agreed to meet us, we described our act to him and showed him some photographs of the two of us in action. I'll never forget what happened next. It was a Wednesday morning, and, after listening to what we were describing, he said: 'Why don't you give me an audition?' By this time I had become the businessman of the team – the one who did all the talking and the negotiating – and I explained that we'd be only too happy to audition, but that it was impossible as I didn't have my table with me, and that the table was an essential part of the act.

He then called in a young man whom he introduced as Harry Saltzman (yes, *the* Harry Saltzman, who, with Cubby Broccoli, was responsible for the original James Bond films), and said: 'Harry, go hire a table somewhere because I want these boys to audition for me.' As Mr Saltzman couldn't possibly have known exactly what kind of table I needed, we went round with him all day until we eventually found one that would suit my purpose. The legs had to be correctly spread, so that it wouldn't topple over when I got to the edge of it. On a couple of occasions in the past, when I had danced too near the edge, I had fallen and twisted my ankle, which meant I had to be off for a couple of days. So I had to be very careful.

Finally the audition was all set. I quickly briefed the pianist about what tunes to play, as I hadn't brought along my sheet music, and we went into our routine for Mr Rottenberg.

He thought we were tremendous.

'How'd you boys like to work on Friday and Saturday at the Casino Deauville?' he said. Just like that. Naturally, we said we'd love to. 'Great,' he said. 'The fee is 1000 francs, plus first-class fares to Deauville and all accommodation paid.'

As you can imagine, we were very excited. A thousand francs was about £8 – which, admittedly, wasn't a fortune, but it wasn't bad. Besides, in the time-honoured tradition, we were able to supplement that by cashing in our first-class tickets and travelling tourist. But money couldn't have been further from our thoughts. Just seeing a place like Deauville was exciting enough. To be playing in the world-famous casino there – and on such short notice – was a real miracle.

When we arrived we were told to report immediately for rehearsal, as there was a show that afternoon. We didn't realize there were two performances a day – one in the afternoon, called the Tea Dance, and one in the evening. This didn't bother us in the least. We were just delighted to be there. In all we did four performances: two on the Friday and two on the Saturday. As we were leaving the casino on Saturday night, the manager came to pay us, and handed over 4000 francs. What Rottenberg hadn't explained was that our salary was to be a thousand francs a performance! Such a windfall!

So, with the money we saved by trading in our first-class tickets, plus our 4000-franc fee, we had enough to return to London, and arrived back with the same amount of cash that we'd had when we left. The whole episode was a terrific eye-opener for us – not to mention a confidence booster – for it made us realize the kind of potential the continent was offering.

But our contract with Convery still had another six months to go. We were on £20 a week, jointly, with all our fares paid. Out of the £20 we had to pay our board and lodgings, so at the end of the week there wasn't a great deal left. I also had to find money to send home whenever I could. Clearly, we needed to improve our financial circumstances, so I said to Al, '£32 a week has to be our absolute minimum. We mustn't work for less.' Al, as he always did, said he'd leave that side of our partnership entirely to me. I immediately approached Convery with a request for more money. He was sympathetic, but kept stalling. Finally, with only two more weeks left to go on our present contract, I said to him, 'Look, this can't go on. If you don't want to renew our contracts at an increased salary, just tell me so we can look for another job.'

'All right,' he said. 'I'll tell you straight. I've just signed a contract with Al Gold. He's going to do a solo act, finishing off with your table routine. So we don't need you. You're through.'

This thunderbolt from out of nowhere was, as you can imagine, a terrible shock to me. I had no idea Al was planning to go solo. Up until then we'd been such good pals. I'm not saying we didn't have the odd row or disagreement, what partnership doesn't? – especially when you're living cooped up in digs together. But I wasn't ready for this kind of betrayal, and I regard it as the first major professional blow in my career. There were to be others, of course, but, when you've been in the business as long as I have, you expect them. This one took me completely by surprise. It was so unexpected. There has been only one other occasion in my life when I experienced a similar sense of betrayal – but more of that later.

After I left the act, Al Gold received £20 a week as a solo performer. He did my table routine. But not, I'm here to tell you, on my table.

What worried me wasn't being on my own again, but how I'd be able to sustain an act of ten to twelve minutes. I simply couldn't dance for that length of time without collapsing.

However, I somehow managed to get my act together – literally. I started with a little song that didn't tax my vocal abilities too badly, then went into a comedy ecentric routine that wasn't too strenuous. I followed this with an even more eccentric dance resembling a sailor's hornpipe. As usual, my big finish took place on the oval table.

Once again I decided to give Paris a try. This time as a soloist. But first I had to get a work permit. And I couldn't get a work permit without having a contract. I therefore asked for a transit visa, as the port of call I had in mind was Brussels which didn't require a work permit.

My transit visa enabled me to go to Paris for fourteen days. If I was lucky enough to find work there, I'd be able to extend the visa with a work permit.

I arrived in Paris with two small suitcases and my table. My music and dance clothes were packed in one of them, and my normal clothes in the other.

The beauty of the city was lost on me this time, for my mind was on getting work – and as quickly as possible. I dumped my cases in a cheap *pension* somewhere, and immediately started on an endless round of visiting agents, mainly in the Montmartre area where most of them were situated. Several of them saw me, and those who could speak English even talked to me for a bit. To those who couldn't, I showed photographs. If I'd spoken better French, it might have been easier, but I didn't so I really had my work cut out for me. Eventually I visited an agency that was owned by Pierre Sandrini, and met a man there by the name of Robert Borkheim. Fortunately, Borkheim spoke perfect English. We got on well, and he seemed genuinely interested in helping me. But, understandably, he wanted a better idea of my act before making any commitments. So I showed him a couple of the steps I did in my eccentric routine. I then told him about my table-top finale, and he asked me to show it to him. I did, and that's another occasion I'll never forget.

He had an office with a hard, stone floor – and not a carpet in sight. I'd worked up a step, now perfected, in which I'd fling one of my legs round the other in a kind of corkscrew fashion, and then fall on my knees. I did this four times, and always at tremendous speed. You couldn't help but be impressed. Borkheim couldn't believe his eyes. He thought it quite remarkable, and asked me to do it all over again. This I did, whereupon he said, 'You have to come in and meet Monsieur Sandrini. Right away.'

He took me into Sandrini's office, which also had a stone floor, and made me do the same step over and over again. My knees were being murdered on those stone floors – but it was worth it, for I was immediately booked into the Bal Tabarin in Paris two weeks from that date. It was the start of my dance career in Europe.

3

Making the Grade

I SHALL NEVER FORGET the help and encouragement I received from Pierre Sandrini and Robert Borkheim. I was at a most vulnerable period in my life and they gave me the confidence to get started in a foreign country.

Sandrini was a brilliant man who, sometime later, became a very close friend. Years after our first meeting in his office, he bought the Bal Tabarin and turned it into the most famous cabaret in France – if not the world. This was due largely to his fantastic designs. Sandrini's sets brought another dimension to the world of cabaret, and, in that particular milieu, they have never been bettered. But all this was in the future. At the time of my second Paris trip – in 1929 – the Bal Tabarin was just another typically Parisian nightspot.

In addition to being an agent, Robert Borkheim was also the stage director of the Bal Tabarin. It was only after I'd signed the contract that I told him my act lasted no longer than between eight and ten minutes. He assured me that wasn't a problem.

When I arrived for rehearsals in the morning, I had no idea who else was in the show, or even what sort of a show it was. All I knew was that I was in Paris, on my own, about to make my solo European début in a well-known Parisian nightspot for a salary of about £30 per week. The money wasn't great, but what a showcase!

I arrived back at the cabaret two hours before anyone else, and was given an enormous dressing room big enough for forty people. Such luxury!

I changed out of my day clothes and into the black silk trousers, grey shirt and red cummerbund I wore in the act. I went on to the stage, rehearsed a few steps, went over my routine a couple of times, and made quite sure the stagehands knew exactly where the oval table should be placed. Eventually the time came for the cabaret to begin, and I was as nervous as hell. After all, apart from a few auditions and some rehearsals, this was the first time I had done my new solo act in public.

Ten minutes later it was all over.

I don't remember much about the performance itself, except that when I walked off the stage I was dripping with perspiration. My clothes were drenched. The stage lights were very strong, and I wasn't used to having them focussed on me non-stop for that length of time.

I rushed into my dressing room to change – and what did I find there but twenty chorus girls completely nude. It wasn't *my* dressing room at all. It was theirs, and I was sharing it!

I immediately rushed out to find Robert Borkheim, who was backstage somewhere, and said, 'Robert, I'll catch pneumonia if I don't get out of these clothes and have a wipe down. I'll never last the week, and you *know* how important this engagement is to me!'

He said, 'So what's the problem? Go to the dressing room and wipe yourself down.' 'But Robert,' I said, 'there are twenty naked girls in there!'

He walked me back to the dressing room, opened the door, and pushed me in. 'Louis,' he said, 'this is Paris.'

I was in the room with the naked girls, and there wasn't a lot I could do about it. I slunk into a corner, took off my shoes and socks, my silk shirt, my silk trousers, until all I was wearing was my jockstrap. I've never felt so embarrassed in all my life. It just goes to show the different attitudes of the French and the English when it comes to nudity.

As soon as I'd finished drying myself with a towel, one of the naked girls approached me. She saw how embarrassed I was, but that didn't stop her from pressing her body next to mine and saying: 'You English boy? I like English boy. You and me, we have some fun?'

And that was my introduction to life in 'gay Paree'!

Happily for all concerned, my dancing was a great success. What I didn't know was that on opening night, the artistic director of the Casino Bellevue, Biarritz, and Oscar Bollinger, the artistic director of the Rialto, Dresden, were in the audience. Later that evening, after towelling down with the naked chorus girls, I met the two gentlemen, and, to my joy and delight, I was booked into the Casino Bellevue, Biarritz, for seven days at 1000 francs per day, plus hotel and food, as well as round-trip transportation. Oscar Bollinger booked me into the Rialto Palais, Dresden, for fifteen days, starting 1 June. This was the break I really wanted, because in 1929, Germany was the biggest continental market – with dozens of theatres and cabarets in every major town.

One of the many agents I saw in Paris was a man called Vincent Massi who booked acts into most of the casinos in the South of France. He saw me at the Bal Tabarin and wanted me to start an engagement at the Casino Municipal in Nice as soon as my commitment in Paris was over.

I really couldn't believe my luck. Suddenly it was all happening. Nice was the kind of millionaire's playground I always imagined was way out of my league. But here I was, being offered work in probably the most prestigious casino in Europe.

I remember that there were nine acts on the bill in Nice, and that I became very friendly with a pair called Henriques and Suzie, who were a married couple. He was a contortionist who did an act on a hanging trapeze, and Suzie was his assistant. After our opening night, at about 11 p.m., all the artistes in the show gathered together and Henriques asked me whether I'd like to go and see a film with them. I thought it was rather late to be going to the pictures, especially after an opening night. But this was France, and nothing surprised me. Or so I thought. The film we all went to see wasn't in a cinema at all, but in a lavishly furnished private house. In the lounge there was a screen and a projector, and, as soon as the 'show' began, I realized, of course, that we were watching blue movies. I was absolutely stunned, and didn't know where to look. Thinking back on those days, I must have been extremely naive and innocent for a grown man of twenty-two, but although I was as attracted to girls as the next man, nothing in my rather humble East End background prepared me for the kind of life style I was experiencing all at once in France!

Anyway, as I looked around the room, and saw the faces of

that select little audience absorbing what they were watching on the screen, I realized there was nothing I could do, but relax and enjoy it all as casually as they were. At the end of the film there was an announcement that 'everything you have seen can be experienced upstairs'.

But I'd had quite enough for one night and was glad to return to my hotel – alone.

Incidentally, when I became an agent myself, Henriques and Suzie were one of the first acts I booked for a long tour of England.

From Nice I proceeded to Biarritz to fulfil my contract at the Bellevue Casino, and was enchanted with the town. The accommodation was perfect, the casino was charming, and on the bill was an English act called The Barry Twins. They were two beautiful blondes, aged eighteen, who did a song-and-dance act, and were well known in France. Their mother travelled with them as a chaperone. Both girls were equally pleasant, and were extremely kind and helpful to me. I really was very taken with them.

We were doing two shows a day – just like Deauville – and, again, you'll forgive my lack of modesty when I say I was an outstanding success. Now I have never had any delusions about my abilities as a dancer. I knew I could charleston well, but that was about it. What, I think, audiences in Europe were responding to in 1929 was the charleston itself. It was something of a novelty, and people in Deauville, Paris, Biarritz and Nice were seeing it performed on a stage for the first time. There is no doubt in my mind that the same act I was doing wouldn't have meant tuppence in New York or any other big American city, where the charleston was no longer a novelty. But in Europe they lapped it up, and who was I to complain?

As I was taking my bows during a tea-dance performance one of the many middle-aged women in the audience that afternoon took a diamond ring off her finger and threw it to me. I picked it up, smiled, walked over to her, and returned it. I'll never forget the look on her face. No one had warned me it was the practice there for people to throw gifts on to stage as a token of their appreciation. The Barry Twins and their mother had been watching me from the wings, and told me afterwards how foolish

I was to return the ring. I assured them that the next time it happened I'd keep it. But it never happened again. I kept waiting for women to throw gifts at me, but they never did. So that was that.

After the week in Biarritz was over I travelled back to Paris with the Barry family. I was staying at the Moncey Hotel in the rue Blanche, while they were at a small *pension*, called the Olympic Hotel in the rue Fontaine, which catered mainly to theatre-folk.

We arrived in Paris early on Sunday morning and I went straight to my hotel. Around noon the phone rang, and it was one of the Barry twins. 'Louis,' she said, 'we've met a marvellous American man here. He's a millionaire, and his name is Mr Bray,' she said. 'He wants us all to go to the races with him at Longchamps this afternoon. So how about it?'

I refused the invitation. Racing really didn't interest me, and besides, all I'd managed to save after Nice and Biarritz was about 7000 francs which had to last me a couple of months until my next engagement on 1 June in Dresden. But she was so insistent that I finally agreed to accompany them.

I called for the girls at the Olympic Hotel, which was only a couple of minutes' walk away from my hotel, and was introduced to this Mr Bray, who was aged about forty-five, and wore a big gold chain on his waistcoat. He seemed pleasant enough, and produced a large limousine which took us all to Longchamps.

As soon as we arrived, I felt it only correct that I should pay for one of the girls, but Mr Bray refused to hear of this. 'You're my guests, today,' he said, 'and I want you all to have a good time on me.' Whereupon he gave each of us a pair of binoculars and escorted us on to the course.

Though I had no reason to doubt this man's integrity, something at the back of my mind worried me about him, and I couldn't help feeling suspicious. There was something odd about him which I didn't like, but couldn't explain. This mysterious millionaire . . . it all seemed so strange. For a start, what was a millionaire doing living in the Olympic Hotel? By now the race meeting had begun and, after a couple of races, Mr Bray came to me and said, 'Louis, I've lost all the cash I brought along with me. There's plenty more in travellers' cheques back at the hotel,' he said, 'so could you just lend me a couple of thousand francs until we get back?'

I was getting increasingly nervous about this man – but I loaned him the 2000 francs all the same. The race took place, and when it was over he came back to me carrying a bundle of notes. 'Louis, the horse won,' he said. 'Here's your 2000 francs.' Maybe I was wrong after all, and Mr Bray was perfectly 'kosher'.

After two more races, he came back to me and said: 'Louis, I've lost it all again. Can you lend me 3000 francs?' As he'd paid back my previous loan so promptly, I reluctantly handed him 3000 francs.

Towards the end of the afternoon, and with only one more race to go, he approached me yet again. He'd lost the 3000 francs and needed 2000 more for the last race. 'The moment we get back to the hotel,' he said, 'I'll pay it all back to you.'

Believe it or not, I fell for this and gave him 2000 francs more, which left me with exactly 2000 francs and a few odd coins.

He lost the last race as well and suggested we all return to the hotel. So we piled into the limousine and arrived back in great style. As soon as we got there, he invited me up to his room for a wash and brush-up. I'd rather have spent the time talking to the Barry twins, but he was so persuasive that I went along with him. 'Look,' he said, once we were in the room, 'I'm going downstairs to get the travellers' cheques, but meanwhile I'd be grateful if you could lend me another 2000 francs.' He didn't say what for, and stupidly I didn't ask. All I know is that with great trepidation, and against my better instincts, I handed over my last 2000 francs. As we walked downstairs together, he suddenly said, 'Louis, today's Sunday. It's silly to carry around all that money with you. Why don't we wait until tomorrow? You can't get them cashed until tomorrow, anyway.'

'Okay,' I said. 'Just give me the cheques, and tomorrow I'll cash them myself.'

'No no,' he said. 'It's foolish carrying all that money on you. You might get your pocket picked or lose the cheques. You're better off taking them first thing tomorrow morning and going to American Express.'

Again I allowed myself to be persuaded, then went with him, the girls and their mother to a cinema. We sat in a special box, but I really couldn't concentrate on the film at all. My mind was on my 7000 francs, which was all I had in the world.

It was a very strange evening indeed. The twins and their mother didn't talk or even smile at me. Not once. They seemed completely lost in thought.

After the film was over, Mr Bray dropped me off at my hotel, and then took the Barrys back to the Olympic. His last words to me were: 'I'll see you first thing in the morning.'

Needless to say, I couldn't sleep a wink. At 4.30 a.m. I got out of bed, dressed, and walked over to the Olympic Hotel. I climbed the stairs to his room, and knocked on the door several times. But there was no answer. Eventually, I turned the door knob and the door opened. The room was empty. Not a sign of the mysterious Mr Bray anywhere.

I was shattered. Nothing like this had ever happened to me before. Not only was I devastated at having lost all my money, but I was thoroughly humiliated at having allowed myself to become such an easy con man's victim.

I rushed down to the Barry sisters' room, which was on the floor below. By now it was about 5.00 a.m. I banged on the door shouting, 'Girls, wake up. Bray's gone.'

They opened the door, but before I even had a chance to open my mouth, they burst out crying, and told me their sad story. What had happened was that on the Sunday morning, just as they were preparing to go to Longchamps with Mr Bray, they were about to put their own money into a suitcase and lock it up for safe-keeping. Bray saw what they were doing and insisted they were making a mistake. 'The only way you can be sure your money won't be stolen', he said, 'is to put it under your mattress in an envelope. Nobody will find it there.'

They did this. But on Sunday night, just before they went to bed, the money, they discovered, had gone. Bray had clearly stolen it, and had evidently left as soon as they parted for the night.

So we were all in the same boat. None of us had any money. Naturally, we went to the police. But there was nothing much they could do about it. We were victims of our own gullibility. When I think back on the whole incident, it's hard to believe I could ever have been that naive. I vowed that nothing like that would ever happen to me again, but I still had another lesson to learn.

Meantime, though, I was pretty desperate. Fortunately, the twins, who felt a bit responsible for what had happened, persuaded the owner of the Olympic Hotel, with whom they were quite friendly, to put me up until my Dresden engagement a couple of months away.

So I moved into the Olympic, which was to become my home from home. I had no money at all, and nowhere to turn. I'd never ever been in such a situation and the only thing I could think of doing was wiring my brother Bernie – collect – and asking him to send me £15 as soon as possible. I then went to see Vincent Massi and told him about my predicament. He was most helpful and immediately fixed me up with an engagement for seven days at the Palm Beach Casino in Cannes, another of the top venues in the South of France. On the bill with me was a wonderful pair of ballroom dancers called Deze and Artini. We became good friends, and whatever free time I had was spent in their company, touring the local sights.

Just as I was beginning to get over the Bray incident, I received yet another shock. A cable arrived from Dresden saying that my contract to appear on 1 June was postponed due to a clause in the agreement of force majeure. What this meant was that should any unusual circumstances arise, they could cancel or postpone the engagement.

The 'unusual circumstances' in this unfortunate instance was that the weather in Germany was swelteringly hot, and that the management had decided to close the Rialto Palais for a couple of months as from 1 June.

Another catastrophe. The Dresden engagement was crucial to me. Without it there were absolutely no prospects for earning a living during the summer.

I told Artini what had happened. He was very cool about it all. 'Don't worry,' he said. 'Just get a 5000-franc advance from the Palm Beach management, and in no time at all I'll show you how to double it.'

Here we go again, I thought. But I felt so deflated at this point, I figured I may as well see what he had in mind. So I went to the management and drew a 5000-franc advance. Artini then took me to the casino in Cannes, where there was roulette, chemin de fer and baccarat. He was highly confident about it all, and assured me he'd made a great deal of money at the tables and saw no reason why I shouldn't do so as well. 'All you have to do', he said, 'is say "Banco!" '

The next thing I knew I was handing over my 5000 francs. Bearing in mind how much money my own father had lost gambling, I should never have gone anywhere near the place. In retrospect I realize that losing the 5000 francs in Cannes was the best thing that could have happened, because it made me aware of one of the crucial facts of life: never gamble unless you have the money to lose.

At the time, of course, I didn't quite see it that way. All I saw was that once again, due to my own stupidity and gullibility, I'd lost money I could ill afford. Fortunately, this time I wasn't entirely penniless. I still had 2000 francs left. Artini was genuinely sorry, and offered to lend me the money I'd lost, but I told him I'd be able to manage on what I had.

As soon as the Cannes engagement finished I returned to Paris and the Olympic Hotel, and once again relied on the kindness and patience of the *patron*, who allowed me to stay on without paying until I was in a position to do so. And once again I started doing the rounds of the agents' offices. It was extremely soul-destroying. All I had was one meal a day, and this consisted of a long French-bread sandwich of veal, and unlimited cups of coffee which the *patron* of the Olympic generously gave me without charge.

Every night I would stay up until 12.00 or 12.30 and then go to bed. But I couldn't fall asleep. Over and over in my mind I kept wondering what was going to happen to me next. My European venture which had started so well seemed to be in ruins. I could have returned to England, of course, and tried to get more bookings there. But I honestly didn't feel my act was ready for England yet. On the continent I was still something of a novelty where the charleston was concerned. In England I was already a fixture, and to be taken really seriously I'd have to have a much better act.

No question about it: I was desperate.

Then one night, around midnight, a short little fellow walked into the Olympic Hotel. He spoke with a broad American accent, and we got chatting. As the Olympic was a *pension* for theatrical performers, he automatically assumed I was in show business, and asked me what sort of an act I did. Before I answered him, I asked him what line *he* was in. He was, he said, in management, and was especially influential with the Moulin Rouge – one of the most famous music halls in the world. 'Is that so?' I said. 'And I'm the world's greatest charleston dancer.' I really thought the fellow was a bit of a nut, and I didn't take him at all seriously. Having been bitten twice in as many months I was in no mood to be taken for a ride yet again. My gullible days were over.

He then asked to see some photographs of me in action. I was reluctant at first, but I thought, 'What have I got to lose?' and I showed him a few. The next thing he said to me was: 'How'd you like to play the Moulin Rouge?' 'Great,' I said, going along with the joke. 'But only if my name is up in lights, if I get star billing, plus 1000 francs a day.' He said, 'Right. You've got it. I'll get you a contract.'

'Fine,' I said. 'You do that.' And off I went to bed, amazed at how many lunatics there were in show business.

At 2.30 a.m. there was a knock at my door. I said, 'Come in,' hoping against hope that it would be one of the Barry twins, who were still staying at the hotel.

Well, the door opened, and in walked this fellow. I was a little worried because I thought he might have other ideas, or something. He was something, all right: an angel from heaven. In his hand was a signed contract, for a fifteen-day engagement at the Moulin Rouge. *How* he got it, I never found out. Paris, I knew, was a city that never sleeps . . . but this was unbelievable. I looked at the contract, and it clearly stated that I was to receive 1000 francs a day, plus a guarantee of major publicity. He then told me I was to be co-headliner with Rosita Barrias, a famous Spanish singer. I simply couldn't believe it.

In case he should change his mind, I signed the contract there and then, and agreed to pay him the customary 10 per cent commission. In addition, I had to pay a further 10 per cent to the house agent, who, I later learned, was a close friend of his. But this still left me with 800 francs a day – enough to live on, and to pay off my debt to the *patron* of the Olympic Hotel.

I still couldn't believe it, but it was all true. My main concern now was to make my act as good as it could possibly be, and most of my spare time was spent rehearsing. A few days before the opening night, a big article about me appeared in the *Paris Midi* – a very important newspaper at the time. It was great publicity and encouraged me to rehearse even harder. The only thing was that the writer of the article had spelt my name incorrectly. Instead of Louis Grad, it came out as Lew Grade. I liked the look and the sound of it – and Lew Grade it has been ever since.

The night before I was due to open, I walked past the Moulin Rouge, and there, up in lights, next to Rosita Barrias, was my name. I'd been joking, of course, when I said to the little fellow that I'd only play the Moulin Rouge if they put my name up in lights. He, however, had clearly taken it seriously. And who was I to argue?

It also makes you wonder whether there is anything to fortune-telling. For, as you may remember, barely a year earlier my landlady in Newcastle predicted all this would happen.

The following morning I arrived at the Moulin Rouge very early. I couldn't stop looking at my name up there in lights. It really was a thrilling experience. And the fact that it was all happening at the Moulin Rouge turned it into some kind of fantastic dream.

After the morning rehearsal, which went very well, I felt confident I was going to be a great success. I rehearsed again in the afternoon, and again, just before the show. I was determined to be as good as I possibly could.

My youthful enthusiasm, however, didn't take into account that I only had a certain amount of energy on tap. The result of all my rehearsing was that by the time it came to the actual opening-night performance, I was, to put it mildly, exhausted. So much so, that during my finale on the table I was barely able to finish the routine. My act ended to only a fair amount of applause, and I limped into my dressing room distraught. I really believed I'd blown it. But the management came round afterwards and told me not to worry about a thing. They'd seen me at my best in rehearsal, they said, and knew what I was capable of. They suggested that I find something to do before going into my finale – in order to give myself a breather.

This presented me with something of a problem. The following day, however, I hit on an idea which I thought might just work. Once, in a circus, I'd seen a clown sewing his fingers together with an imaginary needle and cotton. It was extremely effective. I devised a variation on this, making it look like I was sewing a button on to a jacket with an invisible needle and thread. (By this time I was no longer wearing a silk shirt. I kept my black silk trousers and wore a white shirt, dinner jacket and black tie.)

That night, I incorporated the mime into the act, thereby giving myself about a minute and a half's breathing space – certainly enough to regain my strength before going into my big finish.

It worked like a dream, and the act ended to terrific applause – the kind I'd rather hoped to get on my opening night. The management were delighted, and the next two weeks were among the happiest I have ever spent. Everyone at the Moulin Rouge was supportive and friendly. Backstage, among the other artistes, there were no rivalries or petty jealousies, while the 'front of house' staff couldn't have been more helpful. The management treated everyone as equals. It didn't matter whether you were a stagehand or a headliner. No one played favourites, and this resulted in the most agreeable working atmosphere I think I've ever known. It was all so different from what I'd experienced in England, where, in most instances, the managements didn't give a damn about anything – except whether or not you put bums on seats. At the Moulin Rouge we were one big happy family, and to this day I think back on my engagement there with tremendous nostalgia.

Those, indeed, were the good old days.

4

Doing the Continental

DURING MY TWO WEEKS at the Moulin Rouge, I finalized a contract to work in Spain for the month of September, and another to work at the Alcazar Theatre in Hamburg, commencing 1 January 1930. Until September, however, I once again found myself with nothing in hand. This was the main problem about 'freelancing' around Europe. The work was so irregular. The money – when I *did* work – wasn't at all bad, and if I'd been guaranteed fifty-two weeks' employment every year, I'd have been laughing. But that was not to be, so, after every engagement, I had to take stock of my financial situation and put aside enough money to live off during the weeks I was unemployed.

At the Moulin Rouge, I'd got to know an acrobatic team who were on the same programme. They knew about my Dresden cancellation, and suggested I join their act and go to South America with them, where they were guaranteed several top bookings. I was sorely tempted, but, in the end, decided against it.

The acrobats were due to sail for South America on 30 May. After waving goodbye to them and wishing them the best of luck, I suddenly fell into a depression. With no work on the horizon, the next three months looked as though they were going to be very bleak indeed. I didn't feel like going back to the hotel, and decided instead to go to the Paramount Cinema, where I knew they showed English-speaking films. At least it would help me forget my troubles for a couple of hours. So I jumped into a taxi. But halfway there something told me to call in at the hotel to see if anyone had left any messages, as I'd now been out for most of the day.

Back at the hotel I almost collapsed with excitement. There, waiting for me, was a cable saying that the Rialto Palais in Dresden had decided to keep open throughout the summer, and that my contract was still in order.

With the help of the *patron*, I checked the times of the Dresden trains – and found there was a train leaving Paris at midnight. I was all packed and ready to go, when suddenly I realized that I needed a visa for Germany. I didn't know what to do. Once again the *patron* came to the rescue. He discovered that my train stopped at Brussels, and suggested I see the German consul there to arrange for a visa. It was, he said, a mere formality.

Unfortunately, I arrived in Brussels at 6.00 a.m., three hours before the German Embassy opened. There was nothing I could do but travel on to Dresden and hope for the best.

The train duly arrived at the German border where it was met by the usual customs and passport control.

Apart from not having my visa, I had a problem with my oval table, which had been left in the baggage van, and which had been taken directly to the Customs Hall. I knew I dared not enter the Customs Hall or go through Passport Control because they'd notice immediately that I didn't have a visa. So I walked up and down the length of the platform for forty-five minutes, beside myself with anxiety. I can't remember what concerned me more: the fear that I might be sent directly back to Paris, or that something might happen to my table. And talking about my table, this is as good a point as any to tell you just how problematic that damn piece of furniture turned out to be.

As it was the highlight of my act, and not all that easy to replace, I lived in constant fear of losing it, or damaging it. And as it didn't fold in half, it was extremely cumbersome to carry around with me wherever I went. In fact, now that I think about it, it was the single most worrying thing in my life, and to this day I still dream that I'm about to go on stage somewhere, and that the table is missing, or that it hasn't been correctly placed. Actors, they say, dream about forgetting their lines. With me, it's the table I dream about forgetting. I was only a professional dancer for about seven years, but, at least twice a year, I still have this recurring nightmare. Which just goes to show what an important part it played in my life.

However, to return to the German border. There I was, walking up and down the platform, immaculately dressed in plus fours, and hoping not to be too conspicuous, when I noticed a man looking at me. After passing him for about the thirtieth time, he suddenly said: 'Excuse me, but you seem to be at a loss. Is there anything I can do to help?'

He was nicely dressed, spoke good English – although I was sure he wasn't English – and seemed genuinely concerned, so I decided to take a chance and pour my heart out to him. I told him all about the cancellation of the contract, the fact that I had no visa for Germany, that I was worried about my table, but frightened to go into the Customs Hall, that I had a deadline in Dresden the next night, and so on.

Meanwhile, during the ten minutes or so it took me to relate my story, a strange thing was happening. Uniformed soldiers and customs officials were walking by, and saluting me. Now that really was puzzling. Perhaps they'd never seen a young man in plus fours before, and thought I must be a titled aristocrat, or something. While they kept saluting, the man who was listening to my story kept reassuring me that everything would be satisfactorily resolved. He asked me where my compartment was, and I showed him. Then he offered to buy me a cup of tea.

By now I was totally confused. It wasn't tea I needed, it was a visa. And the assurance that my table would be returned to me in one piece!

At last the train was ready for departure. I went back to my compartment, and there, standing in front of it, were two uniformed men. 'This is it,' I thought. 'This is the end of me.'

They saluted yet again, and one of them said, 'Please come with us.' Obviously I was never meant to dance in Dresden!

Between them they carried my cases, and, to my surprise, escorted me to a first-class compartment marked PRIVATE.

By now I was more intrigued than ever, and decided to ask them what was going on. I couldn't speak much German, but I managed to make myself understood by speaking Yiddish, which is quite similar. They told me that the gentleman I'd been talking to was the Chief of the Secret Police, that he'd telegraphed Dresden, and that I'd have no more problems.

Finally, I arrived in Dresden, and there, waiting to greet me at the station, was Oscar Bollinger, the artistic director who'd booked me into the Rialto Palais. With him was the Dresden Chief of Police.

Oscar couldn't have been more welcoming or warmer, and I was taken into a private office where the Chief of Police stamped my passport with a visa that allowed me to enter Germany officially.

Luck was with me yet again.

Years later, whenever I think about this whole incident, I cannot help wondering what a different ending there might have been had it all taken place in 1939 rather than in 1929 . . .

Oscar Bollinger had arranged lodgings in a small apartment, and the people who ran the place were very nice to me. If there was any anti-Semitism in Germany at the time – and, of course, there was – it somehow managed to pass me by. I was not really aware of the atrocious political situation that was brewing, and, as far as I was concerned, I was simply a cabaret performer fulfilling one more engagement. I can't even remember whether the name Hitler meant anything to me at the time or not. Or whether I'd even *heard* of such a person. Politics, you see, could not have been further from my thoughts.

My opening night at the Rialto Palais went well. The Chief of the Dresden Police and his family were there, and seemed to enjoy it all enormously. Everybody did, because no one in that part of the world had seen the charleston before. It was all so new and fresh to them.

In fact, it was such a novelty that soon after the performance Oscar Bollinger came up to me and said, 'Starting from tomorrow, I want you to do four shows a day. I want you to do two here in the main room at the Rialto; one in the afternoon and the late-night show at 11 p.m. During the day you'll work the downstairs room at the Rialto, then go on to the exhibition centre six miles away.' He promised to provide a car to get me back from the exhibition centre to the Rialto in time for the eleven o'clock performance.

This was to be my first experience of what was called 'doubling', or, in this instance, 'quadrupling'. The main problem was that each time I finished a show I had to rush to the next venue and make sure my table was correctly placed. It was really tough

65

going, but I was so excited about my success I somehow managed to cope. I also knew I'd be getting extra money for these additional performances, though, at the time, it didn't occur to me to ask how much. In fact, they doubled my salary.

After about the third late-night performance at the Rialto Palais, I noticed a beautiful girl in the audience. She was there the following night, and the night after that. I told Oscar about her and asked him what he thought she was up to. 'She probably fancies you,' he said. 'After all, you're a slim, attractive young man, so why shouldn't she? Tell you what,' he said, 'I'll bring her backstage to your dressing room if she comes again.' Well, sure enough, the following night she was in her usual place, and after the performance Oscar brought her round to meet me. She really was a very pretty girl, and I must admit I fancied her. We struck up a relationship, and I walked back to her apartment every night after my last performance. But I never went to bed with her. After four shows a day, all I had the strength for was a cuddle on her doorstep and a bit of a canoodle, even though she kept inviting me up.

Well, this ritual went on for almost two weeks, until the fourteenth night when I couldn't resist her any longer and agreed to go up to her apartment.

As soon as we got inside, she undressed and sat down on a settee. Then, while I was undressing, she casually picked up a pack of cards and started turning them over. Just as I was about to take off my underpants, she said: 'I see I've got money coming to me. . . .'

I quickly pulled up my trousers. 'Not from me, *liebchen*,' I said.

She must have realized what I was thinking. She gently touched my cheek and murmured, 'No, not from you, *liebchen*.'

After that night she didn't leave my side. She came to all my shows and gave the impression that she would like to come with me when I left for Berlin. I realized that I had got myself into a real fix, and in desperation asked Oscar Bollinger what he thought I should do. Oscar, being a man of the world, was extremely helpful, and suggested I take the midnight train.

'Good idea,' I said, 'but it means I'll have to miss the 11 p.m. performance.' 'No problem,' he said. 'We'll find someone else to take your place.'

And that's exactly what happened. Oscar found a replacement, and I took the midnight train to Berlin alone.

In case anyone reading this thinks that I behaved like a complete heel, I agree with them. I did. And I'm not in the least bit proud of it. In my defence all I can say is that I was a young twenty-two-year-old, and that nothing quite like that had ever happened to me before. I was taken by surprise and simply allowed my passion to outweigh my sense of reality. At any rate, as the train sped from Dresden to Berlin, I wasn't happy with what I'd done. In fact, I hated myself, and my only consolation was that I knew she wouldn't be alone for very long.

*   *   *

Berlin in 1929 was considered to be the most decadent city in Europe. Or so I've been told. But as far as I was concerned it was just another thriving town which offered me the prospects of work. The threat of Nazi-socialism, and the numerous propaganda revues and satirical cabarets which the political situation was supposed to have created, made no impact on me at all. My brief stay in Berlin was taken up seeing agents and landing a seven-day contract to appear at a glittering ballroom called the Barbarina. Besides, I really didn't have the money to spend on entertainment. In Paris it was slightly different. After I'd appeared at the Moulin Rouge and established a bit of a reputation, I could frequent every cabaret and nightspot in that city without having to pay. The Bal Tabarin, for example, always provided me with a loggia, or box seat, and champagne on the house – which, though I didn't drink, was much appreciated by the girls I brought there. In Paris I was something of a celebrity. In Germany few people had ever heard of me, and that made quite a difference to my social life. I was, you might say, living from hand to mouth.

I spent about ten days in Berlin, including the week at the Barbarina, for which I was paid the equivalent of about £8 a performance – which was the going rate at the time. Then, with no other work on the horizon, I returned to Paris where Vincent Massi found a ten-week spot for me in the Palace Theatre Revue.

The Palace Theatre was very famous in Paris, and similar in

style to the Folies-Bergère. I'd been hired to replace Hal Sherman, the well-known American eccentric dancer. Sherman, you may remember, was the man who first introduced eccentric comedy dancing into England, and was one of the few dancers who influenced my own style. He had to leave the Palace to take up a commitment in America, and that's how I got the job.

Accepting the Palace engagement meant cancelling my booking in Spain, but I didn't really mind. The management at the Palace gave me star billing, and, as an added attraction, the show boasted several dozen beautiful chorus girls, most of whom walked around backstage in the nude. This no longer embarrassed me, and I made friends with many of them. I was growing more and more confident every day, and the combination of my success in this area, plus my undisputed ability as an eccentric dancer was, as far as I was concerned, a winning one. I felt on top of the world.

Despite my success in Paris, though, during the run at the Palace Theatre Revue I started to think about returning to England, and wrote to an agent called Tom Rice, a representative of the Walter Bentley Agency. I described my act to him, and enclosed photographs, reviews and publicity material. A week later I received a nice reply which, to my surprise, was followed by a telegram offering me a booking at the Stratford Empire beginning Monday, 11 November 1929. The Stratford belonged to the Moss Empires circuit, and was one of the better houses in London. I was thrilled.

So, as soon as my engagement at the Palace came to an end, I packed my bags, checked out of the Olympic Hotel and sailed for England.

Returning to the drabness of London was a bit of a jolt after my colourful experiences in Europe, but it was something I had to do. Making a reputation on the continent was one thing, but I knew that if I really wanted to become a star, it would have to be in London.

Understandably, I was nervous and anxious about the Stratford booking. I knew my routine worked well enough abroad, but was it solid enough for audiences who had grown up in music halls? Well, we'd soon see.

Most performers find that their first night on a variety bill is never all that good because, although they've rehearsed the music, the orchestra isn't always perfectly in step, and it takes a couple of performances for everything to go right. Of course, this doesn't apply to established stars who have their own musical directors.

And I wasn't in that league, yet. In fact, when I arrived at Stratford, I discovered I was the opening act on the bill – which is, traditionally, as low down as you can get.

And this, after being a headliner in Paris!

Still, the money wasn't bad – £27 10s a week, which was quite an improvement on the half-share of the £20 I was earning when I worked with Al Gold.

At any rate, I weathered the opening spot, and, despite the number of latecomers who arrived during my entire act, received some solid applause.

During the intermission, Tom Rice came into my dressing room and told me he was with a Mr Wingrove, the chief booker for the Moss Empire circuit, which, together with Stoll Theatres, had all the music halls in Britain tied up. 'Wingrove saw your act,' Rice said, 'and liked it so much, he's booked you into the Victoria Palace next week. He wants you to open the second half.'

Considering I'd only been back a couple of weeks, this was quite an achievement, and I honestly believed I was well on my way to stardom. Opening the second half is far more prestigious than opening the show, and the Victoria Palace was far more prestigious than the Stratford Empire. So, naturally, I was thrilled.

My act improved throughout the week at Stratford, and by the time I played the Victoria Palace I was on pretty safe ground. Tom Rice, who was not only an agent but a friend, brought the booker of the Stoll circuit to see me, and the result was a tour commencing in May 1930.

My next engagement, however, was at the Alcazar Theatre, Hamburg, on 1 January. This time my travelling documents were all in order, and I arrived without incident in Hamburg late in the afternoon of 31 December. The theatre had arranged lodgings for me in an apartment block, which was a lot more pleasant than the usual theatrical digs. My room was nice and large, and had a separate entrance to it, as well as a second door which led into the main area of the apartment.

Knowing I had to be up bright and early for rehearsals the following morning, I had a light snack, then went to bed around 8.00 p.m.

While I was sleeping I dreamed that someone was kissing me. I woke up, but there was nobody there. I went back to sleep again. A little while later the same thing happened, and I thought this most strange. I remained in bed – wide awake by now – and about a half an hour later, I suddenly saw the door to the main apartment opening. I immediately switched on my bedside lamp, and there, framed in the doorway, was a very attractive young lady. A year earlier I might not have known how to react to the situation. Now, however, I was receptive to her charms. What a great way to start the New Year, I thought.

I spent the next fifteen nights in Hamburg making passionate love to this gorgeous woman and never, for a moment, felt worried about being tired in the morning because, unlike Dresden, I was only engaged to do one performance a night. I had the whole day in which to relax and regain my strength.

My Hamburg engagement at the Alcazar went well enough. As far as my dancing was concerned, I was as good as I was ever going to be. I had no ambitions to increase my range or add different routines to the act, and as long as audiences applauded, I was blissfully content.

The headliner at the Alcazar was Dante the Magician, whose magic extravaganza comprised the whole second half of the programme. His son and daughter were part of the act as well, and I got to know and like them all. It was a superbly staged act, and I asked Dante whether he'd ever appeared in England. He said he hadn't, but hoped to some day.

My fifteen days (and nights!) in Hamburg came to an end – and I returned to London where Tom Rice had arranged some extra bookings for me.

It was at about this time that I was introduced to an agent called Will Collins, better known in the business as Joe. He was the son of the renowned Will Collins, also an agent, and he was the sole booker for a very high-quality cabaret club called the Ambassadeurs, which was situated in a turning off Regent

Street. Joe managed to get me an engagement at the Ambassadeurs at a handsome fee, and he became a good friend.

During the course of several conversations about the business, I told Joe that while working on the continent I'd seen many wonderful acts which I thought would be suitable for England. He seemed interested in everything I had to say, and suggested I send him written details of these acts. If they sounded right, he said, he'd think about booking them into the Ambassadeurs and some of the other places he handled.

Every act I recommended, Joe hired. They all did well, and he kept asking for more.

In fact, what was happening was that slowly, and imperceptibly, I was beginning to enter the agency business.

Little did I know at the time that scouting for Joe Collins was, once again, about to change my entire life.

Taking Stock

IN THE MIDDLE OF 1930, I decided it was time to work in England on a more regular basis, I had 'done' the continent and needed a break from overseas travel, so Tom Rice arranged two massive provincial tours for me – one with the Stoll group, and one with Moss Empire. It was a thirty-week commitment, and the start to what I really believed, at the time, was a permanent career as a dancer in Great Britain.

And believe me, there was no shortage of work. Music halls and cabarets were greedy for my kind of eccentric dancing, and so were the numerous cinema circuits. At that time, many of the larger cinemas presented stage acts as part of their supporting programme and often I found myself playing two cinemas on the same day – and always having the same problem about getting my damned oval table from one venue to the next without mislaying it or damaging it.

One of the cinema circuits I played was the Granada, owned by Sidney and Cecil Bernstein. I didn't know it then, of course, but one of the longest and most fruitful relationships of my life was to be with the Bernsteins.

Around about this time too, I often shared the bill with a rising young comedian by the name of Tommy Trinder. Again, little did I know that one day, Trinder would become the host and compere of the first 'Sunday Night at the London Palladium', presented, in the early days of commercial TV, by my company ATV.

But that was well into the future. Meantime, my relationship with Joe Collins went from strength to strength, and, whenever I discovered a new and exciting act, I'd let him know about it.

As for my own career, I had no complaints. Tom Rice kept

booking me on the circuits and I found that there were about thirty engagements I could play on a fairly regular basis.

Gradually, however, some of these venues started dropping me, and the reason, not surprisingly, was that I was becoming old hat. They'd seen everything I had to offer and were looking for something fresh and different.

Tom Rice, who was aware of what was happening, suggested that I should change my act. But this was easier said than done. The fact is, I *couldn't* change my act, because there wasn't much more I could do with it. Not as a soloist, anyway. That's when he said I should think about getting a partner. But after my experience with Al Gold (who, by the way, had teamed up with – and later married – a girl called Lola Cordell), I didn't want to have another man. So I thought I'd look for a girl partner.

I found one – and her name was Anna Roth. I'm not sure how we met. I think I advertised in *The Stage*. At first I wasn't a hundred per cent sure she was what I was looking for. Anna was a quiet sort of girl who, in her heart of hearts, really wanted to be a classical dancer. But she was very attractive, and I thought that the contrast between my eccentric stuff and her gentler bits would work very well. And they did. We were known as Grade and Roth.

With a whole new act to offer, Tom had no difficulty in booking us for a thirty-week tour of the circuit. After that we went to Europe playing many of the same dates I had worked as a single – as well as six weeks in Holland on the Tuckinski circuit.

When we returned to England Tom said that the only way he could guarantee more work for me was if I changed the act yet again. In other words, he thought I should get a new partner. So I did, and her name was Bobbie Medlock. She was eighteen years old and I was twenty-seven. Bobbie, a very sweet young blonde, was basically a contortionist and an acrobat, and her solos gave the act an entirely fresh look to it, although my routines never changed and I still did the big finish on the table. We worked up an enjoyable act together and Tom booked us into all the places Anna Roth and I had worked the previous year, except that this time we didn't go to Europe. We were billed as Grade and Medlock – 'Those Superb Dancers' – and some of our London dates included the Metropolitan, Edgware Road, the

London Pavilion on Piccadilly Circus, and the old Alhambra. The Pavilion, I remember, was a particularly strenuous engagement, because of the theatre's non-stop policy. The first show of the day was at 2.15 in the afternoon, and went on continuously until 11.15 at night. The ticket prices, as I recall, ranged from 1/3d to 5s, and audiences could arrive and leave whenever they liked. In other words, we were doing about four or five shows a day, which was incredibly tiring.

Bobbie remained with me for about eight months in all. It was a strictly business relationship, and, though I found her attractive, we were never romantically attached. She married a man called Vic Marlow, and for years they did an act called Medlock and Marlow. I believe they retired in 1964.

Not long after Bobbie left the act, I went to the London Hippodrome to see a show called 'Bow Bells'. One of the girls in the company was Marjorie Pointer, and I was immediately struck by her good looks and her talent as a dancer. Like Anna Roth, she was classically trained and, I thought, had a lot of style. So I arranged to meet her and asked her whether she'd like to work with me. I made no secret of the fact that I really fancied her, and she obviously fancied me too, because as soon as we started working together a great romance blossomed. I'd bought a car shortly after meeting Marjorie and I remember driving with her across the country from one booking to another. It was all very romantic – and our act was really quite classy. We'd begin with a kind of tap dance duet, then, while Marjorie was changing her costume, I'd do one of my eccentric comedy numbers. I'd go off, and Marjorie would do her big solo spot – a jazz ballet, or something equally 'modern', as I recall. Inevitably the act ended with my big finish on the table. It was simple, but quite effective.

All the same, though, I suddenly began to feel that my own career as a dancer was coming to an end. By 1934 the charleston was no longer the craze it had been in the 1920s, and I had nothing to replace it with. My limitations were becoming more and more apparent. The Fred Astaire and Ginger Rogers films were all the rage by now, and each week the musicals that were coming out of Hollywood introduced some terrific new dancing talents to the world. I really felt that I couldn't compete. My range was just too narrow. Even my brother Bernie was more versatile now than I was. In fact, by 1934 he was doing extremely well for himself. He and Al Sutan had split up when Al got married, and, after starving in Europe for a while, Bernie met a beautiful girl called Toko, who was half-Japanese, and they formed a successful partnership together called Delfont and Toko – Syncopated Steps Appeal. They stayed together until 1937, which is a long time for a dance duo, and gives you some idea of how good they were.

As for my brother Leslie, he was sixteen years old, and doing well for himself in the rag trade. In fact, he was making quite good money until he got into some financial trouble. He'd gone into business on his own, which, at that age, was very enterprising of him. But he made the mistake of buying things on credit, and overextending himself. When I heard about this, I got so angry that I really read him the riot act. Now I don't often get that angry – but I just couldn't restrain myself. He owed his creditors about £500 and that, in 1934, was a fortune. I immediately took over his financial responsibilities, and personally promised to pay every one of his creditors. And I did. It took a while, but, in the end, everyone got their money. There was no way I was going to allow Leslie to continue in business on his own, so I got him a job as an office boy with a woman called Florence Leddington, the booker for the Syndicate Theatre Chain who had the Metropolitan in Edgware Road, as well as the Chelsea Palace, the Palace in Walthamstow and the Palace Watford – about seven theatres in all. It was the best thing that could have happened to him because it provided him with a direct introduction to show business and the agency game. After that Leslie never looked back.

Just to complete the family portrait, my sister Rita was about nine or ten at the time, and very much the spoiled baby of the family. But with three grown-up brothers, that was only to be expected. My father was still working for Jack Isow's in the Commercial Road, near Bow, and barely earning a living. Bernie and I helped as much as we could and, somehow, my parents managed.

Then tragedy struck. In 1935, at the age of fifty-six, my father died. He'd never been a particularly healthy man and he came down with Hodgkin's disease. He was confined to Hammersmith Hospital, and to see him deteriorating over a long period of time, getting weaker and weaker, was absolutely heartbreaking for the family. Bernie and I visited him whenever we could, but often weeks went by when we were on tour without our managing to see him. This made us feel guilty, of course, but by now we were the sole breadwinners of the family and we had to keep working, no matter what. All in all it was a very distressing time – especially for my mother, who suddenly found herself a widow at the age of fifty-two.

My father wasn't the kind of man to concern himself with insurance, so it was entirely up to us to keep my mother and Rita provided for. Which we did. In fact, the money the three Grade boys managed to contribute to the well-being of the family was sufficient to buy a modern de luxe flat in Pullman Court, Streatham, not long after my father died. It had three bedrooms, a sitting room and a nice little balcony. It was certainly the most pleasant home we'd had since arriving in this country years earlier.

By mid-1934, the time had come for me to take stock of my situation. I was twenty-seven years old, and not getting any younger. The charleston, as I say, was on the way out, and I had water on the knee by now, which could be extremely painful. Most nights I'd come off stage with bleeding kneecaps and would have to put ointment on them. At the beginning of my career, I should have had the intelligence to use kneepads. But I didn't. And later, when I tried to pad myself a bit, I found the pads restricted my movements and slowed me down. So, one way and another, I realized the time was coming to call it a day. The only thing about my act which could possibly change was my partner, and, as Tom Rice correctly said to me, there was a limit to the number of times I could tour the country pretending to have an entirely new routine.

Deep down I knew I should be thinking about some other aspect of the business for myself: like becoming an agent. I've always had an instinct for what will or won't work in the theatre – as my recommendations to Joe Collins successfully proved – and there was no reason at all why I shouldn't put these instincts to good use.

The friendlier I became with Joe Collins, the more I realized that the agency business was definitely worth pursuing, and when Collins asked me to sit in for him at his office one day, while he attended to some business in the provinces, I was only too happy to do so. It felt great, sitting behind his desk. One afternoon, the telephone rang, and the voice at the end of the phone said he was a cinema manager looking for an act. I suggested Grade and Pointer. I was all buoyant and excited and rather pleased with myself, until I discovered the whole thing was a gag perpetrated by an agent-friend of mine called Brian Roxbury. Naturally, I was deflated, but I took it all in good spirits.

One day I was walking along Charing Cross Road, heading towards Soho where most of the agents' offices were located, when a man approached me and asked me if I knew the way to the IVTA offices. IVTA was an agency that booked artists for South Africa, as well as representing a few acts of their own. 'Certainly,' I said, 'I'm going that way myself.' Making conversation, he asked me whether I was in show business, and I told him I was. He introduced himself as Harry Smirk and casually told me he'd just bought the Winter Gardens in Morecambe and was looking for acts. 'Well,' I said, 'I hope some day I can play your theatre. But more important, I hope I'll get the chance to book a few acts for you as I intend to become an agent.' 'Fine,' he said. 'If you succeed, get in touch with me.' We reached the IVTA offices, said goodbye, and that was that.

A short while later Joe Collins mentioned to me that the Alhambra Theatre, which then occupied the site of the Odeon, Leicester Square, needed an attraction for two months. I told Joe about Dante and his Magical Extravaganza and suggested he try and sell the act to the Alhambra, which was part of the Stoll Theatres Group.

He did, and Dante stayed the eight weeks and was an extraordinary success. As soon as the Alhambra engagement was over, Collins signed up Dante and his troupe for a major provincial tour. After this I had no doubt in my mind that my future definitely lay in being an agent.

While all this was happening, I'd been seeing a lot of my brother Bernie's ex-partner, Albert Sutan, whose stage name was now Eddie May. One day, Albert came to me and said: 'Lew, I know you've always wanted to be an agent. Well, so have I, so why don't we become partners?' He then flashed a bundle of notes at me. 'I've got all the backing we need, so how about it? You can book the dates and run the office, and I'll stage the shows.' As he was so convincing, and so enthusiastic – and seemed to have the money – I agreed.

The first thing Albert did was put together a band show called 'Eddie May and his Hollywood Serenaders'. In Europe I'd seen a wonderful trumpet player called Louis D. Vries, whom some people considered even greater than Louis Armstrong. I suggested him to Albert, who thought it a terrific idea, and he now billed the show 'Eddie May and his Hollywood Serenaders – with Louis D. Vries'. They did the whole second half of the show.

Our opening date was Oldham, where we lost a bit of money. But it was a useful try-out for the show. Besides, money, it would appear, wasn't a problem. Albert seemed to have stacks of the stuff. He also doubled as conductor and dancer in front of the orchestra.

Our next date was Belfast. The box-office take wasn't bad, but not good enough to pay out the full company, or the transportation and scenery costs, which were quite hefty. But still Albert didn't seem too concerned. He continued spending money as if it grew on trees, and when I asked him where it all came from, he said he had a backer who'd won the Irish Sweep Stake. This was true, for I later discovered that the girl singer in the show was the backer's sweetheart. I also learned that the amount of money our backer had won wasn't all that tremendous.

After Belfast we went to Cork. It was pouring with rain when we arrived and the theatre was flooded. Not surprisingly, we played to nearly no business at all. I was worried to distraction. But Albert Sutan remained totally unconcerned. On the Saturday night I couldn't stand it any longer and demanded to know where the pay-out money – about £550 – was coming from. 'We'll pay them by cheque,' he replied. I gave everyone in the company enough cash to pay for their digs, and the rest I paid out in cheques.

Later that night, after we'd returned to our digs, Albert told me the cheques, which were his mother's, weren't any good.

There was no money in the bank.

Well, I just didn't know what to do, and thought it was the end of the road for me and my show-business aspirations. I was reminded of that time in Paris when Mr Bray did me out of my earnings, and I was at the end of my tether. I can cope with anything except lies and dishonesty. Indeed, throughout my entire life I have been known for my straightforward, up-front approach to business. My word has always been my bond. I have never reneged on a promise or gone back on a deal – and, believe me, there have been many occasions in my life when it would have been easy to do so, as I have often entered into major negotiations without the benefit of a contract. From the earliest age, my parents, who were tolerant about most things, only lost their tempers if they caught me lying. As a result, I always told the truth. Even when it wasn't in my best interests.

I can remember an incident in my childhood when my father knocked on my bedroom door and asked me what I was doing. I was about seven years old at the time, and it so happened I was playing 'doctor' with a little girl my own age. We were in bed together, and I told my father the truth. In that particular instance the truth really hurt because he gave me a hiding I've never forgotten. It would have been so easy to have said we were playing with some toys – but I didn't, because I'd always been told never to lie.

At any rate, with regard to those bad cheques, I just couldn't face the prospect of having them returned, unhonoured, to a company I was associated with, and I found out from Albert who his backer was and where he lived. His name was Abrahams, and he lived in Jersey. I told Albert I had to go to Jersey as soon as possible. 'It won't do you any good,' Albert said. 'I've had all the money I can get out of him. You haven't got a hope in hell.' All the same, I said, 'I've got to give it a try,' and I flew to Jersey in a small, two-seater plane. I'd never flown before, and I was petrified. But I knew that, somehow, I just had to get the money.

I arrived in Jersey, and met Abrahams. He was about my age, perhaps a little younger, and I explained the whole situation to him. He was sympathetic, said that he appreciated my concern, and although he only had about £2000 left, offered to give me four hundred of it. This meant I was still £150 short.

I flew back to London, banked the £400, then tapped everyone I knew for a loan in order to meet the balance of the debt. Finally, when every penny was accounted for, I told Albert Sutan I didn't think we had a future together, and we split. At the time, we had a little office in Charing Cross Road and I decided to keep it on and to run it as economically as possible with an assistant called Dena Waldman. The idea was that I'd look for a few acts to handle, and gradually ease myself into the agency business.

Towards the end of the year, I got a theatre on a guarantee-and-percentage basis in Southampton, and provided my own bill. I was in the show too, without Marjorie Pointer, and after the performance each night – at about 11 o'clock – I'd motor back to London in order to be in the office at seven o'clock the following morning. Then, at four in the afternoon, I'd leave London and drive down to Southampton and repeat the whole tiring process all over again.

At the end of the week, not only was I broke, but I also had debts of about £60, and couldn't even pay for my digs – at least, not out of the theatre receipts. Added to all this was the fact that by now my knees were really killing me, and I'd walk off the stage each night looking bloodied and bruised.

It was at this low-spot in my career that I decided, once and for all, to give up dancing altogether, and to concentrate on becoming an agent. I conveyed my feelings to Marjorie Pointer, who wasn't all that upset by my decision. Marjorie was much 'grander' than I was, and although for the eighteen months or so we were together we worked well enough, I think she felt that she was cut out for better things. I suggested to her that she should form an act with two other girls, that they should call themselves The Pointer Trio – and that they should let me handle their bookings.

I entered the agency business with no artistic collateral, so to speak. In other words, I had no one on my books of any note. I did, however, hear of a young harmonica player called Louis Almaer. Thanks to Larry Adler, harmonica players were very popular in Britain at the time, and I was convinced that I could get work for Almaer. I became his manager, and although I didn't yet have the clout to book him directly into a theatre, I managed to find him work through Joe Collins, with whom I split the commission.

Collins, incidentally, had suggested I join his agency. I'd be happy to, I said, but only as a partner. But Joe wouldn't hear of this. He wanted me as an employee as he didn't feel I was experienced or important enough to warrant a full partnership.

I must also add that at this stage of my career I was considered a bit of a joke. I'd always be in my office by 7.00 a.m., and, even though the mail didn't get in until an hour later, I used the time to relax, to think about the day's work, and generally to get my day into some kind of perspective. It's a practice I've adopted for over fifty years.

Though my phone hardly ever rang, I proved to be an excellent manager to Louis Almaer, taking care of his harmonicas, his clothes, and anything else I thought necessary. He earned good money, and, as his personal manager, I took a respectable commission.

One morning a circular letter arrived from the Winter Gardens Theatre, Morecambe. Apparently it had been sent to every agency, and it said, 'We need an act for next Monday, to open the second half of the programme. Please call my home any time or the theatre at night.' It was signed Harry Smirk, the same man I'd directed to the IVTA offices a few months earlier. I read this circular and racked my brains to see if I could come up with anything. Suddenly, I recalled an act called Beams' Breezy Babes, which consisted of twenty-four little girls aged between twelve and fourteen, with a lead singer-dancer who was fourteen years old, but looked twelve. This girl was Kathleen Moody. It was only much later on that I met her – and even then I didn't realize that she was the lead singer in the first act I'd booked into the Winter Gardens Theatre.

I telephoned Mrs Beams and found that the act was available for Monday, then called Harry Smirk at his home, and he booked them.

I went to Morecambe for the opening night, which was the following Monday, and the act was an outstanding success.

Harry Smirk and his other directors were extremely pleased and impressed that I'd bothered to come all the way to Morecambe just to see an act open the second half of a programme.

They invited me to supper, and we all got on very well. I told them a little about myself, reminded Harry of our first meeting, then suddenly found the courage to say, 'Why don't you let me become the exclusive booking agent for your theatre?' 'Because,' said Smirk's directors, 'all agents are crooks.' 'Okay,' I said, 'you're entitled to your opinion. But why don't you give me a chance to prove you wrong.' 'Fine,' they said, 'we'll give you a trial period.'

Being the exclusive booking agent for the Winter Gardens Theatre made a huge difference to me. It enabled me to find acts belonging to other agents, and to book my own few acts into the theatres they represented. However, because I was still a virtual unknown in the agency business, I was rarely able to make personal contact with the booking managers of the principal circuits. I couldn't even get some of them on the phone! It was therefore often necessary for me to book the acts I handled through one or two reputable, well-established agents, and Joe Collins became my principal go-between.

I then decided I'd try to drum up some business at the Argyle Theatre, Birkenhead. The Argyle was a famous little house in which many stars made their reputations, and often took smaller fees than those they were used to just so they could be seen by all the provincial bookers. The owner, Mr T. D. Clarke, was very tough, or so I was told. But I decided to tackle him anyway. I went to see him personally, and persuaded him to allow me to put in a full programme for two weeks at a fixed sum of money. He was so pleased with the results, he let me have an additional twelve weeks.

Next, I tried the Theatre Royal, St Helens. I saw a Miss Mary Newcombe there, and talked her into giving me six weeks a year.

The word soon got round that I was putting in good programmes at Morecambe, Birkenhead and St Helens, and I was able to make the same arrangements with the Hippodrome, Wigan.

It was suddenly all coming together for me, I was learning fast, and definitely moving in the right direction.

6

Enter Kathie

B Y 1936 I ALREADY HAD the nucleus of an agency, although I still wasn't able to book directly with any of the major circuits – Stoll Theatres, Moss Empires and General Theatres Corporation (including the London Palladium). In addition, there were the ABC, Granada and Gaumont Cinema circuits. Most cinemas, quite apart from showing films, booked anything up to three or four acts a week.

I now felt I had to strengthen my catalogue of acts, and decided to go to the continent again. It was at this point that my career really moved forward.

I arrived in Europe knowing just how difficult a task I had if I wanted to represent a large number of acts. The principal agent in England for continental artistes was a man called Stanley Wathon. He had a great reputation, and booked nearly all the attractions for the Tower Circus, Blackpool (which played for thirty-two weeks a year). He also serviced several other circuses, including Bertram Mills and Olympia. Wathon had been at it for many years now, and 'specialty' acts, you might say, were his thing.

Undaunted, I set off on my first trip which was to be quite extensive. I started in Paris, then went to Belgium, Switzerland and Germany, often seeing as many as three performances a night.

But it was definitely worth the effort, and I returned to England three weeks later with several exciting new acts to promote.

Almost as soon as I started in the agency business I developed an instinct for what would or wouldn't work, and it wasn't long before I was so proficient at talent-spotting, I could smell a headliner a mile away. And my judgements were rarely, if ever, wrong. Not only could I recognize talent when I saw it; I could assess its worth on any bill. More important, I knew which theatres would be best for certain acts, and in what order the acts should be presented on the bill. Early on in my career I discovered you could kill a show stone dead if the running order was wrong.

As soon as I returned to England, I discussed with Joe Collins all the acts I'd signed. Joe, having so much confidence in my judgement, used his connections to book them with the major circuits for a minimum of eight weeks each. They were all successful and proved how richly endowed the continent was with novelty acts. So much so that, Wathon notwithstanding, we were determined to go after the European market ourselves.

At this point in our relationship Joe finally offered me the full partnership I'd always wanted, and we became the Collins and Grade Agency. Our premises were at 41 Charing Cross Road, facing the London Hippodrome and the offices of Moss and Stoll Theatres, which, incidentally, ATV (the company I was later to found) subsequently owned. Thus continued the circle of coincidences which have occurred throughout my career.

I wasn't at all surprised that Stanley Wathon harboured a tremendous hatred towards me. He had never had a real competitor before, and refused to take me seriously at first. But after I'd managed to persuade the Bertram Mills and Blackpool Tower circuses to book a few of my acts, I was suddenly a real threat.

I now realized I had to spend weeks at a time on the continent, and found myself increasingly involved with circus people, cementing friendships and building relationships. Even in those days, a good working relationship with the people you did business with was the most important thing of all.

The circus proprietors were very nice to me. My enthusiasm was infectious and they all knew I genuinely wanted to learn the business. In the entertainment game you're always learning, no matter how old you are or how long you've been at it.

During my visits to Europe I built up a fine relationship with Circus Krone in Munich, Circus Scott in Sweden and the Knie family of the Circus Knie in Switzerland. I also got to know the Circus Schumann of Copenhagen, who were famous for their incredible horses.

By now the agency of Collins and Grade represented about a hundred acts. But I did more than just book these acts.

I used to meet them at the railway stations when they arrived, take them to their lodgings (nobody stayed in hotels), and, as I was naturally adept at figures, do their tax returns at the end of their engagements. In fact, come to think of it, for the 10 per cent commission they paid me, I gave them a service nobody else could provide.

My main problem, as far as the circuses were concerned, was a logistical one. At the beginning of each season, all the European circuses started at approximately the same time and I had to make sure I forestalled Wathon by getting to some of them a day or two earlier than he did. Fortunately, I had a close friend who had a small, but good circus in Denmark. He opened two days before the Circus Schumann, and I persuaded him to do a preview to which he invited all the town's celebrities. That way I was able to be one step ahead of Wathon whose anger with me got worse and worse.

Some years later, when the Second World War had commenced, Stanley Wathon, who was German, was the subject of an enquiry and he was interned for the duration of the war. By that time, however, the managements of the Blackpool Tower and Bertram Mills circuses knew that if they wanted the best continental talent, they had to come directly to me for it.

Being a fully fledged partner of Joe Collins provided me with instant access to all the managements who hitherto hadn't given me the time of day. My reputation as a spotter of quality acts grew, and I was fast making a name for myself in the business.

As I mentioned before, in those days most of the cinema circuits, such as the Granada, Rank, ABC and Union Cinemas, had stage acts sandwiched between the films, and I arranged a meeting with Miss Stephanie Anderson who was the booking manager for the ABC and Union cinema circuits. I'd just returned from Europe, and recommended one of my acts to her. Sight unseen, she booked it.

The act was called Satsuma and Ona and it was a 'perch' act. For the uninitiated, a perch act is one in which the man lays on his back on a little stand on the floor, balances a pole about forty feet high on his feet, while his partner climbs to the top of the pole and performs a succession of balancing tricks. The finale of this act had the man at the top of the pole dropping a big, sharp knife in the direction of his partner, who would then catch it in his hand. While this was going on, the stand would be swaying out towards the audience.

Satsuma and Ona did three performances a day, including a 2.00 p.m. matinee. I remember I was out at lunch one afternoon when Joe Collins received a telephone call from Miss Anderson asking him to meet her immediately at the Carlton Cinema, Islington. Joe was in a panic, and as soon as I returned he said: 'You've got us into terrible trouble. Stephanie's received a call from the manager of the theatre to say the act is horrible and she's insisting we get there immediately to see the 4.30 performance.'

I couldn't bear it. I was in a state of shock. Was this my first failure as an agent? As soon as we arrived I said to the manager, 'I don't know how you can say this act is horrible. Personally, I think it's one of the most sensational acts I've ever seen.' The manager then said: 'I didn't say it was horrible. I said it was horribly frightening!'

It just shows how easily a person can be misunderstood! And the trouble it can cause.

Well, we saw the act with Miss Anderson, and it was phenomenal. The press gave it tremendous coverage and audiences were thrilled by it.

The following week Satsuma and Ona were due to go to Birmingham where they had to win the approval of the Watch Committee who checked out every act to see whether or not it was suitable, or how dangerous it was. Mr George Black, then the head of the General Theatres Corporation, and Mr Val Parnell supported the duo, and once again they were a sensation. So much so, that for several years they were one of our regulars.

After I'd established a solid reputation booking foreign circus and specialty acts, I decided to branch out a bit and find some performers more suited to a theatre or cabaret than a tent. In Paris, for example, at the Hot Club, I saw a fantastic group called The Quintet de Hot Club de France, whose stars were Django Reinhardt and Stefan Grappelly. Without doubt, Django was the greatest guitarist I'd ever heard, while Stefan was probably the finest jazz violinist of all time. I returned to London full of enthusiasm, and, such was the high standing of our office, we were immediately able to book Reinhardt and Grappelly as headliners. They opened at the Ardwick Theatre, Manchester, which was part of the Stoll Theatre Group, and were so well-received I had no trouble getting them a full circuit booking. This was the first time I'd engaged such a quality act, and its popularity convinced me to cover the whole spectrum of entertainment on the continent, and to sign such stars as Edith Piaf, Jean Sablon and Patachou. After that, I created a two-way traffic and began booking English acts into Europe.

With the impressive list of attractions we now had on our books, Joe and I decided to stage our own programmes. We'd get a guarantee and a percentage from the theatre owners, and take the risk of either losing or making money.

We were becoming really important agents now, and it looked as though our partnership was all set for a long and healthy run. We even managed to book a few acts into the prestigious London Palladium, which occasionally had short variety seasons featuring local headliners. Most of the Palladium's artistes, however, were American.

A Collins and Grade act was fast becoming a fixture with almost every management in the country, and one of our most lucrative outlets was pantomime. In London, for example, no pantomime ever had less than two of our artistes on the bill. In addition to our specialty acts, we represented several excellent comedians, including Issy Bonn, a Jewish comedian with a wonderful singing voice. And whenever we booked him, we supplied the rest of the programme as well.

One of the biggest agencies in the country was Fosters Agency because Harry Foster represented the mighty William Morris Agency of America in Europe. In 1938 Fosters booked an act into the London Palladium called The Diamond Brothers, who were a smash hit. They were one of the best comedy knockabout acts ever seen in Britain, and I got quite pally with them. Towards the end of the year I suggested we did a revue together called 'Running Wild'. They liked the sound of it, and, after discussing the general outline of the show, we completed negotiations. They needed a leading lady who could sing, dance and

87

feed them gags, and the following day they telephoned me and said, 'Right. We've found the girl.' 'Fine,' I said. 'Send her up to my office.'

A while later in walked this lovely young girl. She looked fourteen but was actually seventeen, and her name was Kathleen Moody, the very same girl who sang for Beams' Breezy Babes.

There was something charming and vulnerable about this girl, and I found myself becoming very protective towards her – which is why I told her she wasn't right for the part.

She was terribly distressed by this and said she'd been especially picked by the Diamond Brothers. 'That's all very well,' I said, 'but we're paying the salaries and taking all the responsibility.' Naturally, she wanted to know why I wasn't giving her the job, and I told her I thought she looked too young. Actually, the truth of it was that I felt the Diamond Brothers' gags would be far too coarse and crude for this sweet, innocent girl, and I didn't think she would be able to cope with them. She pleaded with me, but I flatly refused to change my mind. Later, I had quite an argument with the Diamond Brothers about this, and told them they needed a much more mature singer. In the end, the job went to someone else, the show went on tour, was a big success and we made money.

In addition to 'Running Wild', we had several major attractions touring in theatres throughout the country, and we were fast establishing a reputation as one of the leading agencies in England.

The Quintet de Hot Club de France were a tremendous hit and, because I knew I'd have no difficulty booking them all over the country, I agreed to stand surety for Django Reinhardt who wanted to buy a new car, but didn't have sufficient funds. He was a safe bet, I thought, and, besides, that's what agents are for. Grappelly, meantime, was living in style at the White House apartments, near Regent's Park, and enjoying his first English summer enormously.

It was 1939 and life couldn't be better.

Then, on 3 September, I woke up to the terrible news that war had been declared. My immediate concern was for all the foreign artistes we had working in Britain, many of whom were German.

There was no time to lose, and we quickly made arrangements

for all those who wanted to leave the country.

The Quintet de Hot Club de France were due to start an engagement on the following Monday at the Finsbury Park Empire, but I received a call from Stefan Grappelly to say that Django and the rest of the group had left the country just as soon as they had heard the news about the war. They returned to the continent in Django's new, unpaid-for car, and, as I'd agreed to stand surety for him, it was up to me to pay for it. Needless to say, Django had left without a thought of making good his debt.

Stefan remained in London for a while, but eventually he, too, returned to France.

Meanwhile, throughout all this time I had kept up my relationship with Morecambe. Harry Smirk had become a close and valuable friend, and I continued to provide complete programmes at Birkenhead, Wigan and St Helens. I'd also built up a relationship with the Broadhead circuit, who owned theatres in Manchester, Salford and Preston.

Every four weeks I made a tour of the circuit. I'd get up at four in the morning, drive first to Birkenhead, then on to Manchester, St Helens, Wigan, Oldham and Preston, which was the headquarters of the Broadhead circuit. It was important to keep in touch, for the whole of show business relies on the building-up of relationships, no matter in which branch you happen to be involved.

When the war began, nobody really knew what would happen to the entertainment industry, but at the beginning it seemed to go on unchanged for quite a while. For me, at any rate, it was business as usual.

One afternoon I popped into the Quality Inn in Leicester Square for a cup of coffee and saw Kathleen Moody sitting there with a group of girls. I didn't know what to do. I couldn't forget that I'd turned her down for the Diamond Brothers' revue, and felt a bit embarrassed. But there was no way I could avoid her.

I smiled in her direction, and got a sort of half-smile back. It would have seemed cowardly not to say hello, so I walked over to her table and asked the group whether I could join them for coffee. After a bit of awkward small talk I began to relax, and so did she. In fact, by the time I'd drunk my coffee, we were getting on so well together that I invited her to watch me play table tennis at a club in Frith Street. I explained, all over again, why I didn't think she'd have been suitable for the Diamond Brothers' show, managing to avoid the *real* reason – that I was secretly very attracted to her and didn't like the idea of her being exposed to smutty jokes and suggestive routines. She was, she said, touched by my concern but assured me she could look after herself.

It was the beginning of a love affair that was to end in the best deal I ever made: marriage.

7

At War with the Army

AS THE WAR GOT into its stride, business slackened off a bit.
Most theatres remained open, though, and Joe Collins and I
worked hard to maintain the agency. We decided to move to
Regent Street, as our original offices were not big enough for our
developing business. The new set-up was much more impressive, and consisted of a small, outside office for our two secretaries
and a larger one which Joe and I shared. The room was domin-
ated by an enormous desk, which we also shared.

We managed, somehow, to keep our heads above water, but
were forced to change our style of business because so many of
our specialty and novelty acts had left the country. Those that
remained were from parts of Europe not yet involved in the war.
All the same, we still had quite a formidable list of attractions on
our books, including several well-known singers and comedians
who were in the semi-star category. We also decided to get more
heavily involved in promoting our own programmes, and, considering we were in the middle of a war, we did exceptionally well.

During the early war years, I would go to Morecambe every
second week for the opening night of each new programme there.
Looking back on those days makes me realize just how important
Morecambe was in my life, and what a debt of gratitude I owe to
Harry Smirk. It was entirely due to him that my career as an
agent took a major step forward.

In August 1940, the musical director of the Winter Gardens,
an ex-army man called Colonel Hodgkinson, asked me what I
intended to do in the war. I said I'd do whatever I could. He
then told me a long story about how badly the army needed
entertainment prior to the men going overseas. The Pioneer
Corps was the section in which he was especially interested. He

said the men attached to it worked the hardest, did the dirty jobs, and were all rather depressed – a case of all work and no play. He wanted me to enter the services as an entertainment officer for them.

I kept pointing out that I was nearly thirty-four years old, had water on the knee, and wouldn't be able to do any physical activity such as marching or training. He said he understood this, but, knowing my reputation in the entertainment industry, felt I was the best person for the job. In the end I decided not to wait to be called, but enlisted voluntarily – despite my bad knees – hoping I wouldn't have to do too much walking. In due course I received the usual telegram advising me of my army number and that I was to be stationed at Preston. They said they'd let me know when my presence was required.

By now Kathie and I were officially engaged. I say 'officially', although I'd not yet received her mother's blessing, but I was working on it. I knew, however, that she liked me a great deal and had a high regard for me, and we got on well together. They lived in Maida Vale, and I was a frequent visitor there, always bringing flowers for Mrs Moody.

Although I knew that Kathie could sing, I'd never heard her myself. She had appeared on many radio shows for both the BBC and Radio Luxembourg, and had been a leading lady in a revue with Ted Ray. She now felt she wanted to extend her range and do a variety act. I had no idea what her voice sounded like but I arranged a rehearsal room with a pianist and left her to work something out for herself.

Every evening at 7.30, after her rehearsals were over, she'd pick me up from the office and we'd go out for a meal. One evening, however, I thought I'd surprise her. I left my office early, and as I walked into the rehearsal room I heard this wonderful, pure coloratura soprano voice singing 'The Blue Danube' to a jazz rhythm. I asked the owner of the rehearsal rooms, 'Whose is that sensational voice?' He said, 'You must be kidding. That's your fiancée, Kathleen Moody.' I rushed into the room and said 'Was that *really* you singing "The Blue Danube"?' She then showed me what she'd been rehearsing, and sang three more songs for me, finishing up with 'Lo, hear the gentle lark'. I couldn't believe how wonderful she was!

It so happened I was looking for an act to appear at a Sunday concert at the Regal, Kettering, which was then owned by Nat Cohen and his partner, and I immediately booked her for that engagement. I went up to Kettering with her, and she was an instant success. I was absolutely thrilled, and of course became her official agent. She toured all over the country, and continued her radio work as well. When television transmission recommenced after the war, the first TV variety show televised was on the Saturday, 8 June 1946. It was produced by Cecil Madden from Alexandra Palace and Kathie was selected to be one of its stars. On the same programme were The Beverly Sisters. We were all very excited about this and would have gone to the studio to watch the show, but Kathie's young sister Phyllis had been ill with a severe chest infection and we thought it would give her a tremendous boost if she could watch the show on television.

As we didn't possess a television set in those days, I racked my brains trying to think of where to find one, and suddenly remembered I'd seen a Baird in the rehearsal rooms Kathie used. I asked the owner if I could borrow it for one day and rushed round to our flat in Cavendish Square. All Kathie's family were assembled there to watch her appear on television for the first time. It was a thrilling and proud moment for us all.

Nat Cohen and his partner owned several cinemas which featured stage acts, and we were their exclusive bookers. We were also exclusive bookers for the Kay Brothers, whose pride and joy was a modern cinema in Barking in the East End. One incident springs to mind in my dealings with John Kay at that time. We were handling an act called Max and Harry Nesbitt. For some reason or other, Johnny Kay wouldn't let us book them into any of his cinemas. We could never understand it, because we were sure they'd do well. Once a week Johnny would come up to our office after lunch, sit down in the chair, and while we were talking to him about various different acts, he'd be snoozing away and every now and again would nod his head. So we thought this was a great opportunity to book Max and Harry Nesbitt while he was asleep. 'Can we put Max and Harry Nesbitt into the cinema at Barking?' I said. He nodded his head, so we booked the act.

About a week later, when we sent in the poster billings, Max and Harry Nesbitt were included as the headliners. Johnny came rushing round in a frenzy. 'I told you we don't want the Nesbitts,' he said. 'But Johnny,' I replied, 'you distinctly nodded your head when we suggested them. You definitely gave us the go-ahead.' When he realized he was licked, he was good-humoured about it, and let the booking stay. The Nesbitts were a hit and continued to play several return engagements.

Although the Germans were dropping their bombs on London, people still carried on working. At that time I had a flat at the White House, where there was a swimming pool on the lower ground floor, and a gymnasium on the floor below that. When the sirens went off signalling an air raid, all the residents would shelter in the gymnasium until the all-clear sounded.

Kathie was still living with her mother and sister Phyllis in Maida Vale.

At that time one of the acts on my books was a comedy-pantomime duo called Eddie Gordon and Norah. Eddie Gordon was a talented American who did mime and all kinds of tricks. What I didn't know was that the Norah of his act was another of Kathie's sisters. They had been working in Paris and it was only during the time of Dunkirk that Norah managed to get back to England after a really terrifying journey, and was now living with her family.

I felt it was no longer safe for the Moodys to continue living where they were, so I found them a house in Primrose Hill, near Regent's Park. It had concrete walls about three foot thick, was three storeys high, and had a small garden.

Late in 1940, just after Dunkirk, Kathie's brother Jimmy returned to London. He, too, moved in with his family. And so, after a while, did I. I thought it would be much safer in Primrose Hill than at the White House. But as it happened, it was horrendous. The first night I was there the bombs dropped ceaselessly and the garden was in flames. As the bombs continued to fall all around us, Jimmy and I would take buckets of water to douse the flames.

The same thing happened the following night. I couldn't stand it any longer. At six o'clock in the morning, I gathered the family together and said to Kathie's mother, 'Look. You've got to leave

London now. Pack a few bags, leave all the rest of your things in trunks and I'll bring them later. Here's a map of Devon. Stick a pin in it somewhere and that's where you'll go.' Her mother did just that and made off for a place called South Moulton. 'Go to a small hotel for a few days,' I said, 'then find some comfortable accommodation and I'll come and visit you in a fortnight.'

At that time I knew I'd shortly be going into the army, and there wasn't much time to lose.

After a couple of days they found a lovely farmhouse and they approached the couple who owned it to see if they could stay there for a while.

The man and his wife happened to be Plymouth Brethren, and the first thing they asked Kathie's family was what religion they were. They said they were Catholics. 'We really don't care for Catholics,' the lady said, 'but if you promise to go to our church on Sundays, we'll take you in.'

They promised.

Two weeks later I telephoned Kathie to say I'd be coming down, and that although I'd be staying at a hotel, I'd come straight to the farmhouse and take them all out for a slap-up meal. What I didn't tell her until after I arrived was that their beautiful house in Primrose Hill had suffered a direct hit in an air raid, and had been razed to the ground. I had gone to the house to collect some cases and baggage, intending to bring them down to Devon with me, but when I arrived, there was no house. Just a pile of smoking rubble.

Was it just luck – or a premonition – my insisting that the Moodys move out of London to Devon? Impossible to say. What I did discover, though, was that the house in Primrose Hill was close to the gun sites in Regent's Park, and was therefore in an extremely vulnerable spot.

The family accepted what had happened as philosophically as they could. Kathie seemed far more concerned about how the owners of the farmhouse would react to me. If they hadn't much cared for Catholics, what would they feel about a Jew? But she needn't have worried. When the couple heard I was Jewish, the lady of the house said: 'Praise the Lord! We'll certainly welcome one of God's chosen people.'

Kathie told them I was planning to stay at a local hotel, but they wouldn't hear of it. 'He's got to stay here,' they insisted. 'We'll be honoured.' And they meant it, for they gave up their own bedroom, made it look beautiful and welcomed me like a long lost son. They also asked me whether I'd like to visit their church. I said I'd visit it from the outside but wouldn't go inside. I didn't go to the synagogue, so why should I go to church?

After the service almost everybody in the congregation came up to me outside the church and shook my hand. It was a great feeling being Jewish in that situation – and so unexpected.

A few days later I was told to report to Preston to commence my army training. I was quite confident I'd only be there a short time before being transferred to the Pioneer Corps.

The Royal Signal Corps, the unit I was assigned to, was based in an old mill. I was allocated my number, and immediately sent a telegram to Colonel Hodgkinson giving him the details. I expected to be out of there within three or four days to do the job for which I had really enlisted. But I heard nothing for a week. In the meantime, I was wearing those heavy army boots and my legs were giving me hell.

We did some marching exercises and almost immediately my knees began to swell. But nobody took any notice. This was the army. Not only did we have to get up at five in the morning and wash and shave in icy water, but the food was inedible. Nothing in my hard, East End background had ever prepared me for anything like this! The only thing that kept me going during the first few days was the knowledge that any minute now I'd be getting a telegram confirming my transfer.

But still nothing came. After ten days of real hardship, I managed to contact Colonel Hodgkinson and I asked him why my transfer was taking so long. 'We have rather a problem,' he said, 'and I'm afraid there's not much I can do about it. You see,' he went on, 'you're in a senior regiment in the army, and we can't just pull you from the Royal Signal Corps.'

I felt suicidal. I honestly didn't know how I was going to survive in that atmosphere. I was having to sleep and eat alongside boys who were half my age – and I needn't have been there in the first place!

One day I was asked to go and see the adjutant, and the first thing he said to me was, 'Why aren't you sending your mother any money out of your army pay?' I said, 'I don't have to. I still get my salary from my company, Collins and Grade, and she gets her money out of that.' He flared up and said, 'You're in the army now and you have to do what everybody else does.' From this moment on, he took an instant dislike to me – the feeling was mutual – and I was given all the hard duties.

I decided this couldn't go on. I had to eat properly. So I had my car sent from London to a garage near the barracks, and made arrangements for the garage to leave the car outside the barracks at 6.00 p.m. each day. I would then drive into Preston, which was about five miles away, and have a good meal at the Bull and Royal Hotel. I knew the proprietor very well, as I always used to stay there when I was doing business with the Broadhead theatres. The adjutant, it turned out, didn't live in the barracks. He lived at the Bull and Royal. One day he saw me eating there, and went straight to the proprietor. 'I see you've got Gunner Grade eating here,' he said. 'Well, I won't allow it.' To which the proprietor smartly replied, 'As long as Gunner Grade, or anybody else in the army, has enough money to pay for their meal, he's welcome here.' 'Then I'll move out of the hotel,' he said. And he did.

I happened to know that the adjutant went to see the show at the Palace Theatre, Preston, every week, and after the perform-ance, went backstage to meet and talk to the artistes. I told Percy Broadhead, who was the owner of the Broadhead circuit, all about my problems with the man, after which he barred him from going backstage ever again. This wasn't such a good idea because it meant the adjutant disliked me even more!

One day I was told to go down for motorcycle practice. 'But I've never ridden a motorcycle in my life,' I said to the sergeant. 'What do I do?' 'You drive a car, don't you?' he said. And when I replied that I did, he said, 'All you have to do is get on the bike, start the motor, turn the handlebars and kick off. Nothing to it.' I got on to the motorbike, turned the handlebars and woke up in Preston Hospital. I had driven into a tree. I was in hospital for about two weeks and eventually one of the doctors came to me and said, 'We can't understand why you're in the army at all. We've checked your grading and find you're Grade III. Go back to your barracks and get an immediate discharge.' Music to my ears! I went back to Preston Mill Barracks and waited for my discharge but, yet again, nothing happened – except that from now on I was given light duties, such as sweeping the floor, and was allowed to wear slippers. No discharge.

After it seemed that I'd be remaining at Preston for some time, Kathie and her family rented a little house in Windermere, almost on the edge of the lake. When they left London they had taken Nat Cohen's dog with them because Nat said his dog was petrified of the bombing. I drove up one weekend in my army uniform, looking spick and span. It was vital that army boots gleamed at all times and the routine of 'bull' – keeping one's webbing, buckles and boots, etc., spotless – was a neverending ritual. I arrived at Windermere to find that Nat's dog was in a terrible fight with a neighbour's dog. Being the gallant gentleman that I am, I immediately rushed in to separate the animals, and, in the struggle to tear them apart, they had a go at my boots and really made a mess of them, not to mention the rest of my uniform. I finally prised them apart, but I looked such a mess that I was frightened to report back to Preston for duty because I didn't know what would happen when they caught sight of my precious boots! Fortunately, by that time I was well acquainted with the major in charge of my division, and he sympathized with me because he knew what a hard time I was having with the adjutant. He managed to find me a new pair of boots and the incident passed off without any problems.

Two months went by and still I had not been transferred to the Pioneer Corps. We used to sleep on three-tiered bunks – about sixty people in a room – and one morning, at about 4.00 a.m., the sergeant burst in. 'Everybody up. Everybody up,' he said. 'Full pack and kit, and rifles. I want you ready and assembled in one hour.' 'What's it all about?' I asked. 'You're going to Harrogate,' he said.

I wore my full kit. We marched part of the way, went part of the way by train, then finished with yet another march to the barracks in Pennypot Lane. On the way I found out that we were being sent to a dispersal centre for overseas action. I was shocked, and scared stiff because I knew there was no way I could keep up with the eighteen-year-olds I was surrounded by. If only my knees had been OK, it might have been different.

By the time we arrived in Harrogate, I collapsed. My legs were swollen, my knees were like balloons and I was suffering the most agonizing pain. When they saw the condition I was in, they immediately put me into the sick bay, where the staff were wonderful to me. I was then sent to York Military Hospital, which was the permanent army hospital in the North of England. All the time I was there, I kept receiving flowers and letters from friends in the entertainment industry, many of whom were big stars. My postbag was soon the talk of the hospital.

The head of the hospital, a brigadier general, came to see me and said, 'We can't understand why you're here!' I told him I'd been asked a similar question when I was in Preston Hospital and related the whole saga of how I came to be in the army in the first place.

'Well, I've got to give you a discharge,' he said. 'However, are you sure you wouldn't like to do the job you originally intended to do?' 'No,' I said, 'I've had it. I want my discharge, and that's that.'

Then he told me that Harrogate was a base where the recruits came in for an intensive six-week training period before being posted for services. 'Every six weeks, four thousand soldiers are sent overseas,' he said, 'and, frankly, we have a problem. The War Office is continually getting complaints that they're overworked with not nearly enough diversion in their lives. All they do is train and get ready for duty. It really would help, you know, if they had a bit of entertainment.'

Once again I said positively no. Not after what I'd been through.

Then he said, 'Well, won't you at least come and have a good look round the Harrogate Training Centre?'

Reluctantly I agreed, but again repeated that nothing would make me change my mind. I'd had it up to my neck with the bloody army!

The brigadier general came to Harrogate with me, where we were met by the colonel in charge of the barracks – who wore a red band on his cap which signified he was attached to the War Office – and the regimental sergeant major, who said, 'We know how you feel and that you want out, but the complaints are getting so bad, and the morale so low, we really do need your help. Why don't you come and have a look at our theatre?'

It would have been unreasonable to say no, so I walked into this huge hall which could seat approximately two thousand people. It had a nice-sized stage, and, as I looked it over, I thought if I brought in a few spotlights, put a couple here and a couple there, and maybe some curtains and a few small sets, I might just be able to make it look like a proper theatre.

'Okay,' I said, 'I'll do it for six months. But you've got to give my discharge papers to the colonel and whenever I decide to leave, he must promise to fill them out for me.' They agreed, and I now found myself in charge of entertainments.

I immediately went into action. I arranged for some curtains, lights and basic scenery to be sent from London to Harrogate, and contacted all the artistes I thought would be willing to lend their services. The response was fantastic, and every Sunday night the men were treated to an outstanding variety show – but only those who had passed their various training tests were allowed in.

There were several other army installations nearby, and all their colonels and captains asked for tickets. I told them they were exclusively for the Harrogate Barracks, and refused to let them have any. The colonel in charge wanted to give me three stripes and make me a sergeant, but I said one stripe would be sufficient. My official title now was Lance Bombadier Grade – but everyone from the colonel downwards called me Lew – and I had complete freedom to do whatever I wanted. I had my own private room, and at ten in the morning the RSM would knock at my door and say, 'Lew, what would you like for breakfast this morning?' I was always allowed into the officers' mess, and could mix freely with the two hundred regulars who were the training staff for the new recruits. They were a group of experienced young men, all in their early twenties, who were specially selected because they were on the permanent staff and therefore exempt from going overseas. They were short, but strong, and I became friendly with quite a few of them.

I had my car with me and would often drive into the town of Harrogate. I never bothered to wear a gas mask and wore my jackets loosely. One evening I was suddenly surrounded by four six-foot-tall members of the military police. They gave me a bad pummelling, apparently on the pretext that I was incorrectly dressed, saying, 'You think you Jew bastards can do what you like.' Fortunately, six of my small, tough pals happened to be passing, sized up the situation and came near to murdering those four military policemen. I was proud of my relationship with all my camp buddies, because I realized they cared. After this I had complete freedom to go anywhere I liked, even in civilian clothes. I was also free to go to London whenever I chose, and would combine these trips with a visit to the Collins and Grade offices to do a spot of business.

Although I only agreed to take on the job for six months, I was so elated with the reaction the shows were getting that I decided to continue my contribution to the war effort indefinitely.

In May 1942 I was asked by Mrs Churchill to put on a special show called Aid to Russia at the London Coliseum. Meanwhile, Kathie's mother had finally given her approval to our getting married. But we hadn't set a date.

The Coliseum show was staged at the beginning of June and, naturally, Kathie was included in the cast. She was tremendous, and I was thrilled with her. After the finale I went backstage to congratulate all the artistes and, after telling Kathie how good I thought she'd been, I said, 'So, when are we getting married?' She said her mother had agreed the wedding could take place on her twenty-first birthday, which was 23 June. I grabbed her hand, rushed upstairs to the bar where all the dignitaries were assembled, including my colonel, and said to him, 'I'm going back to camp with you tomorrow morning, and I'm going to fill in the date of my discharge. Then I'm coming straight back to London.' 'Why?' he asked. 'Because I'm getting married,' I said. He couldn't argue with that.

Kathie and I married at Caxton Hall Registry Office on 23 June 1942, and Joe Collins was my best man. Everyone said the marriage would last about six months. To date it's lasted forty-five years, proving all the doubting Thomases wrong.

After the ceremony, we had our wedding breakfast at Oddenino's Restaurant in Regent Street. The colonel, the senior officers and the regimental sergeant major, together with representatives of the War Office, all came. The regulars, and senior officers from the camp, gave us a beautiful tea and dinner service, and Kathie and I were both tremendously moved by their generosity.

We spent our honeymoon at the luxurious Imperial Hotel in Torquay. We were only there for four wonderful days, because at that time that was all I could afford.

It was a very happy time for me, marred only by the fact that my dear mother chose not to attend our wedding. The problem, of course, was that Kathie wasn't Jewish. All Jewish mothers want their sons to marry into the faith. Unfortunately, in this respect, my mother was to have no luck. The first of her sons to marry a Gentile was Leslie. His bride's name was Winnie Smith and they married in secret in 1940 when Leslie was twenty-four years old. He was too scared to tell my mother what he'd done because, as her favourite son, he knew how much pain it would cause her. For a while she was absolutely distraught and nothing we said nor did eased her disappointment. Things only began to heal when Lynda and Michael, Leslie's two children, were born. But the marriage didn't last and Leslie divorced after the war. In 1948 he married Audrey Smith. By now, though, my mother must have resigned herself to the fact that her daughters-in-law were not to be Jewish, for Bernie had also married out of the faith – happily, as it turned out. He and his wife Carole, like Kathie and I, continue to enjoy a wonderful life together.

Fortunately, my sister Rita did the right thing as far as my mother was concerned. In 1949 she married a Jewish doctor! His name was Joe Freeman and he became an indelible part of all our lives. He was a wonderful, caring man who, during my brother Leslie's long illness in 1966, was a tower of strength. Sadly, Joe passed away in 1979, leaving behind two sons, Ian and Andrew.

As far as Kathie and my mother were concerned, over the years they became inseparable, as I knew they would. Considering the initial resistance on my mother's behalf, it blossomed into an extraordinary relationship. So much so, that until the day she died my mother convinced herself that Kathie had Jewish blood in her!

Kathie continued with her regular radio appearances after we got married, but reduced her other engagements to eight to ten weeks a year, and only worked in London. She kept up these occasional London appearances when I was away a fair amount of the time after the war. Wherever I was I always spoke to Kathie every day, and one day she told me that my brother Leslie had called her and wanted her to be a headliner out of London. He told her it was a beautiful summer resort with a beach and it would be a good holiday for her. Although I was not keen on her working out of town, I agreed that she could do it. She then discovered the venue was actually in a little place called Wednesbury – nowhere near a beach and certainly no summer resort. It was just that Leslie had been stuck for a headliner and knowing how I felt about Kathie playing out of town, he had pitched his story to make it sound like an attractive venue. She had rather a depressing week, but we both realized that Leslie wouldn't have done it unless he had been in a real fix.

When Kathie was working in London I used to pick her up on the Saturdays when she had finished her engagement, and help her bring all her luggage back home. At that time we had a little dog called Cinders, a miniature Pekinese, and while I was waiting in the wings, holding the dog and listening to Kathie singing 'Lo, hear the gentle lark', the dog suddenly jumped out of my arms and ran on to the stage. The audience immediately started laughing. Kathie couldn't understand what had happened, then seeing Cinders, picked her up and held her in her arms. Each time she hit a high note, the dog howled in unison. Kathie finished the song to terrific applause and, needless to say, the audience thought it was all part of the act.

It's true what they say: children and animals are the biggest scene-stealers in show business. Particularly animals!

8

Getting There

AFTER MY HONEYMOON, it was business as usual at Collins and Grade, though I began to sense a change in the relationship between Joe Collins and myself. We just weren't getting on as well as we used to. Little things began to irritate us about each other – and every now and then there'd be a row over something.

One example: I was friendly with Jack Hylton and he gave me the exclusive bookings to put one of his musical revues into theatres throughout the country. Both Joe and I booked dates for this particular show. As usual, we were sitting at opposite sides of the large desk in our office and he was on the phone to a theatre in Widnes asking for a guarantee of £150. While he was in the middle of this conversation, I said, 'Joe, it's ridiculous for you to accept a guarantee of £150 for the show when you know the theatre can't take more money. It costs Jack Hylton £250 a week to run the show, which means he'll end up having a definite loss of £100!'

At that moment, Joe threw the telephone on to the floor and said, 'Right. You run the business,' and he stormed out of the room.

I knew I couldn't possibly allow a personal friend of mine to run the show for a week just to lose money! From that day onwards, things got worse and worse between us and I knew it was only a matter of time before we would split up.

My brother Leslie, meanwhile, was also making quite a name for himself in the agency business. From his humble beginnings as an office boy with the Syndicate Theatre Chain, he had become an extremely successful agent in his own right, and, among other things, was a booker for the 2500-seater Stoll Theatre, Kingsway. During the war years, when times were lean and people were frightened to leave their homes, Leslie came up with a marvellous gimmick to entice people back into the theatres. The custom, normally, was to feature only one big headliner on each variety bill – but, because at the time there were so many top stars out of work, Leslie was able to persuade about four or five major names all to appear on the same pro- gramme, and with no extra cost to the public. With such value for money on offer, the public flocked in.

The amazing thing was that he was able to cope with all this added activity at the same time as being stationed in the air force at Hendon. Leslie's clients included Billy Cotton and his Band, then the most popular show band in the country, as well as a major attraction in its day called Troise and his Mandoliers. He also handled a marvellous American xylophone player called Teddy Brown, and a top radio star by the name of Hal Monty. Monty did a very funny routine about life in the services, and it was only much later that I discovered he was really Albert Sutan – my brother's ex-dance partner, and my very first business partner (then also known as Eddie May)!

While I was still part of Collins and Grade, my brother Bernie had finished his Delfont and Toko act, and he, too, decided he wanted to give the agency business a try. It seemed to be working well enough for Leslie and me – so why shouldn't it work for him too? So, he joined Collins and Grade. But he only stayed with us for about a year or so – although he did well (for example, he brought the pianist Charlie Kunz on to our books), he was very much the junior partner, and it was apparent, right from the start, that he had bigger things in mind. In 1939, with some financial backing from Carl Heimann, the Chairman of Mecca, he started out on his own and became Mecca's exclusive booking agent.

My differences with Joe Collins didn't stop Kathie from liking Joe's wife, Elsa. Everybody, in fact, adored Elsa. She was so warm and generous and didn't have an enemy in the world. I remember when she had her first baby in 1933. Joe and I weren't partners then, but we were good friends, and I can still recall arriving at the hospital in time to hear Joan Collins's very first cry!

In January 1943 Leslie was suddenly called for active service overseas in the Middle East. He knew that my relationship with Collins was souring fast and asked me to take over his business while he was abroad. 'I've got quite a lot of money in the bank,' he said, 'five shows touring the country, and lots of star attractions.' So I agreed.

I moved in straight away. Leslie's offices were at 62 Shaftesbury Avenue, overlooking the Queens and the Apollo Theatres – another coincidence as they were part of the Stoll Moss Group, which by now had merged with the General Theatres Corporation, owners of the London Palladium.

My little brother, I was soon to discover, did not believe in paying income tax, and for the next couple of years I had to work particularly hard to pay off the tax debts he'd incurred.

I was also extremely nervous of the stars he handled. Up until now I'd been used to dealing with acts who did exactly what I told them to do. I fixed their engagements, paid their salaries and that, as far as I was concerned, was that.

With stars it was a whole new ball game. I had to consult them on every detail and every decision, massage their egos, and generally make them feel important and loved. It took quite a bit of getting used to. It also required the kind of finesse which, at the time, I just didn't possess. I was equally intimidated by Val Parnell, who'd become the Managing Director of the Stoll Moss Theatres Group and one of the most powerful men in the business.

Kathie, who has been a tremendous influence throughout the whole of our happily married life together, knew about these anxieties of mine, and, for £6, bought a box of cigars off Stanley Black, the well-known orchestra leader who happened to be a good friend of ours. She brought the cigars into my office one morning and said, 'Why don't you offer these to some of your stars when they come in and see you. Perhaps it'll put you at your ease with them.'

I agreed, and put the box, unopened, into a drawer in my bottom desk.

I forgot all about it until a few weeks later, when I opened the drawer and saw the box of cigars. I was suddenly overcome with curiosity. I wondered what it would be like to smoke one.

So I opened the box, pulled out a cigar, cut off the tip (as I'd often seen people do) and lit up.

It just so happened that, precisely at the moment I was taking my first couple of puffs – and enjoying it enormously, I might add – the telephone rang. It was Val Parnell.

'Yes, Val,' I said, cigar in hand, and no longer intimidated by this formidable man, 'what can I do for you?'

That was the day the *real* Lew Grade was born!

Ever since then, of course, cigars have played an enormous part in my life. In one respect, they're my 'security blanket'. In another, they're my trademark. They give me something to clutch on to, and they give me confidence.

When I first started smoking Montecristo cigars, I'd go through about two or three a day. But as the business escalated, and required major decisions involving large sums of money, my anxieties and tensions increased, and so did the number of cigars. In fact, for as long as I can remember, I smoked about fifteen a day. Today, I've reduced that by about half. On top of this I give away almost as many as I smoke. It's the perfect gift. There are people I know who've kept the cigars I've given them as souvenirs. 'Do you mind if I don't smoke it?' they'd say. 'I'd just like to be able to have a Lew Grade cigar for a keepsake.'

In the end, though, the pleasure I've had from smoking my cigars can't be measured in money, which reminds me of something that actually happened, and wasn't just apocryphal, like so many stories about me tend to be.

There was a young man working for the Grade organization called Peter Pritchard. He wanted a raise in salary, and when I asked him what he thought he was worth, he said, 'As much as you spend a week on your cigars.'

'My boy,' I said, 'if you gave me as much satisfaction as these cigars, you could have it. Now get out.'

God forbid there should ever come a time when my doctor or my wife – because those are the only two people I listen to – make me stop smoking. I just can't imagine what it would be like going through life without a cigar first thing in the morning, last thing at night, and half a dozen times in between. It would be murder, I'm sure, because I'd have to chew sweets all day. Or eat chocolates. The only thing that really keeps me calm is a cigar. Who knows what I'd get up to without them. . . .

*   *   *

At the time we formed Lew and Leslie Grade Ltd, there were only two other agents in the office working for us, and Bert Knight, who was our general manager and producer. Unfortunately Bert was away on duty in the air force, which meant that I had to work all hours of the day and night to keep things going. In 1944, however, Bert was discharged from the forces and rejoined the agency. He was a tremendous help to me and undertook full responsibility for several of the shows we were hoping to produce.

I personally looked after the star acts. One incident that always stands out in my mind is the time Billy Cotton came to see me. 'Lew,' he said, 'I want to work thirty-six weeks this year and I want all the bookings to be in London.' I said, 'Bill, that's impossible. There aren't enough first-class theatres in London for you to play thirty-six weeks.' To which he replied, 'Well, in that case, if you can't get me the thirty-six weeks I'll go to another agent who can.' With that he started towards the door, opened it and was halfway through it, when he turned and came back. 'Well, how many weeks *can* you get me?' he asked. 'Twenty-four,' I said. And he said 'Fine.' Throughout my entire career, I have never promised to do anything I wasn't confident of being able to fulfil.

During the war, Kathie was becoming an important star in her own right. She was the leading lady in a show called 'Variety Bandbox' which was broadcast every Sunday by the BBC from the Queensberry Hall Services Club, which was later the London Casino and is now the Prince Edward Theatre.

The famous American orchestra leader Glenn Miller used to come to the rehearsals on Sundays, and particularly admired Kathie's singing.

Meanwhile, Kathie's sister Norah also became very well established as a variety act and leading lady. She was an actress and a wonderfully talented impressionist – her specialty being that famous film star Charles Boyer.

In 1944 Kathie was appearing in the Christmas pantomime at the Winter Garden Theatre, Drury Lane (now the New London), for a ten-week season, with Bobby Howes as the principal star.

I always used to pick her up at the theatre each evening but I would arrive just before the end of the performance in order to telephone the various theatres I'd booked acts into – to find out what the box-office takings were like.

Early in January 1945 the sirens were still sounding and bombs – those dreaded V2s – were still falling. You'd hear the noise of the engine and suddenly there'd be silence. Then the rocket would fall to earth causing the most terrible damage and destruction. But the horror was that you never knew when the engine was going to cut out until the second it stopped, so there was no time to take cover.

I had a pantomime on at the Ilford Hippodrome at that time, the same theatre, in fact, where I'd won my first important charleston competition. I phoned Ilford for the figures and they told me a bomb had just fallen there. I was worried sick because I knew that Norah was the principal girl in the show. When Kathie finished her performance I told her to come quickly to my car with me. She couldn't understand why I didn't give her the usual time to take off her stage make-up and it wasn't until we were on our way to Ilford that I told her about the bomb.

I drove like crazy through a nightmare air raid and we found that Norah had indeed been injured, and had been taken to hospital. We quickly drove to the hospital, and found her dazed and bloodstained with injured people all around her. We carried her back to the car and drove her to our flat in Cavendish Square. Norah's husband, an independent theatrical agent called Solly Black, had a brother – Dr Louis Schwartz – who was an eminent physician in Paris and happened to be in London at that time. We called him and he rushed round with his wife Tony and picked all the bits of glass out of her face. Happily, she made a complete recovery.

As soon as peace was declared, Dr Schwartz returned to Paris to open the British hospital there, and was awarded the Légion d'Honneur for his magnificent services during the war.

I, too, returned to Paris in 1945, on the first available civilian flight. Kathie was very excited, and when I asked her what she'd like me to bring back for her she said a brassière and some nylon stockings, because both were difficult to get in London at the time.

I was met at the airport by George Le Roy, who had become our French representative in 1937. Whenever I was in Paris I used George's office as a base, and I remember an occasion involving Yves Montand (whom George handled) and a weekend engagement at the Casino Knocke in Belgium. Yves said he wouldn't fulfil his commitment there unless he could travel to Belgium in a sleeper. Unfortunately, there was none available.

In desperation George called the Gare du Nord in Paris and said he wanted a sleeper for Yves Montand. 'Impossible,' they said. 'There aren't any.' 'Look here,' said George, 'this is the Chef du Gard du Nord speaking. Fix a sleeper!' And they did!

Thereafter, whenever I travelled on a French train and someone else came into my compartment, I always said, 'This compartment is reserved for the Chef du Gard du Nord', and it always worked.

When the Germans invaded France, George Le Roy was with the Resistance. In the early part of 1943 he joined de Gaulle in England, as he was a high-ranking officer in the French Army Reserve. He returned to France at the same time as de Gaulle, but not before arranging to reopen his agency in Paris in partnership with Lew and Leslie Grade. It was a relationship that lasted until his death in 1952.

As soon as I mentioned to George that I wanted to buy a brassière and some nylons for Kathie, he said, 'Fine. I'll bring my girlfriend Minouche along to help you choose.'

As we were all walking towards the Rue de la Paix in the direction of the lingerie shops, George said, 'What size bra does Kathie wear?' I said, 'I've no idea.' 'The same as Minouche?' he asked. I said, 'I really don't know.' 'Tell you what,' he said. 'Feel Minouche. That'll give you some idea.' I blushed and said I couldn't possibly do that. 'Lew,' he said, 'this is Paris!' Somehow I managed to buy the right size without feeling Minouche.

While in Paris I called on my old friend Pierre Sandrini at the Bal Tabarin, and was surprised to see what a transformation the place had undergone. The Bal Tabarin had been just an ordinary Parisian cabaret. Now, however, it was a really spectacular nightspot with great stage effects and international cabaret acts. One of these was The Andrea Dancers, a Hungarian group who had lived in Italy for a long while. They were, without doubt, the classiest adagio act I'd ever seen, and performed in immaculate evening dress. The Sonys, a brother and sister dance team, were also on the bill; as were The Amin Brothers, who were what is known in the business as a Risley Act. They went in for acrobatic balancing tricks and were fantastic.

Watching these extraordinary people perform once again filled me with tremendous pleasure and admiration, and with Sandrini's help I became their exclusive representative worldwide, giving each a twelve-week guaranteed contract to commence just as soon as they became available. They were all acts of outstanding calibre and I knew I'd have no difficulty keeping them in work for years.

George Le Roy mentioned another act he thought I should see called Robert Lamouret and Dudule. Lamouret was a ventriloquist, and Dudule, his dummy, was a duck. I was overwhelmed by them both, and arranged to bring them to England in 1946.

Then I travelled to Switzerland to see my old friends Rolf and Freddie Knie of the Knie Circus, and while there saw the fabulous Pierre Elysée Trio, a remarkable flying trapeze act. Pierre Elysée was the first man I'd ever seen performing a triple somersault, and I immediately signed the trio for a thirty-two-week season at the Tower Circus, Blackpool.

The Knie Circus also featured an amazing lion act, called Trubka. I signed that too, and booked it for Blackpool.

At that time, a lady called Kathleen Williams was the chief booking manager for all the Blackpool attractions. In addition to the Tower Circus, she booked summer shows for the Winter Gardens, whose producers were George and Alfred Black, sons of the original George Black, the founder of the General Theatres Corporation.

Kathleen Williams and I made three trips to Europe every year in order to search for new talent. Each trip lasted about ten days, during which time we'd often see as many as three circuses a day. Kathleen was always worried that Bertram Mills would get there first, and our main concern was to be one jump ahead of them, which we usually managed to be.

This whole period was probably the most strenuous of my life. There were very few planes going directly to the places we needed to be – especially the more out-of-the-way places where the smaller circuses were situated. But we knew that some of the finest talent was to be found in the smaller towns, so we just had to get there as best we could, even though it meant taking several trains and buses. People to this day ask me if I've ever been to Venice, or Florence or Lyon. And I say, 'Yes. For half an hour waiting for a train connection to somewhere else.'

I never ceased to marvel at Kathleen Williams's energy. As if traipsing round Europe looking for talent wasn't enough, she always insisted on going shopping for her husband and daughter – usually just before a long train journey. Inevitably, I tagged along with her, so, by the end of the day, I was exhausted.

Nothing perked me up faster than a marvellous act, though. Seeing really great talent was better than being given a million pounds, because talent and skill, as far as I'm concerned, are priceless. And when I think of some of today's youngsters who become millionaire pop-stars with just one hit record, I realize there is no justice in this business. Most of the circus performers I met began their apprenticeships almost as soon as they could walk. It took them years of practice to perfect their skills, yet the money they earned was nothing compared to their talent. Today it's just the opposite. There are some kids who are in a position to retire before they turn twenty-one, although many of them, of course, go on to become talented song writers and great performers.

*   *   *

My brother Leslie was discharged from the air force towards the end of 1945. When he returned, we decided that our offices in Shaftesbury Avenue weren't large enough to accommodate our ambitions. So we moved to 241 Regent Street and rented two floors in that building, which, as I mentioned before, is directly facing the London Palladium, via Little Argyll Street.

We then decided to acquire several other agents and agencies of reputation, each agent or agency having a number of acts which fitted comfortably into the Lew and Leslie Grade agency. Among our new acquisitions was Dennis Selinger (one of whose clients was Peter Sellers), now the Managing Director of International Creative Management. He had been in the air force during the war and was on his way back to England from India by troopship. His ship picked up several more air force personnel from the Middle East, including my brother Leslie. They became friendly and it was shortly after this that Dennis joined our company. Others who joined up with us were Dennis's uncle, Montague Lyon, who had his own much-respected agency; Brian Roxbury, for whom I had a high regard, particularly for his judgement on specialty and circus acts; Cyril Berlin; Elkan Kaufman – a young man who I thought had the makings of a good agent; and Solly Black. Solly had been in the army for about the same time as me, and when he was discharged he formed his own highly successful agency. Comedian Spike Milligan was one of his clients; as was Digby Wolf, who later went to America and was heavily involved in the hugely successful American television show 'Laugh-In'.

Solly Black was not only married to my sister-in-law, Norah, he was also my best friend. He was British, but had been brought up in France and was a French boxing champion in his young years, so considered to be extremely fit. We were very close indeed, worked well together, and loved to play snooker together whenever we had the time.

We used to play regularly on Sunday afternoons and one Sunday – 18 October 1959 – we were at the Empire Billiards Club in Frith Street, Soho. At about six o'clock Solly said, 'It's time to go. I'll drop you off at your flat, then I'll go home for some supper because I want to watch "Sunday Night at the London Palladium" at eight o'clock.' At about 8.30 p.m. his son Philip, who was then nearly nine years old, telephoned and said, 'Daddy's not well. You'd better come round quickly.' Kathie and I rushed there immediately and found that Solly had suffered a major heart attack. Thank goodness he was still conscious and was able to talk to me for a while, even discussing the artistes he had been watching on television that evening, and then he peacefully passed away. His wife and family were absolutely distraught, as indeed we all were. He was my dearest friend and I missed him terribly, and still do. In fact I have not played snooker since that day. Philip, incidentally, is now working as an independent film and television producer.

By the end of 1946 we had about twenty agents working for us, including a young man called Alec Fyne. They were all paid a salary, plus a small percentage, leaving Leslie and me free to concentrate on the development of the company.

Meanwhile, my brother Bernie was progressing too. His agency, headed by Billy Marsh, was growing daily more important and was heavily involved in producing plays and musicals, such as Charles B. Cochran's *Bless the Bride* and Richard Tauber's *Old Chelsea*. Bernie also ran several theatres of which he was part-owner, including the London Casino. He later renamed this The Prince Edward, which became the home of *Evita* for five years, and, more recently, the hit musical *Chess*.

During this time I continued to develop relationships with the circus proprietors I was doing business with, and booked the Knie Circus which was noted throughout the world for its superb elephant acts, as well as the Schumann Circus of Copenhagen, famous for its horses. I also established a good working arrangement with Jerome Medrano of the Cirque Medrano, Paris, the Bougliani Brothers of Circus Bougliani, also in Paris, and the Circus Togni in Italy, whose representative I'd become.

Most of these circus proprietors acted as unofficial representatives on my behalf. Whenever they saw a good act, they'd let me know about it, even if it were more suitable for music halls or cabarets than the big top. And, because I really valued their judgements, I'd always follow up their recommendations.

These relationships I established after the war continued for as long as I was in the agency business.

When Leslie returned, I was able to spend much more time abroad and it was then that I started bringing out such people as Edith Piaf, Charles Trenet, Jean Sablon and Patachou. Although I had no contact yet with the United States, and had never been there, I had the foresight to sign these stars for America as well.

At the end of 1946 a new show was due to open at the Prince of Wales Theatre in London, starring England's best-known and best-loved comedian, Sid Fields. The producer needed a novelty act and naturally came to see me. I booked Robert Lamouret and Dudule. I was unable to meet Lamouret on his arrival, so Kathie went instead and took him to the Piccadilly Hotel in London. We had booked the room in the name of Mr and Mrs Lamouret, as he told us he'd be travelling with his girlfriend. But when the receptionist saw their passports, he refused to register them as man and wife and insisted that they occupy two separate rooms. After all, this was England, not Paris!

They flatly refused to do this, so Kathie had no alternative but to take them home to Cavendish Square. When I arrived back late that night, I found them comfortably ensconced in our bedroom, and Kathie and I had to sleep in the guest room, not just for one night but for six weeks. It was the time of food rationing in Great Britain, and we took them out to dine every day of the week except Sunday. Lamouret's girlfriend said she thought we lived such a glamorous life, always eating in restaurants. She never realized that our total food ration for the week disappeared on the Sunday and we had no alternative but to eat out the rest of the time. Well, that's show business!

It was quite usual for big shows to have a try-out in the provinces, and we opened for two weeks in Birmingham. Present at the opening was Harry Foster, who, because of his connections with William Morris, had the biggest agency in Europe. Lew and Leslie Grade were acknowledged to be the second largest, although we had no American connections whatsoever.

After the opening night there was a supper party at the Queens Hotel in Birmingham and Harry Foster came to me and said, 'Lew, Robert Lamouret is wonderful. I'm going to book him in America, just as soon as the show finishes its London run.' I was thrilled and said, 'Harry, I'm very grateful to you. Thank you very much.' He then said, 'But, you must make your own commission arrangements.' 'Exactly what d'you mean by that?' I asked. 'Well,' he said, 'Fosters Agency gets five per cent and the William Morris Agency gets five per cent.' 'Harry,' I said, 'my artistes only pay ten per cent. What you choose to do with your five per cent is your business entirely.' 'In that case,' he told me, 'you'll never book Robert Lamouret in America,' and he walked off.

The show subsequently opened in London and was a smash. Lamouret was the talk of the town, and I kept brooding over the fact that he was missing out on America.

And then I had an idea. One of my better ones, as it turned out.

I spoke to George Le Roy. 'George,' I said, 'I've decided I'd like to go to the States and I want you to come with me. We'll try and work out an arrangement with an agency in New York to be their European representatives, and, at the same time, see if they'd be interested in representing Lew and Leslie Grade Ltd in America.' George thought it a great idea, and said he'd love to go with me.

Val Parnell, with whom by now I had an excellent working and friendly relationship, gave me letters of introduction to the three leading New York agencies, namely, William Morris, MCA (Music Corporation of America) and GAC (General Artists Corporation). He also gave me an introduction to a Mr Balaban who owned the Roxy Cinema in New York – a huge picture-palace which seated five thousand people and had a forty-five minute stage show between films. Charles Cochran, the producer, gave me a few introductions as well, and so did Binkie Beaumont, the powerful head of H. M. Tennants, the biggest producers of stage plays in England.

It wasn't immediately obvious at the time, but another important chapter in my life was about to begin.

9

Long-Distance
Traveller

GEORGE LE ROY AND I left London on the *Queen Mary* shortly after Christmas, 1946, and arrived in New York on 3 January 1947. We planned to be there for two weeks and were full of expectations. A trip to New York in 1947 was a major undertaking and an expensive one. Transatlantic travel wasn't nearly as popular as it is today, and New York City nowhere near as accessible. Currency restrictions were a terrible problem for a British tourist, and although we were given four dollars to the pound in 1947, the number of pounds we were allowed made it impossible to take advantage of everything the city had to offer. I cannot remember exactly how much money George and I had between us when we arrived, except that it wasn't nearly enough.

Like most visitors who arrive in New York by sea, our first sight was the fabulous Manhattan skyline. Though I'd seen pictures of it many times before, nothing prepared me for the real thing. There were no skyscrapers in London at the time – certainly nothing to compare with the Chrysler Building or the fabulous Empire State – and my first view of the city literally took my breath away. So did the Statue of Liberty, and Ellis Island – through which so many immigrants passed at the turn of the century. I couldn't help wondering, as the *Queen Mary* came in to dock, how my life would have turned out had my parents chosen to emigrate to America and not Britain . . . .

George and I were booked into a hotel overlooking Central Park called Essex House. We shared a tiny room, but as we didn't plan to spend much time in it, it didn't really matter.

Sadly, almost from the minute I arrived in Manhattan, I

became a bit disillusioned with the city, and a bit intimidated by the size and pace of it all. I felt like a real 'greener' and slightly out of my depth. I wasn't prepared for the brashness of the people, and what I thought to be their lack of warmth. In Europe, wherever I went I was welcomed like a member of the family. Not so in New York. I was a stranger and very much made to feel so.

One of the first places George and I went to was a famous theatrical restaurant near Times Square called Lindy's. They had a reputation for having the best delicatessen food in New York, so we thought we'd go and try it. Well, there was such a queue of people waiting to get in it would have taken at least an hour before we were seated. Some people, though, were just walking in and being seated immediately. They were obviously from the show-business fraternity and well known to the establishment, hence their preferential treatment. Ordinary people, like myself, had to take their turn. After about five minutes I spotted a man who had just paid his bill and was leaving. He looked like an important actor to me, so I approached him, introduced myself and George and said we were agents from England. I asked him if he could use his influence to get us a table. 'Sure,' he said. He snapped his fingers, and, talking to no one in particular, said, 'Give the bums a table.' And he walked away. Needless to say, we didn't get a table, and I was so furious at that man for treating us like a joke I vowed I'd never go back to America again. Suddenly I hated the place. If I'd had my way, I'd have left there and then. But we had work to do so I just had to stick it out.

Business-wise, things weren't any easier. The first meeting we had was with William Morris, who, of course, headed up his own agency. He was a charming man, but told us he had had a long and successful association with the Foster Agency in London, and didn't want to change that.

Several phone calls later, we finally managed to make an appointment with MCA, and met one of their top people – a man called Sonny Miller. He, too, was courteous to us, but during the half an hour we were supposed to have with him, he never stopped taking telephone calls. In all, I think we managed to talk to him for about five minutes. It was a case of don't call us, we'll call you. He said he'd contact us at the Essex House, but never did.

All the letters of introduction we'd been given turned out to be worthless, and I soon realized that America wasn't exactly waiting for me.

It took us several days to fix up an appointment at GAC with Tom Rockwell and one of his senior people, Thomas Martin. The first available date they could offer was 16 January, the day before we were due to sail back to London. By now we were both depressed and felt that the entire trip had been a failure – a complete washout. We weren't even able to take advantage of what the city had to offer in the entertainment line, as we were getting lower and lower on funds.

In 1947 the New York Theatre had many more hit shows than it does now, and, walking down Broadway I saw advertised such wonderful attractions as *Annie Get Your Gun*, *Carousel*, *Oklahoma!*, *Life With Father* and *Born Yesterday* with Judy Holliday. Unfortunately I didn't see a single one of them. For a start, I didn't have the money, and, even if I had, at that stage in my life I was far more interested in individual acts than Broadway shows. Broadway was my brother Bernie's territory – and he was welcome to it.

As the days slowly passed, my dislike of New York increased even more. I couldn't wait to get home. The number of rejections we were getting really undermined my confidence and I could barely bring myself to make an appointment with Mr Balaban of the Roxy Theatre because I was convinced we'd meet with the same kind of negative response from him as we'd had from all the others so far. But I did phone him, and he agreed to see us on 15 January.

As soon as I arrived in his office I gave him the letter of introduction which Val Parnell had written, then told him all about Robert Lamouret's marvellous ventriloquist act. I've always had the ability to describe the acts I handled in great detail, and vividly, and when I was through, Balaban seemed quite impressed. He sent for his booking manager and, without any ceremony, said: 'Give Lamouret four weeks at the Roxy starting January 1948 at $2750 a week.'

I couldn't believe it. Was I hearing correctly? I was – and left his office elated. For the first time in almost two weeks New York didn't look so bad after all.

The following day – which was our last – I went to see Mr Rockwell and Thomas Martin at GAC.

They were very gracious and seemed genuinely interested in everything we had to say. They were also very cautious, though, and wouldn't commit themselves to anything. Mr Martin, however, did invite George and I out to dinner that night, and, given that we had hardly had a decent meal in two weeks (because of the strict currency restrictions in those pre-credit-card days), we were only too happy to accept. He made reservations at an expensive New York restaurant, and topped a pleasant evening by giving me an enormous box of chocolates, which I brought back as a gift for Kathie – a tremendous luxury because we had sweet rationing in England at that time.

The following day we took a cab to the docks, boarded the *Queen Mary*, and returned to London. Long before we docked in Southampton I'd made up my mind that, despite my own little success with Mr Balaban and Robert Lamouret, America was definitely not for me.

Little did I know how heavily involved I was eventually to become with that marvellous and exciting country. Not all my first impressions have been right!

*   *   *

Soon after the Lew and Leslie Grade agency was formed, I had a habit of setting a target for the amount of business I thought we should be doing each week. If by Friday morning that target hadn't been reached, I'd call the various managements I did business with and persuade them to book some additional acts so that I could achieve my financial goal for the week. I'd frequently raise my target, and enjoyed the challenge.

I soon stopped this practice, however, because the business was progressing so well.

In April, 1947 there were reports in the trade paper *Variety* about a number of top American stars being booked for London at astronomical salaries – anywhere between $10,000 and $15,000 a week.

Some of the names quoted were Abbott and Costello, The Ink

Spots, Allan Jones, Sophie Tucker, Chico Marx and Gloria Jean. The reports claimed that the man responsible for these bookings was a Hollywood agent called Eddie Sherman. I took no notice, but the reports were fairly frequent. Certainly the Harry Foster Agency didn't know anything about it; neither did Val Parnell.

One day I received a telephone call from a man called Foster (no relation to Harry) who said he wanted to talk to me about these reports. I said I'd be only too delighted to see him, and he came, showed me the contracts which were all countersigned by Sherman, his guarantor, and asked me to find a theatre suitable for these star attractions. I said I'd be quite willing to do as he asked, but I'd need the sum of $50,000 placed in escrow in a bank.

He said: 'Fine. It's yours.' We then made several appointments to meet at Berners Hotel, off Oxford Street. Each time, he failed to keep the appointment. He did, however, always telephone with an excuse. We kept arranging fresh meeting places, and it was always the same story. He didn't show.

By now I had the feeling that Eddie Sherman was being taken for a ride, and that Foster was perpetrating some terrific con-trick.

In the middle of May I telephoned Sherman's office in Hollywood – a *real* long-distance call in those days! – and was told he was on his way to London from New York on the *Queen Mary*. I telephoned him on the ship and said, 'Mr Sherman, I hate to say this, but I think you're being taken for a ride.' I then told him all about the mysterious Mr Foster, and how he'd asked me to find him a theatre. I suggested to Sherman that, as soon as he arrived in London, we should meet.

As I'd suspected, it *was* a con-trick. Foster, it turned out, had been wined and dined in Hollywood by Sherman and several of Sherman's stars, some of whom were contracted to appear in Britain in February 1948. The contracts had all been underwritten and guaranteed by Sherman.

Understandably, Sherman was in a terrible state about this, and, because I'd taken to him from the moment we met, I had to think of a way to get him out of the spot he was in.

I went to see my brother Bernie, who, at the time, had a show

121

on at the London Casino which he planned to close in the middle of March 1948, and persuaded him to turn the Casino into a music hall headlining Sherman's list of American stars.

By rearranging the prices of admission, we worked out that the venture with Sherman could end in profit – though, given the salaries some of the stars would be getting, not a large one. Bernie saw the deal as a challenge – which he was happy to take on – and the day was saved.

After that Kathie and I became very friendly with Sherman and his wife Lillyan. They remained in London for three weeks and were extremely grateful that I'd managed to get him out of a jam.

In November 1947, I received a letter from Beryl Formby, whose husband George Formby was probably the biggest star in England at the time. They were in Australia (he was the first star I ever booked there), and in her letter Beryl suggested that I should take a trip down under to meet David Martin, the owner of the Tivoli circuit, whose business she felt I could get.

It has always been my habit to discuss the main events of the day with Kathie, whose influence on my career has been tremendous, and Beryl's letter was no exception. My own feeling was that it was ridiculous. I couldn't afford the time or the money such a trip would entail, and there was nothing in Beryl's letter to suggest that it would be anything other than speculative. I went to bed that night convinced I wasn't going to go.

At about 3 o'clock in the morning, Kathie switched on the light and woke me up. 'Lew,' she said, 'you've got to go. I know if you do go you'll get the contract and it will improve your business even more.'

I still wasn't convinced, but, as I say, I've always taken Kathie's advice, and decided to go to Australia in the first week in December. I telephoned Eddie Sherman (with whom I was on long-distance terms!) and told him what I'd decided to do. He thought it was a great idea and suggested I go via California in order to break the trip and spend a couple of days 'seeing the sights'.

My second trip to America was altogether more pleasant and more relaxed than the first, and I realized what a tremendous difference it makes if you have someone you know and like to escort you everywhere.

Two days isn't a great deal of time, but it was enough to give me an impression of Los Angeles, which I instantly liked. The climate was great, the people were friendly, and the 'laid back' atmosphere of the place appealed to me much more than the frenzied pace of New York. It was fun driving down Hollywood Boulevard and seeing such landmarks as Graumann's Chinese theatre, with its famous collection of cement footprints.

I spent one of my two evenings in California in Palm Springs having dinner with Rudy Vallee, who, in the 1920s and 1930s had been a top singer and saxophone player. He had a beautiful home, and we all had a most pleasant evening until he asked me where I was going on to from Los Angeles. I told him Australia. He wanted to know how I was getting there. Via San Francisco, I said. By what means? he asked. I said I was flying, of course. Whereupon, for the next hour or so, he put the fear of God into me telling me how dangerous long flights were and suggesting I cancel immediately. 'What happens if the pilot has a heart attack?' he asked. 'Or develops stomach pains? Or faints? Or has had a row with his wife and is feeling suicidal? What if he's got a hangover and can't think straight?' He went on and on, and really got me worried! But I flew to Sydney just the same, arriving there at about eight on a Saturday night.

It was a long, exhausting flight with several stopovers. Beryl Formby was at the airport to meet me, and we drove straight to my hotel where I checked in and unpacked. 'Let's go on to the theatre and see the finish of George's act,' she said. 'I know George's act,' I replied. 'Where's David Martin? He's the man I've come to see.' 'Don't worry,' she said, 'we'll see him tomorrow.'

The next day, however, David Martin was nowhere to be found, and it wasn't until Monday afternoon that we discovered he was in Melbourne.

I immediately caught the next plane to Melbourne.

Martin knew all about my visit, and, after checking into the Australia Hotel, I finally met up with him at about 7.30 in the evening.

Naturally, I wanted to get down to business immediately. After all, I'd travelled a long way for this moment, but before I could say anything, he said, 'Let's go down to my theatre and catch the show.' Seeing a show was the last thing I was in the mood for, but I couldn't really say no. As luck would have it, it was one of those interminable revues and it ran for over three hours. After it was over I was introduced to his charming wife, Isla, and we all returned to my hotel at about 11.30 for some supper. At twenty to one he suddenly yawned and said, 'Time to get to bed,' and he and his wife got up to leave. By now I couldn't contain myself any longer. 'Mr Martin,' I said, 'do you know the real reason why I came to Australia?' 'To see George Formby?' he enquired. 'No,' I said, 'to see *you*! Now I know it's twenty to one in the morning, but I just have to tell you that I came here especially to persuade you to give me the exclusive bookings of the Tivoli circuit in Australia. It's very late, I know. But I'd be grateful if you'd give me another half an hour of your time – or however long it takes to tell you the life story of Lew Grade, variety agent.'

He looked at his watch. 'How about tomorrow?' he said. 'Mr Martin,' I said, 'tomorrow I'm going back to London.' 'Okay,' he said. 'Go ahead.'

I heaved a sigh of relief, and told him as much about myself as I thought necessary, with special emphasis on my relationship with the Winter Gardens, Morecambe, where, after twelve years as their booker, they'd discovered I wasn't a crook and still allowed me to represent them.

At half past one, these were the words he uttered: 'We'll get the 8.00 a.m. plane to Sydney tomorrow morning, which means we'll be in my office just after 10.00 a.m. The agreement should be ready by midday, and after that I'll take you to the airport.'

I had clinched the deal!

When I had arrived at my hotel in Sydney on the Saturday I had found a telegram from Eddie Sherman. He'd arranged a meeting with Jules Stein (the founder and major owner of MCA), Lew Wasserman and Taft Schreiber, and suggested I made a stopover in Los Angeles.

I thought it would be a waste of time, but rescheduled the flight to include a stopover in Honolulu, which I'd always been fascinated to see. We had a four-hour wait for the connecting Los Angeles flight and during that time I must have eaten three whole watermelons and three pineapples. Such luxuries were not available in England as we were still on food rationing.

When I arrived at Los Angeles, I was met by Eddie Sherman who had booked me into a small room at the Beverly Hills Hotel on Sunset Boulevard.

My meeting with Jules Stein, Lew Wasserman and Taft Schreiber went off better than I could possibly have hoped for, and we completed an arrangement whereby I would be the exclusive representative of MCA in Europe for personal appearances of all their talent, and that they would represent and book for the States whatever talent Lew and Leslie Grade had to offer. There was no written agreement. I didn't need one. They were people of such high repute that they respected my word, as I respected theirs.

The following day I flew home to London in time for Christmas.

The way my business was now going, I realized I'd have to spend a great deal of time in the States, not only acquiring American attractions for England, but making sure – in the two-way traffic – that my own acts were well looked after.

Leslie, by that time, was proving to be an absolute wizard, and, possibly, the greatest agent in the business. He got the best deals, in the best theatres, and produced the best line-up of talent imaginable. We had twelve shows on tour each week, which has to be something of a record.

Shortly after my return from California it was decided that I would definitely concentrate on the American market, and that Solly Black, together with Brian Roxbury, would be responsible for finding new acts from the continent, thus relieving me of the burden of having to go there myself so often – even though I did make the occasional trip to Paris, Rome and Milan.

By this time Bernie had announced that the London Casino would open as a music hall with star attractions, the first being the comedians Abbott and Costello. The London Palladium, meanwhile, had a big spectacular which included three of the acts I'd recruited from Europe – The Andrea Dancers, The Amin Brothers and The Sonys.

Val Parnell came to see me one day and said, 'Lew, when the present Palladium show finishes, I want to run a series of variety shows there. It's got a much bigger capacity than the Casino, which means we'll have a better chance to meet the kind of terms the artistes are demanding. I'm sure Bernard will understand.'

He did, and agreed to run only a twelve-week season at the Casino before putting in a musical. But he wanted to open two weeks earlier than announced. This meant another trip for me to the States, not only to find an attraction prior to Abbott and Costello for the Casino, but to sign up some additional big names for the Palladium.

New York, the second time round, wasn't nearly as daunting. By now I was a bit more used to Americans and their methods than I was on that first trip in 1947, and, besides, after my deal with Lew Wassermann and MCA, I could no longer be ignored. What I had now was credibility – which, in America, is the name of the game. I was no longer a 'greener' and walked down Broadway with a lot more confidence this time.

In New York I met Eddie Elkort and Joe Sully, two men who acted as a liaison between the artistes MCA represented, and Lew & Leslie Grade. I told Eddie that one of the main reasons for my trip was to find an artiste for the opening show at the London Casino, and on my first night in town he took me to Bill Miller's Riviera Club, whose starring attraction was Lena Horne. I met Bill Miller himself, and after the show he took me backstage to meet Miss Horne and her manager. Eddie didn't take part in any of these discussions because Lena wasn't an MCA client.

As beautiful as Miss Horne looked in films like *Cabin in the Sky* and *Stormy Weather*, two all-black musicals she'd made a few years earlier, in real life she was even more stunning. There was a star quality about her that was unmistakeable – off stage and on it – and it was a great thrill for me to meet her. When, however, we came to talk business, she was extremely cautious and needed a great deal of persuading. One of her main concerns was England's racial climate. All her life, she explained, she'd been up against racial prejudice and, at this stage of her career, she wouldn't, she said, go anywhere if there was even the remotest chance that she would come across discrimination. I assured her that London was absolutely free from that kind of prejudice, and that there would be no problems whatsoever.

She still needed convincing and said that what she really wanted was a good holiday after her Riviera engagement.

I told her she'd have a great holiday in London, and, as a further inducement, offered to put her up in the River Suite at the Savoy Hotel. Not only that, but I'd supply her with a limousine and a chauffeur to go with it. I assured her she would have the time of her life, and that British audiences would adore her.

We talked until the early hours of the morning after which I realized that maybe I should have been a salesman instead of an agent, because, finally, she agreed. Perseverance, caring and inspiring confidence, I was to discover, was a winning combination when dealing with major stars.

Bernie was absolutely thrilled when he heard the news and admitted he couldn't have done better himself!

With Lena Horne safely under my belt, I flew out to California to see what kind of a line-up MCA could offer me for the Palladium. I felt we needed a real super-star – someone like Jack Benny, whom Lew Wasserman and Taft Schreiber personally handled.

They arranged a meeting with Jack, whose radio show, incidentally, was one of the hottest shows on the air.

Like Lena Horne, Jack needed persuading. And, again, it took perseverance and flattery. His main concern was that, not having made all that many films, he wasn't all that well known in England. I assured him that his radio shows – which also starred his wife, Mary Livingstone, Phil Harris and Rochester – were as popular in Britain as they were in America, and that audiences absolutely adored him. There was no way, I said, that he could miss.

He still wasn't convinced. In the end, though, I must have worn him down with my assurances of how well received he'd be, because he finally relented and said yes. A date was fixed for a Palladium opening at the end of May 1948. His wife Mary would be coming along too, of course. And also Phil Harris. I promised them first-class accommodation at the Savoy, and that clinched it.

Once I'd signed Jack Benny, everything fell neatly into place and I had no difficulty securing the services of several other big names at the time. Johnny Ray, the pop star, was one of them, Nat King Cole another. Nat was particularly popular in England, and, in due course, toured the provinces as well as the continent for me.

After a really successful stay in the States, I returned to London. Lena Horne opened at the Casino and was a sensation, as I knew she'd be. The combination of her brilliant voice and dynamic personality thrilled her audiences, who gave her a standing ovation every night. She was delighted to be in London, she said, and particularly happy in the River Suite at the Savoy. Indeed, everything worked out so well for her that she agreed to return at a later date to play the Palladium, and to tour some of the principal cities in the provinces.

In the middle of May, Jack Benny and his entourage arrived. He received tremendous press coverage, which must have done wonders to waylay his initial concern that he wasn't particularly well known here. He loved London, and, to judge by the reaction his show received, London loved him.

All the same, though, on the opening night he was as nervous as hell. All the old doubts about audiences not really knowing who he was, or being on the same wavelength, kept flooding back, and, ten minutes before he was due to go on for the entire second half of the programme, I found myself in his dressing room repeating all the things I had said to him when we first met in California. I kept reassuring him it would be a night to remember, and a wonderful engagement. But he wasn't satisfied. Suddenly, I said to him: 'Look, Jack, when you get on stage, after you receive your first round of applause, look at the audience, stamp your foot, and wave a finger at them. It'll work wonders.' He thought I was crazy.

Finally it was time for him to go on. I accompanied him to the side of the stage, and wished him good luck. His wife Mary kissed him on the cheek, at which point he looked at her mournfully, took a handkerchief out of his pocket, waved it and said, 'Goodbye, Mary – it was nice knowing ya.' Then he walked on stage.

The most thunderous applause I have ever heard for any artiste, at any time, greeted him. Jack couldn't believe it. For a moment he just stood there in silent amazement.

He looked into the wings where I was standing with Mary, then looked back at the audience. When the applause died down a bit, he stamped his foot, waved his finger at them, and the ovation started up all over again.

After that he was home and dry. The critics raved, and the entire run was a sellout. As the song says, 'Who could ask for anything more?'

10

America, Here I Come

ONE OF MY DREAMS was to bring Dorothy Lamour to England, and I spoke to her personal representative at MCA – Herman Citron, a charming man and a terrific agent. He said he had tried to persuade her to come to England, but she said she wasn't ready for that kind of exposure yet – and wanted to try out a new act at the Shamrock Hotel in Houston first. 'Why don't you try asking her yourself?' he said. I said I'd be delighted to and he arranged a meeting at Paramount studios where she was completing a film. It was love at first sight for me, and at the end of our meeting she told me she was opening her new act in Houston in ten days' time. 'Tell you what,' she said, 'why don't you come to Houston to see it? If you like it and think it's right for the Palladium, I'll accept the engagement.'

I agreed, but told her I could only stay one night and would have to leave early the next morning as I wanted to go to New Orleans to catch an act called The Weir Brothers, a comedy trio who'd worked in England before the war.

I happened to mention to Phil Harris that I was going to Houston and then on to New Orleans. Dorothy Lamour and Phil both insisted that I stay at the Roosevelt Hotel in New Orleans, and Dorothy said she'd make the reservation for me.

In Houston, meanwhile, I saw Dorothy Lamour's act and liked it very much. I told her she need have absolutely no qualms about it. 'In fact,' I said, 'all you have to do is come on in a sarong and they'll love you.' Like Lena Horne and Jack Benny, she too needed reassuring – but not as much – and in half an hour or so the deal was settled.

Next day, with very little money (thanks to the still prevailing currency restrictions), I left for New Orleans.

I arrived at 6.00 a.m. and there waiting for me was one of the biggest limousines I'd ever seen. I got into it and was driven to the Roosevelt Hotel, while thinking all the time, 'How the hell am I going to pay for all this?' When I arrived at the hotel, the manager was waiting for me. I didn't have to sign the hotel register. He took me straight up to what I thought would be a single room, but turned out to be a suite as big as a ballroom. There were flowers everywhere, baskets of fruit, and a selection of liquor. Then he took me into the bedroom, which was almost as large as the sitting room and which also had a terrific display of flowers, fruit, and so on. As he left the suite, the manager said casually, 'By the way, the limousine's at your disposal for as long as you need it.' I'd heard about Southern hospitality, but this was ridiculous!

That night I saw the Weir Brothers, who were even funnier than I'd remembered, and immediately booked them for a show Val Parnell was about to stage.

The next morning a gentleman turned up at the hotel to see me. He was evidently a prominent member of the New Orleans community and said he'd been told by Phil Harris to be my guide.

He took me to the elegant Garden District, with its stunning collection of magnificent, Southern-style homes, the city's fascinating cemetery, in which, for some reason no bodies are actually buried underground, and, most exciting of all, to the famous Vieux Carre – or Old City – with its rows and rows of nightspots and jazz clubs. My guide didn't miss a trick, and, after introducing me to some excellent Creole cookery in one of the quarter's more famous restaurants, we went on to several clubs and heard half a dozen or so world-class jazz musicians.

At no point were any bills handed to me, and the only thing that marred my enjoyment slightly was still the nagging problem of how the hell I was going to pay for it all.

Well after midnight he dropped me at my hotel and said he'd be round at 6.00 a.m. to take me to the airport.

In bed I began thinking about what the day had cost. As I certainly didn't have sufficient cash on me, and as there were no such things as credit cards, I thought, perhaps, the management of the hotel might accept an IOU, which I'd have to square with

131

the Treasury when I returned to England, and have the cash transferred to the States.

When I came downstairs the next morning the manager was waiting for me. He was, he said, extremely sorry that the owner of the hotel wasn't able to say goodbye to me personally, but hoped I'd accept his apologies.

'Of course,' I said. 'But I'm afraid you're going to have to accept my apologies too. I can only offer you an IOU for payment.'

He looked at me in astonishment. 'Payment? There is no payment. You're here as a guest of New Orleans at the special request of Dorothy Lamour and Phil Harris.'

That's relationship!

*　　*　　*

Dorothy Lamour came to London and proved she was more than just a sarong girl. Her act was delightful, and she returned several times to play the provinces as well as the continent. Whenever I was in California, I'd always call her up, and if she was in town, she would invite me to her home for dinner. To this day we still correspond.

In November 1948 I received a telephone call from MCA to say they'd like to see me at their head offices in California. On this occasion I decided to take Kathie with me.

She hates flying, and has always claimed that she'd only travel by air in exceptional circumstances. It took all my considerable powers of persuasion to get her to come, and I think she was glad she did, for we had a most enjoyable time. We broke our trip in Chicago to spend some time with Meriel Abbott, who used to book acts into the Hilton Hotel chain, and who herself had a wonderful dance team called The Meriel Abbott Dancers.

We arrived in California on the day before the presidential elections, and had a rather glittering dinner that night at Jack Benny's – whose guest list included James Stewart and Claudette Colbert. I remember we all sat up waiting for the election results. Kathie couldn't have cared less and was far more concerned about Princess Elizabeth, who was about to have her first baby! The results finally came through, and, to everyone's surprise, Harry Truman was re-elected. When I asked the assembled guests whom they'd voted for, they all said Truman. 'So why are you so surprised that he's won?' I asked. 'Because we felt so sorry for him we thought we were the only ones who did!' they said. About ten days later Prince Charles was born – on 14 November 1948. Kathie really regretted not being in London on such a happy occasion.

Though she enjoyed her first visit to the States, her heart, as I say, was in England, as she proved when Jack Benny and his wife invited us to dinner at a famous, star-studded Beverly Hills restaurant called Romanoffs. Everyone at our table ordered the most exotic dishes on the menu. Not Kathie. She asked for egg and chips. Everyone thought she was crazy. What they didn't realize, of course, was that eggs were still rationed in England – and therefore something of a luxury.

The real purpose of that particular visit to California was to meet up with Lew Wasserman, Jules Stein and Taft Schreiber, and to see what was on their minds.

And what was on their minds was that they wanted to buy Lew & Leslie Grade Ltd.

'We don't want partners,' they told me when I called on them in their palatial offices, 'and by giving you all our big star attractions, we're building your agency and treating you as a partner. We'd rather buy your company instead.'

I was really quite stunned by their proposal and totally unprepared. I asked them what kind of money they had in mind, and they told me. It was a fortune. On top of that they wanted to give Leslie and me employment contracts for a minimum of ten years at a very substantial salary as well as a profit incentive.

I was very excited and immediately went back to discuss it with Kathie, who, in turn, was rather confused and didn't really know what to think. I then told the powers at MCA that I'd have to go back and talk it over with my brother Leslie.

After our two weeks in California, we returned home via New York, where we stayed for a couple of days in order to meet Larry Barnett, who was head of the New York division of MCA, as well as Joe Sully and Eddie Elkort, my aforementioned liaison agents.

As Larry Barnett was giving Kathie and me a guided tour of his spacious premises, we passed Joe Sully's office. Joe was on the telephone. 'Who are you calling?' Larry asked. 'California,' Joe replied. I then said to Larry that I wanted to talk to Joe for a while, and could he come back and collect me in about fifteen minutes or so.

Joe finished his call, and for the next ten minutes or so the three of us chatted away. Then the phone rang again, and Joe picked it up. Just at that precise moment Larry came back to collect us and saw Joe on the phone. 'Why the hell are you spending so much time talking to California?' he asked. 'It's not California,' Joe explained. 'It's a local call that's just come in.'

Kathie didn't say anything at all, but she suddenly became very quiet and I could sense there was something on her mind.

We completed the tour of the offices, then returned to our hotel. That's when Kathie said, 'I'm sorry darling, but I don't think you should accept their offer. You won't be happy working for a huge corporation like MCA. If you have to account for every telephone call you make – and you know how much time you spend on the phone – it'll drive you crazy.'

I discussed the offer with Leslie – the only person I know who can speak on three telephones at the same time! – and he said: 'Lew, I'll leave the decision to you. Whatever you think is right, you do.'

I gave it a great deal more thought, and, at the beginning of 1949, I finally told MCA I couldn't accept their offer, but would be willing to continue on the same basis as we'd already established.

They told me this was not acceptable, and that was that.

Little did I know at the time that my relationship with Lew Wasserman was far from over. On the contrary, it was to continue and develop in totally different directions, and to our mutual benefit.

With Wasserman, Stein and Schreiber out of the picture, I had to think of something if I didn't want my American operations to collapse into a heap. It so happened that Eddie Elkort, quite independently, had decided to leave MCA. I asked him if he'd like to join my team, and he said he'd be delighted. I immediately arranged for Leslie to get Bank of England permission to transfer the equivalent of $5000 to New York, and, within seven days of the termination of my arrangement with MCA, I had established Lew and Leslie Grade Inc. at 250 West 57th Street, New York. Eddie Elkort was the President, and I was the Chairman. Eddie and I approached two more agents who joined us as employees, and we also took on Hans Lederer, an independent agent, who specialized in circus acts.

Val Parnell, who had become a close personal friend, was aware of all the things we were doing, and promised to give us his full support.

We now had our own offices in New York!

I thought then how proud my dear father, who had died in 1935, would have been to see us doing so well in America – of all places.

I returned to America to consolidate my relationship with several managements there, and, through Eddie Elkort, met Ed Sullivan, who hosted the most popular one-hour TV variety show in the country. It went out every week on the CBS network and, in addition to the four or five celebrities Sullivan talked to, there were several musical acts as well. Three minutes was about the maximum time allowed for every artiste, but the show was so popular and had such large viewing figures, that stars would kill to appear on it. I established a good relationship with Mr Sullivan, and had at least three acts on his show each week. Several British stars I handled, such as Norman Wisdom, Richard Hearne (Mr Pastry) and Tommy Cooper, appeared with Sullivan, after which I had no difficulty at all finding other dates for them across the country. Such was the importance of the Sullivan show.

Through Sullivan I also met William Paley, who founded the Columbia Broadcasting Company. Paley is, without doubt, the greatest TV showman who has ever lived. He is something of a visionary, who took enormous gambles both in the field of light entertainment as well as hard news: a real heavyweight of the industry. We, too, have a strong personal relationship. He helped and supported me a great deal in those early years and I'm proud that he considers me a friend. There has never been anyone quite like Bill Paley.

Every half-way decent act in England had one desire: to make it big in America. At the time we handled a talented star singer called Alma Cogan, who felt she was cut out for American stardom. She used to drive Leslie crazy, threatening to leave the

135

agency unless he was able to get her a booking on the Sullivan show. Leslie asked me what I thought I could do about this, and I told him something he already knew – that America was full of singers like Cogan, and Sullivan had his pick of them. Still, he said, 'See what you can do. The girl's driving me mad.'

One day I was talking to Eddie Elkort and some friends of his and mentioned Alma Cogan to him. 'You'll never get her on Sullivan,' he confirmed. 'He needs unknown girl singers from England like a second head.' Suddenly Alma became a challenge. 'Tell you what,' I said, 'I'm going to make a call to Ed myself and see what he can do.' Eddie and his friends laughed, and said they'd each bet me $10 I'd be wasting my time. 'Even if you *did* get him to agree,' Elkort said, 'he'll change the date a half a dozen times. And he'll only give her a couple of minutes.' I accepted their bet, and went over to see Sullivan personally.

'Ed,' I said, 'there's a fortune at stake on this meeting. Seventy dollars.' I told him all about the bet, and he said, 'OK, Lew, you'll win your bet.' He buzzed for his secretary, told her to type out the contract, and wrote into the contract a clause which said that Alma could sing two songs without any cuts.

Sure enough, Alma Cogan appeared on the Ed Sullivan show. He didn't mess around with the dates, she sang two songs without any cuts – and was quite a success. He even booked her for another appearance with him. That's relationship!

Needless to say, Eddie and his friends were amazed.

In New York I also made contact with Lou Walters, who ran the famous Latin Quarter nightclub. It was a beautifully mounted show featuring top stars in a season of four to six weeks. I recommended a couple of acts to Lou, and when they went down well it was my open sesame to the Latin Quarter. In time we had two or three of our clients appearing in the same show. One of the acts I recommended, The Dagenham Girl Pipers – a group of girls dressed in kilts playing the bagpipes – was a bit out-of-the-way for sophisticated New York. I told Lou they might be a bit of a risk. But I also said I thought they could be a colourful novelty in the show. Like most good showmen, Lou was a risk-taker and he booked them for six weeks. They stayed for twelve and over the years made several return engagements.

Another act I managed to sell Lou was Tommy Trinder.

Trinder's agent, Sidney Burns (who had been my brother Bernie's first agent), told me that Tommy was dying to work in America and asked me if I could do anything about it. I'd always admired Tommy – ever since we first worked together in my dancing days – and I told Burns I'd see what I could do.

I thought Lou Walters might be interested. 'He's an English comedian with a very broad Cockney accent,' I said. 'So how about it?'

Lou wasn't all that keen, but as a favour he booked him for two weeks, knowing that he was helping a friend, and that I was helping a friend.

The opening minutes of Tommy's first appearance in New York didn't bode at all well. The audience couldn't understand a word he was saying and heckled him terribly. But Tommy was absolutely brilliant. He came back at the hecklers and said, 'You seem to forget it was we who invented the language!' From that moment onwards he had that audience in the palm of his hand. His act clicked, and he stayed there much longer than two weeks.

Later that year, Lou told me that his young daughter, who was sixteen years old, was going to be spending some time in London, and asked if Kathie and I wouldn't mind keeping an eye on her and making sure she was all right. We'd be delighted, we said. Lou had been a good friend, and it was the very least we could do.

His daughter's name was Barbara. Years later, as Barbara Walters, she became the highest-paid anchor woman in television history.

* * *

To most New Yorkers, Manhattan was the centre of the world, as well as its entertainment capital. I was soon to find out that this wasn't entirely true. There was a tremendous amount of business to be done in California, and in places like Las Vegas and Reno, whose fabulous gambling casinos and hotels were always looking for new acts to accompany big-name stars. Also, there were extensive state fairs throughout the country, and numerous circuses – all of whom were constantly on the lookout for unusual or spectacular new specialty acts.

I happened, at the time, to represent the two best springboard acts I'd ever seen: The Faludys and The Hortobaghi Troupe. I also had a juggler called Rudy Horn who had to be seen to be believed. Rudy sat on a high unicycle, put a saucer on his foot, threw it up in the air, balanced it on his head, then threw up a cup until he had eight cups and saucers balanced on his head. Then he'd throw a lump of sugar into the top cup, and, finally, a spoon. He really was sensational.

With all this new talent, and with the whole of America at my disposal, I decided we really should have a branch of Lew & Leslie Grade in California. I told Eddie Sherman in Hollywood about my intentions, and he gave me office space in his building on Sunset Strip facing the world-famous Mocambo Club.

I decided that the man to run our office there should be Elkan Kaufman, for whom I had high hopes and great expectations.

So, in addition to our New York office, we now had a branch in sunny California.

The Grades had finally arrived.

11

~~~

Seeing Stars

BY 1951 WE WERE RECOGNIZED as being an important
agency in the United States. Val Parnell often accompanied me
on talent-scouting trips there, and on one of these trips we went
to Miami where Lou Walters had opened a second Latin
Quarter. One of the artistes we were keen to see was a comedian
called Harvey Stone whom Eddie Elkort thought would be suitable for the Palladium. We saw him, and were very impressed.

On the same bill with Stone was a singer called Frankie Laine.
Laine's personal manager, a man called Dick Gabbe, knew we
were in the house that night, and asked us, as a special favour, to
stay on and hear Laine's act.

Well, Laine came on wearing the worst toupee you've ever
seen, and, frankly, looked a terrible mess. His singing voice was
fine – but the overall impression he made wasn't at all good.
Naturally, Gabbe wanted to know what we thought. He was
keen, of course, that his client should play the Palladium.

I didn't want to tell the man that I really didn't think much of
the act, and simply said that the Palladium had no vacancies for
several years and that we never made a commitment that far in
advance. I hoped he got the message, for we had no intentions of
putting Frankie Laine into the Palladium – ever.

Sometime later we were short of a headliner for the Palladium.
The people who were available we didn't want, and *vice versa*.
Leslie suggested Frankie Laine to Val. 'Not a chance,' we said,
and told him what we thought about Mr Laine. 'The trouble
with you chaps,' Leslie said, 'is that you don't listen to the radio
as much as I do. Frankie Laine's got two hit records in the charts
– "Jealousy" and "Whiplash" – and I'm sure he'd be a sensation.'

139

We resisted for as long as we could, then, out of sheer desperation, we booked him.

On Frankie Laine's first night at the London Palladium, Val and I did something we had never done before. We took the coward's way out, and, rather than watch the show, we stood on the steps of the Palladium waiting for what we were convinced would be a disaster to be over.

Suddenly we heard a roar of applause that startled us. We rushed back into the theatre and couldn't believe our eyes. Frankie Laine was a huge hit! His toupee fitted, he'd lost weight, his act had improved with the confidence that comes with having two hit records in the charts – and the audience were giving him a standing ovation.

Laine played several return engagements for us, he toured the provinces, took Europe by storm, and, generally, was a huge success. Again, so much for first impressions!

Early in 1951, my telephone rang at 4.00 a.m. I picked up the receiver and a voice said, 'This is John Ringling North of the Ringling Barnum and Bailey Circus. I'd like to see you at the Ritz Hotel in Paris tomorrow.' I said, 'Fine. I'll be there.' As soon as I put down the telephone the thought struck me that it might be a hoax. I immediately called the Ritz Hotel to check that he was actually staying there, and found that he was.

So I went to Paris, met John Ringling North and struck up a remarkable relationship. He had seen Pierre Elysée and his wonderful trapeze act, and Trubka and the Lions, and wanted them for his circus at Madison Square Garden. He had approached them directly, only to be told to contact their agent – Lew Grade. We had a terrific meeting, and I did long-term contracts not only for Pierre Elysée and Trubka and his Lions, but also for several other acts. He appointed me European representative for his circus and I had the freedom to book any acts that I thought were outstanding and suitable. He needed as many acts as he could get; his was the biggest circus in the world with three separate rings. We remained friends up until his death about four years ago. A lovely man.

Meanwhile, in the United States our agency was thriving. One of the greatest of all the artistes we booked there was Edith Piaf. Ever since Solly Black and I had first met this small, frail-looking sparrow of a woman backstage in Paris a few years earlier, I was enchanted with her. Her face seemed to embody all the suffering of the human race, and her extraordinarily powerful voice reflected that suffering. It was impossible not to fall in love with this astonishing woman and the Americans took her to their hearts as soon as she stepped on to the stage. They say that star quality is indefinable. But whatever it is, Piaf had it – in spades!

We also booked Jean Sablon, a real Parisian heart-throb at the time, and Charles Trenet, who wrote that beautiful song 'La Mer'. They too were highly successful. So was Petula Clark, who played the prestigious Empire Room at the Waldorf Astoria in New York.

By now there was no star in the world I was afraid to approach. With my cigar to give me Dutch courage, and my excellent track record to stand surety for me, I usually got who, and what, I wanted.

Through Joe Glazer of Associated Booking Corporation, I signed Louis Armstrong for the Palladium, as well as Lionel Hampton and Cab Calloway. My rival Harry Foster realized he had to work in collaboration with me if he wanted the William Morris artistes he represented to appear at the Palladium. That's how we got Danny Kaye – one of the outstanding successes in the Palladium's history.

Burns and Allen did a season for us, so did Danny Thomas, the brilliant American ventriloquist Edgar Bergen (whom I'd met in 1948, together with a pretty little daughter of his called Candice), Spike Jones and his City Slickers, and Jo Stafford, whose personal manager, Mike Nidorf, became a good friend of mine.

I also brought back Stefan Grappelly, who, since the death of Django Reinhardt in a car crash, had formed his own group. He was still the finest jazz violinist in the world.

I booked Harry Belafonte, who was no trouble at all, and Judy Garland who was. She was also, probably, the greatest female performer the world has ever known – so we just had to weather it. The problem with Judy was that we never knew whether or not she was going to show up for the performance. She always did eventually, but she sometimes made us wait, and we'd often have to hold the curtain for her. In the end, though, it was worth it. She was always sensational. And by now, I think, her fans knew that with Judy Garland one was never sure what was going to happen. It was all part of the excitement of a Garland performance. The main thing was that she always delivered the goods.

In the days of the London Casino, though, we had one star who, half way through her act, would always faint. Her name was Gloria Jean. She was quite a big film star in the 1940s, and made a lot of pictures at Universal with people like Donald O'Connor and Peggy Ryan. She had an absolutely glorious singing voice – rather like Deanna Durbin's – and was an enchanting girl. But she had this problem: she kept fainting. We were warned that this might happen, but we took such good care of her, and mollycoddled her all the time, we were sure she wouldn't let us down. The interesting thing was that it never happened at rehearsals. If it had, we would have just cancelled the engagement. But she was fine until she had an audience, then something would happen and she'd just go to pieces and we'd have to bring the curtain down. It was the most nerve-wracking two-week engagement I've ever known. At least with Judy Garland, there were ways of calming her down and getting her on. But once Gloria fainted, that was it.

We also had a problem with Mario Lanza at the Palladium. He was a neurotic man, and, like Judy, we never knew whether he was going to show up for the performance or not. You had to keep flattering him, telling him how wonderful he was, and that his audiences couldn't wait to see him. And, also like Judy, he always went on in the end – but some nights it was really touch and go, and Kathie and I found ourselves having to be a psychiatrist, wet-nurse, wife and father-confessor all rolled up into one. Handling temperamental stars, I discovered very early on, was an art in itself, and if you didn't learn that art quickly, you could be in big trouble. With Lanza it was a case of pandering to an inflated ego all the time; with Garland it was just the reverse. You had to keep building up her confidence and reassuring her how good she was. Either way, though, it didn't make life easy.

One star who was no problem at all though was the great Bob Hope.

When Bob first appeared in London, the Palladium was committed to another show, so Bob appeared at the Prince of Wales. His entourage included a female vocalist from the States, plus a team of gag-writers, including Larry Gelbart, who has since become famous in his own right as the creator of the hit TV series 'M*A*S*H', as well as several successful plays and screenplays. Mort Lachman, another successful writer-producer, was also part of the team, as was Charlie Yates, without whom Bob never made a decision. Charlie was a close friend of Bob's as well as his personal manager, and they were inseparable.

Bob had a regular radio show in America and while he was in England recorded the shows for transmission at a later date. The only time he could do this was on a Sunday night, and, after spending Sunday afternoon at an American air force base outside London with him, we returned to London together in time for the recording.

When we arrived back at the recording studio, Charlie Yates was nowhere to be seen, which was unusual. It got nearer and nearer to recording time – and still no sign of Charlie. I said I'd dash over to the Savoy Hotel to see what had happened. Perhaps he'd taken a nap and overslept.

I went to the hotel and knocked on his door. But there was no answer. I asked the manager for his pass-key, but we still couldn't open the door because the key had been left in the lock from the inside.

By this time I was really getting extremely anxious, and, after a great deal of persuasion on my behalf, the manager called in his maintenance staff to break down the door.

Charlie was lying on the bed. He'd suffered a massive heart attack.

Bob, of course, was in the middle of recording his show, and was totally unaware of this.

I immediately called a doctor. He looked at Charlie and said, 'There's no hope for him.' I said, 'Let's get him to a hospital.' He repeated, 'He's nearly gone and if we try to move him to a hospital, he'll definitely die.' I insisted. We took him to the London Clinic, got hold of a heart specialist, and after two or three days he started to recover. Of course, Bob went to see him every day, as I did. In fact, it was very strange. We had three

143

physicians and I was present at all their discussions. They evidently thought I was a doctor and I'd occasionally interject with a medical-sounding remark, to which they'd respond in kind. It got to a point where they refused to start their daily consultations unless I was present. After about five days, Charlie made a remarkable recovery. They wouldn't allow him to have a telephone in his room, because they wanted him to remain quiet. Charlie, however, loved to bet on racehorses, and nothing could stop him from doing this. Kathie used to sit with him every afternoon, and as he picked out a horse she'd go outside and telephone a bookmaker with the bets. This went on for another two weeks until Charlie had recovered sufficiently to return to the States with Bob.

After every opening night of a major attraction, Val and his wife Helen would throw a party for the star. When Bob opened at the Prince of Wales, I insisted on giving him a party of my own at the Embassy Club in Bond Street. I was not only commemorating his successful début in London, but a high spot in my own career. Bringing Bob Hope to Britain had been my greatest achievement so far – I think I even had a glass of champagne that night, although I'm not a drinking man and never have been. I first realized this in my early years in Paris. Vincent Massi would offer me champagne and after a sip or two I'd have to go to the bathroom as it really disagreed with me. So I thought to myself, who needs this? Occasionally I have a nip of brandy, but not only does it upset my stomach, it makes me lisp! So Kathie always knows if I've been drinking!

Anyway, the following year Bob Hope returned – this time to the London Palladium. The opening-night party was in Val Parnell's flat.

We were all assembled there when suddenly one of the guests came in and said, 'Bob, there's a phone call for you from America.' Bob rushed over, lifted the receiver and a voice at the other end said: 'This is Jack Benny, goodbye.'

It *was* Jack, and Bob was absolutely flabbergasted. 'What do you think of that Jack Benny?' he said. 'He calls me long-distance from California, doesn't even ask how I am, just says, "This is Jack Benny, goodbye"!' What Bob didn't know was that Val and I had planned all this in advance. Benny had already arrived in

London, and was calling from a telephone in another room in Val's flat.

A few seconds later, Jack Benny walked into the room where we all were. Bob doubled up with laughter. Benny, who absolutely adored pranks like this, had flown over specially to work that gag. Seeing the expression on Bob's face was worth it. It turned out to be a really memorable evening.

At the closing performance of Bob's Palladium engagement, Val and I thought we'd play another couple of jokes on him. One of the gags Bob used in the show had a fellow coming on with a medicine bottle and offering Bob a spoonful of the stuff. Bob would take a sip, turn round with his back to the audience, shake his body, turn round again and say, 'I forgot to shake the bottle.' But that night, instead of Bob's usual stooge going on, Val Parnell walked on. Bob did a double take, and, I have to hand it to him, carried on as though nothing had happened.

Also appearing in the show were Jerry Desmond and a tall, beautiful singer-actress called Marilyn Maxwell. Marilyn and Jerry would come on dancing together, while Bob was in the middle of a song. Then Bob would walk up to them and tap Jerry on the shoulder.

Everyone would then expect him to dance off with Marilyn. But he danced off with Jerry instead. That closing night I persuaded Jerry to let me go on in his place, and I found myself dancing with the gorgeous Miss Maxwell. With her high heels she looked about six feet tall, and there was little me – just over 5 ft 6 ins!

Bob turned, saw us and kept us dancing for what seemed an eternity. Then he came up to me, tapped me on the shoulder and finished the dance with me. Again, it seemed to be going on forever. I whispered in his ear, 'Enough, already!' But still he continued. Then he suddenly stopped, took me by the hand so that we both faced the audience. 'Ladies and gentlemen,' he said. 'This is Lew Grade. He's my agent, and he used to be the world's champion charleston dancer. Tonight he's going to do the charleston for us.' My reply was: 'I'll only do it, Bob, if you do it with me.'

That night Bob Hope and I danced the charleston together – my first and last appearance at the London Palladium!

Val Parnell booked Frank Sinatra into the London Palladium. Frank didn't have an agent, and the deal was done through his lawyer and friend, Micky Rudin. Val asked me to look after Frank's affairs in London – such as work permits, tax details, and so forth, which I was happy to do. Mr Sinatra was no trouble at all and we became good friends.

A couple of years later, I received a phone call one Saturday morning. It was Frank calling me from the Savoy Hotel. He said he wanted to see me urgently. I went over to the hotel and he told me he was leaving for Rome the following day. He wanted to buy something over there, and, he said, he needed $12,000 on his arrival, and could I arrange it for him? In return, he promised he'd play ten concerts in Italy at a later date.

I said I'd see what I could do, and telephoned Ivaldi, my representative in Milan. Ivaldi fixed the whole thing up, and the money was delivered to Frank's hotel the next morning.

Sometime later, I called Frank and reminded him about the ten concerts he'd promised to do. We fixed the dates and he did them. No contract. No written agreement. Just one person's word to another. I always admired Frank for this. That's integrity. And that's relationship.

*   *   *

In August 1952 Kathie and I were both overjoyed when our son Paul came into our lives. Kathie, who at the beginning of our marriage was earning more from her singing than I was from my agency, gave up her career completely to take care of him. Suddenly, our life took on a different aspect – we were experiencing all the responsibilities and pleasures that come from being parents.

Paul's first school was the Lycée Français in London, and at thirteen he joined my nephew Philip at Millfield School in Somerset. This was a school renowned for its sporting achievements and many famous sports champions have come from there.

Paul was a very good tennis player and a great golfer. He had a handicap of 2 when he left Millfield and had won many golf competitions. For a while he thought about becoming a professional golfer, and he was certainly good enough, but his interests lay in the music business.

146

Today, Paul has two children from his previous marriage and we are really thrilled that he is now very happily married to his lovely new wife Beverley, who has become very close to us.

12

Did You Hear the One About ...?

MANY APOCRYPHAL STORIES have been told about me during my years as an agent. Most of them are not true. One of them has me lunching with Leslie at Isow's restaurant in Brewer Street, when all of a sudden Leslie jumps up and says: 'Lew, I've forgotten to lock the safe back at the office.' 'Don't worry, Leslie,' I say. 'We're both here.'

When a little girl asked me what two and two make, I'm supposed to have answered, 'It depends if you're buying or selling . . .' Not true!

Nor is it true that when a beggar came up to me and asked me if I could give him 50p for a bed, I said, 'First send round the bed so I can look at it.'

But my favourite – though also apocryphal – story is this: Sidney Bernstein of Granada goes into the Jack Barclay Rolls Royce showrooms in Berkeley Square and says, 'I want a Rolls like Lew Grade's, with a telephone.' 'Fine,' they say. 'We'll get you one in six months' time.' 'But I'm Sidney Bernstein of Granada,' comes the reply, 'I can't wait that long.' 'Very well, Mr Bernstein, we'll get you one in a week's time.' They do, and I'm driving along Regent Street when the phone in my car rings. 'Hello, Lew, this is Sidney Bernstein. I'm phoning you from my car.' 'Hold on Sidney,' I say, 'I'm just on the other line.'

At that time I didn't have a phone in my car, but it's still a great story.

This, however, *is* a true story: I was at a meeting for the IBA (Independent Broadcasting Authority) and, after outlining some programme ideas to the full council of twenty members, one of the councillors, a respected broadcaster called Mary Adams, said, 'Mr Grade, I expect you'll be telling us next you're doing programmes on misogyny and miscegenation.' 'Miss Adams,' I said, 'I don't even know what those words mean!'

One more true story. I was at a gathering of distinguished people and happened to be chatting to Lord Longford and Lord Willis. Lord Longford congratulated me on my announcement about the production of *Jesus of Nazareth*. Ted Willis turned to me and said, 'Lew, I bet you can't name the twelve disciples.' I said, 'I certainly can.' He said, 'Well, name them.' I said, 'Peter, Paul, Mark, Thomas . . .' and then I stopped. He said, 'Go on. Name the others.' I said, 'I haven't finished reading the script yet.'

There was a theatre in the Edgware Road called the Metropolitan, which belonged to the Syndicate circuit, and whenever I was free, I would go with Kathie to see the first performance on a Monday night, hoping that I would find some new English acts to add to our already extensive catalogue.

Many agents went to this opening performance, but during the intermission time they would go into the bar, have a few drinks and generally miss the act that opened the second half. As neither Kathie nor I drink, we used to stay in our seats. One day we saw an act called Winters and Fielding, who did a kind of Burns-and-Allen routine, and I thought they were amazing. I rushed through the pass-door to go backstage, barged into their dressing room and said, 'I'm Lew Grade. I think your act is great. It's absolutely ridiculous that you should be opening the second half of the programme. You should either be a headliner or co-headliner. You're probably only getting £25 per week. If I handled you, it would be different. I could get you £200 a week. Who are your agents?'

They said, 'Lew and Leslie Grade!'

I then proceeded to get them £200 a week and the right star-billing I felt they deserved.

Another incident happened in Copenhagen. As I have already said, Kathleen Williams, the booker for the Blackpool Tower Circus, was always worried that Cyril Mills of the Bertram Mills Circus would get acts before she did. One night we saw a great comedy acrobatic act. I had my representative with us and I asked him to go round and tell them that I wanted to see them at the Palace Hotel at 10.00 a.m. the following morning.

The next morning 10.00 a.m. arrived, but no act. Mrs Williams was calling me every fifteen minutes. She knew that Cyril Mills was coming to Copenhagen the next day. It was driving me crazy and I just couldn't understand it. Eventually, my representative Ernst Salstrohm turned up at 12.30 to have lunch with Mrs Williams and myself, and I jumped at him and said, 'How could you let me down? I wanted the act to be here so that we could sign them for the Blackpool Tower Circus.' He said, 'It's OK. Just relax. I went round to see them last night and they said, "We can't do anything. You have to speak to our agent Solly Black of the Lew and Leslie Grade Agency"!'

Coincidence, as I have observed, has always played a great part in my life. On one of my visits to New York with Val Parnell, I suddenly had a terrible pain in my groin. We got a doctor, who said I had a strangulated hernia and must be operated on immediately. I didn't want to have this operation. I wanted to get back to England and have it looked at by my own doctor. Val virtually carried me on to the plane. I couldn't move and was in agony. In those days the planes had sleepers. They were Stratocruisers with upper and lower bunks. When we got on the plane both Val and I found we had upper sleepers. Val spoke to the person who had the lower sleeper, explained the situation, and asked if he would be kind enough to change places. He was very gracious and agreed. That was the first time I met General Sarnoff, the founder of RCA, who owned NBC, the National Broadcasting Company, and who pioneered colour on American TV. As I'd already met Leonard Goldenson – and knew Bill Paley, of course – this now meant that I was acquainted with the heads of all three networks!

When I arrived in London my doctor came to see me and dismissed the idea of a strangulated hernia – it was simply a cyst in my groin. I went into hospital and within forty-eight hours I was as fit as a fiddle, which proves that a second opinion is always worthwhile.

A month or so later I was out to dinner with Kathie and some friends when I suddenly developed the most terrible stomach pains. Kathie took me home immediately. By that time we had become great friends with Vincent O'Sullivan, one of the leading gynaecologists in this country, who knew all the leading surgeons in every field. He saw me and immediately diagnosed appendicitis, and called in the top man for that, a Mr Victor Smythe, who operated immediately.

A few days after my operation, I was quietly recuperating in the St John and Elizabeth Hospital. It had a calm, peaceful atmosphere and the nursing sisters were nuns, who were unfailingly gentle and caring.

One afternoon I was told that some visitors were coming to see me from the Palladium. One of the nuns brought in six of the Palladium girls, all smartly dressed in their overcoats. They ranged themselves round my bed, threw off their coats and appeared in their dancing costumes, complete with spangles and feathers, and then proceeded to do a high-kick routine all round my bed.

I thought it was hysterically funny, but wasn't quite sure how the nuns would react. However, several of them were standing in the doorway and they were laughing uproariously. They all had a great sense of humour and fun. I later discovered that this prank had been arranged by my wife Kathie and Val Parnell.

When it was all over, Mr Smythe told me of an extraordinary thing that happened while I was on the operating table. He was about to make his incision in one direction when, at the last moment, he suddenly changed his mind and made the incision in another. He didn't know what made him change his mind, but he said if he had done it the way he planned to originally, I would have died from acute peritonitis.

Which would have been extremely inconvenient, and very bad timing, for my life was to change direction yet again.

PART II

13

Teething Troubles

IN 1953 THERE WAS a great deal of lobbying in parliament for commercial television (as it was called), headed by Norman Collins, who was supported financially by Sir Robert Renwick, one of the heads of W. Greenwell and Co., a major City stockbroking company, and C. O. Stanley, who had founded Pye Electronics, makers of electronic equipment, including transmitters, television cameras, and so on. Eventually the Bill was passed. There was going to be commercial television in Britain. I took no notice.

I did nothing about it until early in 1954. Jo Stafford was appearing in London and Mike Nidorf, her manager, was with her as usual. I received a telephone call from him one morning, and he said he was calling from Suzanne Warner's office. Suzanne was then fully occupied handling the publicity for all the stars we brought over to Britain and she was amazingly good at her job. Mike said, 'Lew, have you read *The Times* this morning?' I said, 'I never read *The Times*. I don't have time to read more than one newspaper a day, and that's the *Daily Express*. Why do you ask?' 'There are advertisements in *The Times* for applications for the franchises for commercial television in Britain,' he said.

There had previously been a lot of publicity when the question of commercial television was first mooted, but the initial capital requirement for each major territory application was mentioned as being a minimum figure of £3 million. I said, 'Mike, I know all about it. Where am I going to get £3 million?'

He said, 'Suzanne says that provided you have a sufficiently distinguished board to make the application, plus £1 million, she has somebody who will put up the other £2 million.' I said, 'Put her on the telephone.' Then I said to her, 'Suzanne, who is going to put up the £2 million?' She said, 'I can't tell you that.' With that, I hung up on her.

She rang me back almost immediately – 'Lew, it's Warburgs.'

I never did read the City pages and I did not know who Warburgs were. I called Sid Hyams, who, together with his brother Phil, owned four of the biggest cinemas in London (5000 seaters) for which we used to book the attractions. They also had a small share in Lew & Leslie Grade Ltd.

I said, 'Sid, are Warburgs good for £2 million?' He said, 'They're good for £50 million!' 'Sid,' I said, 'you're in the television business and I'll let you know more about it later.' I then called Val Parnell and said, 'Val, you're in the television business.' He said, 'Great.'

I followed this up with a call to Stuart Cruickshank, of Howard and Wyndham Theatres, who had eight important provincial theatres, and who used to put on musicals, operas, ballets and other big productions. I said, 'Stuart, you're in the television business.'

Then I called Binkie Beaumont, head of H. M. Tennants, the most important producers of plays in London, and made the same announcement to him.

Next I called Dick Harmel, who was John Schlesinger's right-hand man in South Africa. Schlesinger was an enormously well-connected businessman who owned a cinema chain as well as a huge insurance company. I told Harmel the same thing, and said I'd let him know in due course how much I'd be asking him to invest. Everyone I approached trusted and believed in me and promised to support me.

I wanted to get back to Suzanne Warner with the suggested composition of my board, so that I could meet with Warburgs. This all took about one hour.

Then I received a telephone call from Val Parnell. His name was essential to the possible success of the application, as he was the best-known figure in the entertainment industry at the time. He said, 'Lew, I'm sorry, I can't join the consortium. My contract is exclusively with Stoll Moss and Prince Littler says I can't do it as he's against television.'

By that time Prince Littler had bought control of Stoll Moss and General Theatres Corporation, which included the London Palladium, the Victoria Palace, the Theatre Royal, Drury Lane, Her Majesty's, the four Shaftesbury Avenue theatres (the Globe, Lyric, Apollo and Queens), plus many theatres in the provinces.

'Val,' I said, 'I want to come over now and see Prince.' 'Come over by all means,' he said, 'but I tell you he's adamant. He won't allow me to be involved in television. He feels it'll be going against the interest of the theatre business.'

Well, I went over to see Prince Littler. After about two hours of persuading and cajoling, I came away with his full support – both moral and financial. In an intensive heart-to-heart discussion I made him realize that one can't stop progress, and rather than be overtaken by it, one should join it.

I then called Suzanne Warner and gave her my list of prospective board members. She was very excited about it. Prince and I arranged a meeting with Warburgs, and they appointed Commander James Drummond as their nominee to the board. We called ourselves ITC – the Independent Television Corporation. We had £500,000 in the bank, plus the money from Warburgs and from all the others I'd telephoned.

Leslie and I each invested £15,000. It was make or break for me, as £15,000 was all I had in the world.

We made our application and, naturally, appointed Suzanne as our press officer. But she almost did *too* good a job with the press, for the articles that subsequently appeared made it look as though every single theatre in the country, as well as all the available talent, was under our control. She trumpeted our assets out of all proportion, even to the extent of suggesting that there'd be nothing left over for the BBC! By that time Lew & Leslie Grade Ltd had merged with London Artists, a company that represented actors of the calibre of Laurence Olivier, Ralph Richardson and John Gielgud, and all these star names were, understandably, quoted in the newspaper reports as well.

We completed the application and waited to see what would happen.

Then came the blow. The Independent Broadcasting Authority sent for Prince Littler, Val Parnell and me. I had suggested that Prince should be the chairman and I the managing director. We were informed, however, that there was no way we could get a licence; that we were too strong, and controlled too many theatres. They accused us of having a monopoly on entertainment in Great Britain, and suggested that we should supply programmes to the companies that were eventually given the franchises. It was a bitter pill to swallow.

We had a company called ITC, £500,000 and didn't know where to go from there.

Soon after that I met an American producer called Hannah Weinstein, who had been living in England. 'Lew,' she said, 'I'd like to do a series called "The Adventures of Robin Hood". I want to do 39 half-hour episodes and Official Films, an American TV distribution company, are confident they can sell it in America.' I liked the idea a lot. I asked what it would cost. She said about £10,000 per half hour.

Richard Greene had already accepted the part of Robin Hood, and I said, 'OK. Go ahead.' This was on a Tuesday. By the end of the week I realized that perhaps I should have consulted the other members of the board before making the commitment. I had never had to work with a board before, and wasn't used to making decisions by committee. I therefore called Prince Littler on the Friday and said, 'Prince, it's very important that we have a board meeting. It's something I'd rather not explain on the phone. Can you call a board meeting for 10 o'clock on Saturday morning in my office?' He did, and I told all the members of the board that I'd committed £390,000 out of the capital of £500,000 to make 39 episodes of 'Robin Hood'. The reaction wasn't entirely favourable. How, some of them wanted to know, could I make such a commitment? Because, I replied, I liked the idea and honestly believed it could work. 'We're supposed to be a production company,' I said, 'and this will be a good start for us.' One of the board members then asked me whether I'd signed an agreement. 'No,' I said. 'But I have given the go-ahead just the same.' Much to his credit, Prince Littler then said, 'Gentlemen, if Lew has given his OK, that's as good as a contract and we'll support him.'

'Robin Hood' turned out to be one of the most successful television series ever. The CBS Network in America bought it, and the 165 episodes we made grossed millions of pounds for ITC.

Meanwhile, though, the group of investors were still willing to put up the balance of the money we thought we would originally need for the commercial television franchise – namely £3 million.

We then had a call from the IBA. Sir Robert Fraser, who was its first Director General, and Sir Kenneth Clark (later Lord Clark), who, in addition to being the chairman, was a noted worldwide authority on art, had already announced the franchises. Rediffusion had Monday to Friday in London, the Norman Collins/Sir Robert Renwick group had Saturday and Sunday in London, and Monday to Friday in the Midlands. Granada – i.e. my friends Sidney and Cecil Bernstein – were to have the area called Lancashire, which then included Manchester and Yorkshire, from Monday to Friday, while the ABC Cinemas circuit, who had also applied for a licence, were to have Saturday and Sunday in Lancashire, and Saturday and Sunday in the Midlands. These were the four principal contractors. Others came on to the scene later.

Sir Robert Fraser then asked us to go and see him. He said he realized that the publicity we had received during our application for the franchise had been grossly exaggerated, and then asked if we were willing to consider a merger with the Sir Robert Renwick/Norman Collins and C. O. Stanley group. Apparently they hadn't been too successful in raising the money, and, on reflection, wondered whether they even had the programming expertise. We agreed to join them on a fifty-fifty partnership basis, so that ITC would still remain in existence as a production company and we would have a 50 per cent stake in the new company, which at that time was known as ABC – Associated Broadcasting Company. I proposed that Prince Littler be elected Chairman of the Board, and that he should remain Chairman of ITC. I would continue as Managing Director of ITC.

Val Parnell, Commander James Drummond and I were also to join the board of the new company. As far as Val and I were concerned, it was going to be a part-time job. I could remain with the agency to do whatever was required, while Val could continue running the theatres. We would all be 'one happy family'. Unfortunately, neither Val nor I, nor indeed any of the other members of the ITC board, knew anything about commercial broadcasting. Mike Nidorf said it might be a good idea to get somebody in who did!

At that time a young man called Harry Alan Towers, who was producing programmes for Radio Luxembourg, an outfit that broadcast commercial radio programmes overseas, was suggested. I wasn't too happy about this, but finally had to agree it did make sense to have somebody around with his experienced background.

I then went to the board who said if I wanted Harry Alan Towers, I could have him. So Harry joined the board of ITC, and eventually the board of ABC – which later had to change its name to ATV because Associated British Cinemas, who were awarded the franchise for the weekends in the Midlands and in Lancashire, were known as ABC.

Harry Alan Towers quickly made himself the principal protagonist in all preparations for the opening of our TV station. Val and I were happy to let him perform this role, because we had our own businesses to run. I was still very active in the Lew & Leslie Grade agency and Val was Managing Director of the Stoll Moss Theatre Group.

We therefore formed a management group comprising Val Parnell, Harry Alan Towers, Norman Collins, a man called Richard Meyer, and myself.

And that is how I started in commercial television.

Both Val and I made it quite clear that TV was only to be a part-time interest for us. We had periodic meetings, and, I must say, Harry Alan Towers seemed to be a quite remarkably capable young fellow. He kept on sending us fully detailed technical reports on all aspects of TV transmission and we were convinced we'd picked a real genius to mastermind the operation for us.

The moment the licence came through, I contacted Bill Ward, who, a year earlier, had directed a Bob Hope TV special I'd admired, and asked him to join us. I also asked him to make several other suggestions as to who else we might ask, because the only people in the country who had any knowledge at all about television were committed to the BBC. Bill suggested we take on a brilliant technical engineer called Terence MacNamara, as well as Keith Rogers, who would be responsible for all the transmission details. And, as head of production facilities, he suggested Frank Beale. Later, we acquired another very senior engineer, Leonard Mathews. We decided we had to have a studio, so we bought the ailing Wood Green Empire from the Stoll Moss Group at a reasonable price, and converted it into a television studio. In time, this one studio produced up to nine hours of programming a week, a feat that was only possible because everything, at that point, was done live.

The board of ATV was not a very comfortable one. There appeared to be two separate factions – the Robert Renwick/C. O. Stanley/Norman Collins group, and the Prince Littler/Val Parnell/Lew Grade group. Whenever we had board meetings there were constant arguments between C. O. Stanley and Harry Alan Towers. Towers kept on blaming Pye for delays in the delivery of equipment, and naturally this upset C. O. Stanley very much. The two men disliked each other intensely.

The responsibilities were divided as follows: I was to be in charge of any film series we bought, while Val and I together would look after variety entertainment. Drama was to be in the capable hands of Binkie Beaumont of Tennants, whose staff included Cecil Clarke, one of the ablest producers in the country and a future Head of Drama for ATV. The rest of the programming was to be left to Harry Alan Towers.

We realized now that it wasn't practical to have our offices spread out in so many areas, so we rented a floor from Rediffusion in Kingsway. Val and I continued with our own businesses, content to leave most of the TV work to Harry Alan Towers. C. O. Stanley, however, wasn't happy with the arrangement. So Val and I arranged a private luncheon with him at Scotts Restaurant, which was then in Piccadilly, and during the course of our meal had a frank discussion about the general situation.

The impression he gave was that he liked Val and me very much, but wasn't all that happy with Harry Alan Towers. We tried to convince him he was wrong about Towers, and persuaded him not to continue his open battles with him in the boardroom. From that time onwards, meetings went a little better, but although C. O. Stanley was the dominant force, and Val and I always had a high regard for him, there still seemed to be a major division between the two factions.

The time finally arrived to prepare the programme schedules. We decided that on Sunday we would begin the evening's transmission with 'I Love Lucy', and then do a show called 'Sunday Night at the London Palladium', to be hosted by Tommy Trinder. This would be followed by a drama which would run from one to two and a half hours. At that time the first series of 'Robin Hood' was well on the way to completion, and we kicked off our Saturday night programmes with it at 7.30 p.m., followed by a one-hour variety show called 'Val Parnell's Saturday Spectacular', then a film series, and so on.

We were limited to fifty hours' broadcasting a week and found we had a gap to fill between 6.30 p.m. and 7.30 p.m. on Sunday evenings, just before 'I Love Lucy' started. I suggested we try something that had never been done on television before: a one-hour religious programme.

We were the first company in the world to do this and it proved highly successful. So much so, in fact, that we were later encouraged to initiate transmission of church services on Sunday mornings.

Rediffusion opened its broadcasting service on 22 September 1955 with a huge gala at the Guildhall, then a party afterwards at the Mayfair Hotel. I thought Rediffusion's programmes were very poor and the press agreed with me, particularly the Beaverbrook press.

Lord Beaverbrook was totally against commercial television and continued to wage war against the whole concept. The rest of the press were in favour of it, and believed it a good thing that there was competition for the BBC. But the all-powerful Beaverbrook press was critical of all the ITV companies for many years, and rarely had an encouraging word to say about any of their programmes.

At the Mayfair Hotel, Stuart MacLean, who was the Chairman of Rediffusion, came over to me. He was confident about his programmes and pleased with the fact that he had five days a week in London compared with our two. 'When you go broke,' he said, smugly, 'we'll buy you out!'

Though we only had the weekend in which to do it, ATV changed the whole complexion of television with our adventurous programming.

But the costs were heavy, bearing in mind that only London was on the air at that time. It wasn't until March 1956 that the Midlands came on, then Lancashire in June the same year.

We were not getting sufficient support from advertisers, and our financial position became critical.

Then, in December of that year, Val and I decided that Harry Alan Towers should not remain with the company. He had been presenting a programme called 'Free Speech', which included such prominent figures as Robert Boothby, Michael Foot and A. J. P. Taylor. He had packaged this programme himself, and had a package price paid to him. Val and I felt this was unethical, and went to see Prince about this. He resisted for a while, then finally agreed that we were right. So Harry Alan Towers terminated his employment with both ITC and ATV at the end of December 1955.

When we told Robert Renwick and C. O. Stanley about the termination of Towers's contract, they were absolutely delighted and, for the first time since we began, we became a united board. It was then agreed that Val Parnell and I would have to give over a considerable part of our time to the running of ATV. Val was appointed Managing Director and I was made Deputy Managing Director. Val felt we would still have ample time to devote to our own businesses, but this was virtually impossible, and, apart from an hour at 7 a.m. at the Lew & Leslie Grade Agency, I found myself spending the rest of my time at Television House in Kingsway.

My relationship with Sir Robert Renwick and C. O. Stanley continued to strengthen. They had complete faith and confidence in me and gave me every support.

By the end of March, however, we had run out of money. We had no alternative but to raise more cash, so we invited the Daily Mirror Group to acquire a portion of ATV. There were two structures of shares: voting shares and ordinary shares. This was insisted upon by the IBA, who wanted to prevent a situation in which anyone could come along and buy a TV company outright.

The Daily Mirror put in additional capital. More shares were issued, and the Mirror bought 29 per cent of the ordinary shares and 25 per cent of the voting shares.

The rest of our group were also required to put up additional capital. Leslie and I had to advance a further £5000 each, and, although Leslie had his money available, I had a real job trying to raise my share. Kathie sold quite a lot of the jewellery I had bought her through the years and we were eventually able to find the full £5000.

Which reminds me of an amusing incident. We had a half-hour children's programme which a Miss Anna Lett was in charge of. One day Anna came in to me and said, 'Lew, I need an extra £15 for each programme.' 'Anna,' I said, 'that's impossible. We just haven't got the money.' Sometime later she married Christopher Chataway, who was an MP and had once been a famous athlete. Approximately fifteen years from the time she had asked me for the £15, Chataway was appointed Postmaster General, responsible for all areas of broadcasting. I telephoned Anna and said, 'I've been thinking about that extra £15 you wanted for the kids' programmes. I've decided you can have it.' Of course, by that time she was no longer with the company, and Christopher Chataway, who is now in an important sector of banking, often tells this story.

Once transmission started from the Midlands, advertisement revenues began to pick up. This meant that the programme costs could be shared between London and the Midlands and eventually, when Lancashire came on to the scene, the advertisers gave their full support because commercial TV coverage now comprised about 75 per cent of the country.

For the first time since we began, the money started rolling in. Val and I had agreed to take a nominal salary when we became Managing Director and Deputy Managing Director, which I had negotiated. We received £4000 a year each, and a percentage of the profits. At the time our contracts were negotiated, it looked as if there would never be any profits, but June was the turning point. Large sums of money were being made by all four of the major companies. Needless to say, I renegotiated our contracts to exclude the profit share.

Earlier on, Roy Thomson (later Lord Thomson of Fleet) had been awarded the franchise for Scotland. He came in to see me one morning towards the end of January 1956. At that juncture, we were running out of money again, and he said to me, 'I want to do a deal with you to supply all the programmes for Scottish TV. I'll pay you £900,000 for the first year and £1,000,000 a year for the remaining eight years.' I was thrilled. 'OK,' I said, 'you've got a deal.'

Eventually, after the other companies had been on the air a while, they criticized me for making this deal because two years later, when the whole industry turned round, Scotland's share of the programming costs would have been around £10 million. Fortunately, I had Granada's support. 'Once Lew's made a deal,' said Cecil Bernstein, 'that's it – and we'll support him.'

In time, other companies, like Anglia, Southern and Harlech TV, had to pay figures starting at about £5 million and then reaching a figure of approximately £10 million.

When Roy Thomson purchased *The Times*, the *Sunday Times* and their associated publishing companies, he instigated a series of monthly luncheons to which he invited people prominent in the world of politics and business. I received invitations to these luncheons twice a year and he never ever failed to mention that, thanks to Lew Grade, he was able to buy *The Times* newspapers. He was always very generous, and each Christmas he'd send me a box of glacé fruits, which I hated. But at least he remembered me at Christmas!

At the end of 1957 we acquired a new building at 17 Great Cumberland Place, London, W.1, which was known as ATV House, and later became ACC House. We had a 42-year lease at approximately £1 per square foot, so you can imagine what it's worth today.

After Harry Alan Towers left us, Val and I called a meeting with Bill Ward, Terence MacNamara and Keith Rogers. 'You're the professionals,' we said to them. 'We know nothing what-soever about the television business other than programming. We've no technical knowledge whatsoever – certainly nothing compared to Harry Alan Towers. So you're just going to have to bear with us.' 'What makes you think Harry Alan Towers was so knowledgeable?' they asked. 'Because of these memos,' we said, and showed them the batch of memoranda we'd received from Towers. They laughed, 'Excuse us for a few moments,' they said, and left the room. Five minutes later they returned with copies of memoranda which *they* had daily been sending to Towers – and which he, in turn, had been copying and sending to us! We realized then that we knew everything there was to know about television. All we had to do to be given the information we needed was to press a button on our intercom, and call the appropriate person.

I'll never forget an occasion when, during the intermission of a Royal Variety Performance in the presence of Her Majesty The Queen and HRH Prince Philip, the Duke of Edinburgh turned to me and said, 'Can you explain the difference to me between UHF, VHF, 425 lines, 525 lines and 625 lines?' 'Sir,' I said, 'I know absolutely all there is to know about television. But I can't tell you now. I'll have to send you a memorandum tomorrow.' Then I told him the story about Towers and the memos. He roared with laughter and thought it really very funny.

*   *   *

John MacMillan was the first Programme Controller for Rediffusion, the General Manager was Captain Tom Brownrigg and the Managing Director, Paul Adorian. By this time I had appointed Bill Ward as our Programme Controller, and together with John MacMillan we decided we'd start a schools programme, which eventually went out through the full network.

I introduced the first twice-weekly soap opera, 'Emergency Ward Ten', which was an immensely popular series. It was followed some considerable time later by Granada's 'Coronation Street'.

I also introduced the adventure series 'The Saint', starring Roger Moore, and made 143 episodes of which 43 were in colour. At that time there was no colour transmission in England and it wasn't until several years later, when colour TV proved so successful in America, that it was decided the time had come to have colour TV in Great Britain.

Among the many television adventure series ATV made were 'Danger Man' (known as 'Secret Agent' in America) starring Patrick McGoohan, 'The Champions', 'Man in a Suitcase', 'Man of the World', 'Randall and Hopkirk', 'The Protectors' and many, many more. We also made 'The Prisoner', starring Patrick McGoohan, which has since become a great cult series throughout the world.

At the end of 1957 ATV felt there might conceivably be a conflict of interests between ITC and themselves. Val, Prince and I agreed, at which point ATV bought ITC, making it a wholly-owned subsidiary.

My friendship with Mike Nidorf prospered. There was a television distribution company in America owned by Milton Gordon, and Mike told us that a friend of his, Jack Wrather, who was married to that delightful actress Bonita Granville, was interested in acquiring Gordon's company because they were distributors of three of his series – 'Lassie', 'The Lone Ranger' and 'Sergeant Preston of the Yukon'. Wrather, he said, was looking for a partner. So we decided to go into partnership with him and called the company ITC Inc. Walter Kingsley, who had previously been with one of the big television distributors called ZIV, was made President. We now had our own distribution company in the United States.

After a couple of years I felt that ITC Inc. was concentrating far too much on the sales of Jack Wrather's properties and not nearly enough on our product. So we did a deal with Jack Wrather whereby we purchased his half of ITC, but I still remained on good and close terms with him.

Mike Nidorf was then appointed President of ITC Inc. I began to feel there was tremendous potential amongst the American networks for British product and also for syndication – selling to individual stations.

I then began to develop my relationship with the American networks. After all, I had a head start! I was on good terms with Leonard Goldenson, William Paley and Robert Sarnoff, son of General Sarnoff, who had followed in his father's footsteps and was now the head of NBC and later became the head of RCA.

I now decided that, in addition to ITC as a production company in Europe, we should have ITC the distribution company.

Meanwhile, in mid-1956, I realized ATV was a full-time job and that I could no longer maintain Lew and Leslie Grade Inc. in New York and California. We sold our company to Thomas Rockwell of GAC for a small sum of money, plus a share of the commissions on the acts that we represented, which would be forwarded to us in London.

Strange how the wheel turns. A little while later, Herb Siegel, who as a young man was with Official Films, bought the company GAC and made Larry Barnett his President. Herb is now the head of Chriscraft, a major company in America which has a substantial holding in Warner Communications Inc., and Larry Barnett is his right-hand man.

I needed a top salesman to head the distribution division of ITC for the Western hemisphere, and I put Elkan Kaufman in charge. He had done such a tremendous job for me in America, and I felt he could sell anything. By 1957 I had planned well into the future and was anticipating a steady flow of product. Elkan handled his territory, with the exception of Australia, which I personally controlled, very well.

I then took Alec Fyne, who was with the Lew & Leslie Grade agency and made him Head of Casting for Variety and Comedy Shows. By the beginning of 1959 I was ready to spend three or four days a month in New York where the headquarters of the major American networks were based.

We now realized it was time for us to acquire an important studio, so we bought the British National Studios, renamed it ATV Elstree, and, with the assistance of Terence MacNamara, built the most modern and up-to-date TV centre in the country. It officially opened in April 1961, and everyone who worked there – including stars from America – commented on the superb facilities we were providing.

In those early days, I met a young couple, Sylvia and Gerry Anderson, who came to me with an idea for a puppet series. I loved the idea and we started with 'Supercar', 'Stingray', 'Fireball XL5', 'Joe 90' and 'Captain Scarlet'. Some considerable time later, we did 'Thunderbirds' and 'Space 1999', which was the first science-fiction series to include live actors rather than puppets. We were, therefore, the forerunners of all the science-fiction series and feature films that were subsequently made.

*　　*　　*

While Leslie was still in the air force, and our offices were still in Shaftesbury Avenue, I represented an act called Ted and Barbara Andrews, who were a husband and wife singing team. They said they would like their little daughter to audition for me. 'Fine,' I said. We fixed a date and on came this little five-year-old who astonished me with her glorious, mature voice. Betty Box was doing a film at the time, and I took her to see Tony

Darnborough, the casting director of the Maurice Ostrer Film Company, which also owned a large circuit of cinemas. The casting director, Betty Box and I were present and heard her sing. They were all just as amazed as I had been. But as she was only five years old, we couldn't get a work permit for her, so nothing came of it.

Some years later Val put her into a show at the London Hippodrome, later to become The Talk of the Town, which my brother Bernie ran for Charles Forte.

She was a huge success and later went to America. Her name was Julie Andrews and little did I know at that time how she would influence a change of course in my career.

14

Family Affairs

IN 1957 I ASKED KATHIE what she'd like for Christmas. She said she'd like to hold a Christmas tea party for the old age pensioners in the district of St Marylebone, where we lived. I agreed to do this. What happened, eventually, is that she took the Seymour Hall and we had between eight and nine hundred senior citizens there for a sit-down tea. Each one received a bag which contained butter, tea, sugar, soups, chocolate and many gifts. We engaged a five-piece band under Nat Temple to play for them, and got a star entertainer to perform or sing for them. The first one was Gracie Fields, and then entertainers varied from Vera Lynn, Anne Shelton, Tom Jones, Shirley Bassey . . . What started off as a one-time gesture continued for twenty-four years. Our last party was in December 1980. The hall was always beautifully decorated with Christmas trees and lots of flowers, the Lord Mayor of Westminster came, as did the local MPs and different denominational church leaders from the area, as well as local representatives from the Red Cross and WRVS, plus Kathie's mother and all the family. Everyone helped with the old people. They all had such a wonderful time – and Kathie Grade's Christmas party became a highlight for them each Christmas. And that was her favourite Christmas present from me each year.

Nowadays, Kathie is also Chairman of the Alexandra Rose Day. This is a traditional charity founded by Queen Alexandra in 1912, and it provides funds for a number of the smaller charities in this country. Kathie has also done a great deal of work for the Red Cross and had the privilege of being awarded the Red Cross Badge of Honour. She is a great supporter of the Young Women's Christian Association (YWCA) and for many, many years has been Chairman of their Christmas Fair. In addition, she has always been involved with Age Concern.

It seems to me another of my life's extraordinary coincidences that, because Kathie is Senior Vice President of the Royal Albert Hall, and has access to their archives, she was able to find a copy of the actual programme for the World Charleston Championship which I'd entered in 1926.

On Kathie's sixtieth birthday, she said she didn't want to make too much fuss of it, so we decided we would go to the Ivy Restaurant (which Kathie then owned) for a quiet lunch. We were just a small group: Kathie and I, our son Paul, Kathie's sister Norah and her son Philip, Kathie's youngest sister Phyllis and my Executive Assistant, Marcia Stanton. As we walked into the restaurant, Marcia said that some of the ATV staff from Elstree were upstairs having lunch, and she suggested that we called in to say hello. We walked in, and found the room full of ATV personnel, and then Kathie was presented with a magnificent bouquet of roses, and told that Gregory's, the famous rose growers, had specially cultivated these roses – called The Lady Grade Rose – which were to be presented to Kathie on her sixtieth birthday. Mr Gregory himself made the presentation.

It was a wonderful gesture that had been arranged by the staff at ATV Elstree in appreciation for all that Kathie had done for them over the years, in the way of organizing Christmas and other parties for their children at the studios each year.

And it really was a total surprise to us, because the only people who knew about it were Marcia and Kathie's brother, Jack Moody, the head of the photographic department at Elstree, who had originally joined the company with Suzanne Warner, because he had been the photographer in her publicity business.

Kathie was really thrilled, and so touched, by the staff's thoughtful gesture – and she has always adored roses. Although our Elstree Studios are now owned by the BBC, there is to this day a special area in the grounds where Lady Grade roses are still growing, and each year the gardener presents Kathie with a huge bouquet.

*   *   *

On 28 September 1961, Sir Robert Renwick became Chairman of ATV and Prince Littler remained a Director of the Board. In

September 1962 I was appointed Managing Director. During the previous couple of years Val Parnell had been going through some matrimonial problems and decided he could no longer give ATV the necessary time. In fact, he retired completely, although he remained on the Board for a little while. This was quite a wrench for me. Our association went back so many years, and we had gone through so many exciting experiences together, that I knew I'd miss him terribly.

Over a number of years, I had had a feeling that Prince Littler might want to retire. So I said to him one day: 'If you ever want to sell the Stoll Moss group of theatres, we'll buy them.' He gave me his assurance that we'd have first refusal, and that he had the controlling shareholding. I never took holidays, but about twice a year Kathie and I would take the Golden Arrow to Paris for the weekend, returning on the Monday night.

In the middle of January 1965, while away on one of these relaxing weekends, I asked for the *Evening Standard*, which always arrived in Paris on Saturday morning. It was at lunch-time that I read a piece stating that Prince Littler had sold the Stoll Moss Group to his brother Emile. I was stunned! Although they were brothers, they were not on good terms, due to a business disagreement some years beforehand. I went crazy, particularly when I remembered Prince's promise to me. It took me several hours to track Prince down and I finally reached him at his Arlington House flat in London, near the Ritz Hotel. 'Prince,' I said, 'I've just read the *Standard* and see that you've broken your promise to me.' 'I couldn't help it, Lew,' he said, 'I had 49 per cent of the company, Emile and his associates had 48½ per cent.' Then he explained that Emile had told him he'd bought the remaining 2½ per cent from Paul Gillespie, who was the son of one of the founders of that theatre group. I said, 'How do you know Paul Gillespie has sold his share?' He said, 'Well, Emile told me he was going to acquire it.' 'Check with Paul Gillespie,' I said, 'and I'll call you in an hour's time.'

I called him back and he said he'd spoken to Paul Gillespie, who hadn't sold his shares, but was willing to do so. I said to Prince, 'Get him on the telephone now. Do the deal with Gillespie. Buy the 2½ per cent and then call me the moment you've done it.'

He called me later and said, 'It's done.'

I told him I'd get the Golden Arrow on Sunday morning and come straight to his apartment to work out the deal. He said, 'Fine.'

We arrived at Victoria Station at about 6.00 p.m. Kathie went home in the car and I took a taxi to Arlington House. The deal Prince was going to do with Emile was based on a figure of £6 million for the whole group. I completed the deal and shook hands with Prince Littler. I knew that Emile and his associates wouldn't want to remain in a minority position, and the next day I called Emile. He had no alternative but to sell his shares to me, and the deal was then complete. I now thought it was about time I told the Board. I called Sir Robert Renwick, C. O. Stanley and Hugh Cudlipp, who represented the Daily Mirror's interests on our Board, and they were all delighted.

I then realized that the Stoll Moss Group had about 20 per cent of the voting shares and two million of the ordinary shares in ATV (worth about £2 million). At that time companies were not allowed to buy in their own shares.

Suddenly I had an inspiration. I was on good terms with Sir Max Aitken, who, after the death of his father, Lord Beaverbrook, became head of the Beaverbrook Press. I called Max and said, 'Max. I don't know if it's possible, but if I can get you 12 per cent of the voting shares and two million ordinary shares in ATV, would you buy them?' He said, 'Lew, now that I know you so well, I'd be absolutely thrilled to have the opportunity.' All this happened on a Saturday. I then called Sir Robert Renwick and asked what he thought of the idea. He said he thought it would be wonderful, but that I'd never get approval from the Mirror Group, who were Beaverbrook's great rivals. Nor, he said, would I get approval from the Independent Broadcasting Authority, because the transfer of voting shares had to be approved, first by the Board, then by the IBA, who had the right of absolute veto.

I felt my next move was to call Hugh Cudlipp, with whom I'd always had an exceptionally good relationship. He said, 'Lew, I personally would agree, but you'll never get Cecil King to agree.' I said, 'If Cecil King agrees, is it OK?' 'Yes,' he said, 'but you'll still never get approval from the IBA.' So I called Cecil King. He was known to be a very tough man who had tremendous influence in the political arena. I often used to have lunch alone with him at the Mirror offices and we always got on famously. When I put the question to him about whether he'd accept Max Aitken and the Beaverbrook Press, he simply said, 'Lew, if you want it – you've got it.'

We were half way there. But I had yet to tackle the main hurdle – the IBA. It was 11.30 p.m. before I was able to track down the telephone number of Lord Hill, who was then Chairman of the IBA. He was in Luton. I called him and put the proposal to him. His first words were, 'Lew, you're crazy. It's impossible.' I said, 'Charles, do you realize that if we get the Beaverbrook Press as our shareholders, this will put the final seal of approval on independent television? It would mean that our principal critic had finally come round to our side.' He said, 'I never thought of it that way. And yes – you're right. It sounds reasonable and sensible. However, I can't let you know until Monday morning. I want to discuss it with the Deputy Chairman and others.'

As promised, he called on Monday morning and gave me the go-ahead. So commercial television had reached its ultimate goal – it had become respectable! We gave the Beaverbrook Press 12 per cent of the voting shares and the other 8 per cent was divided between various members of the board with IBA approval.

Sir Max Aitken joined the Board and was one of my staunchest supporters. Some years later he had a heart attack and became severely incapacitated, but I still insisted that he should remain on our board. Eventually he sold out to Trafalgar House and Victor Matthews (later Lord Matthews) became the Chairman of the Beaverbrook Press. They therefore held the voting shares as well as the ordinary shares and Victor Matthews joined our Board. Trafalgar has since sold the Express Group, and it is now owned by United.

When I was appointed Managing Director of ATV, the Board felt that I should have the assistance of a deputy managing director. I certainly had no objection, and the person selected by the Board, mainly on C. O. Stanley's recommendation, was an American, Ed Roth, who was involved with Irish television in Dublin. He stayed with us for about a year and I delegated a lot of work to him.

There was one incident I can recall from that period. We were giving special discounts to advertisers once they reached a certain figure of expenditure, and these terms were published in our advertising rate card. The rate card had a termination date. J. Walter Thompson felt they had a right to this discount, because they had made their bookings well before the termination date. I gave Ed Roth this problem to handle.

About two months had gone by when I had a call from the Chairman of JWT. 'We're still claiming our discount,' he said, 'but we haven't heard about our claim.' I then had doubts about Ed Roth, because this matter was far too important not to have been dealt with instantly. I called in Pat Henry, who was head of our sales advertising division, and Tony Lucas, who was the company lawyer, and I said, 'Are we right in refusing the claim for this discount?' Tony Lucas said, 'Absolutely right. However, the wording of the terms is a bit ambivalent.' 'Give them the discount,' I said. I now knew that Ed Roth had to go. And he did.

Then Robin Gill joined me as Deputy Managing Director. He had been Managing Director of Border Television – a small television company in the north of Scotland. Academically he was very bright, but he didn't have my lifetime's experience in dealing with show-business 'personalities' and we were simply not compatible. After a few years, he, too, left.

I then met a brilliant young man with great knowledge and enthusiasm for television. His name was Bruce Gyngell, and he had been one of the first people actively involved in television in Australia. He came over to London with his family and stayed with me for just over three years. Unfortunately, he felt there were many more opportunities opening up for him in Australia and decided to return home. He is now running TV AM, the Breakfast Television Company, and he has made a huge success of it.

By that time, Jack Gill, who had been the chief accountant of the group, was, at my request, appointed to the Board of ATV. C. O. Stanley was against the appointment, but I insisted and he finally agreed.

In 1973 Lord Renwick (formerly Sir Robert) died. This was a

very sad moment for me. He had been my friend and adviser for so many years, and I was to miss the invaluable guidance and support he had given me during the time of our association together.

Later in 1973 I became Chairman of ATV and appointed Jack Gill as Deputy Managing Director.

It was the high spot of my career so far, and provides me with an appropriate point in my story to fill in some of the activities of my brothers.

After I left the Lew and Leslie Grade Agency in March 1956, Leslie became the top agent in town, expanded his business enormously, and in 1963 went public. His assets included two cinema chains, Elstree Film Distributors, and two prestigious theatrical agencies: London Artists and London Management. In the early 1960s Leslie branched out into film production, and, for the Associated British Picture Corporation, produced Cliff Richard's first two films – *The Young Ones* and *Summer Holiday*. *The Young Ones* was so successful it made its money back in the first three weeks of its run. Then, with Robin Fox, father of the actors James and Edward Fox, he produced *The Servant*, written by Harold Pinter and directed by Joseph Losey.

In 1964, my brother Bernie merged his agency with Lew & Leslie Grade Ltd and it was now called The Grade Organisation. He still retained his production companies and theatres as a separate entity, and became the country's most successful producer of musicals. His shows included Anthony Newley's *Stop the World I Want to Get Off*, *Mr Pickwick* and *The Four Musketeers* with Harry Secombe, *Funny Girl* with Barbra Streisand, *Sweet Charity* with Juliet Prowse, *Little Me* with Bruce Forsyth, and *Promises Promises*. He also produced plays such as *Barefoot in the Park* and *The Odd Couple* by Neil Simon, Frank Marcus's *The Killing of Sister George*, and Joe Orton's *Loot*.

On the first Sunday in April 1966, the day of our first-ever colour recording of 'Sunday Night at the London Palladium', I called in to see Leslie at his lovely new home in Kensington Gardens. He looked well and very happy. Then, just before going to the Palladium to watch rehearsals of that night's show, I dropped Kathie at home in Wimbledon, where her mother and sister lived.

Rehearsals were a bit sticky that night, and, because of the technicians' unfamiliarity with the new colour equipment, we were running a bit late.

Suddenly, Kathie arrived at the theatre, rushed into the control box and said, 'I want you to come with me quickly.' Strangely enough, without questioning her, I followed her out, and as I got into the car she told me the terrible news. Audrey, Leslie's wife, had rung her to say that Leslie was seriously ill, and Kathie felt I should get there immediately.

We arrived at the flat to find Dr Freeman, my brother-in-law, already there, and he told me the news that Leslie had suffered a massive stroke, and was waiting for Dr Joiner – a specialist from Guy's Hospital – to come along and see him. Dr Joiner duly arrived and said there was little point in moving Leslie, but we nevertheless decided to take the chance of getting him to Guy's Hospital. He went off in the ambulance with Audrey and Joe Freeman, and Kathie and I followed in our car. We stayed at the hospital with Audrey all night, and then realized that we still had the dilemma of how to break the news to my mother. Kathie said, 'Leave it to me.'

The following morning, she called in to see my mother casually, as if she was just passing by, and suggested that as she was going to Wimbledon to spend the day with her mother, my mother might like to accompany her. Kathie's mother was a very loving person and over the years she had developed a wonderful relationship with my own mother. So Kathie felt she would be the best person to break the news. When they arrived at Wimbledon, Kathie discreetly left them alone, and in her own gentle way Kathie's mother told my mother the news about Leslie, but assuring that he would make a recovery.

My mother spent most of the day there, and then, feeling full of hope, she came back to stay with us at Cavendish Square, where she remained until Leslie was out of danger.

Leslie had suffered a cerebral haemorrhage and, although he recovered with no signs of brain damage, it was obvious to us all that things would never be the same again.

Bernie then spoke to Leslie's son, Michael, who was at the time a sports writer with the *Daily Mirror*, and told him that it

177

looked as if his father wouldn't be able to work for some considerable time. So in the summer of 1966 Michael joined The Grade Organisation. He was twenty-four years old at that time.

During 1967 Bernie received an offer from EMI for The Grade Organisation. He sold it to them for £8 million – to be divided equally between the three of us. EMI basically wanted the cinemas and the properties, so in 1968 they agreed to a management buy-out by three groups who were integrated into The Grade Organisation.

The first group was Michael Grade, Billy Marsh and Dennis Van Thal, and they called themselves London Management Ltd (a company which is still in existence today, although, of course, Michael has not been associated with it for some long time). The second group was Laurence Evans and his associates, who represented numerous stars, writers and directors. This division was eventually bought by ICM (International Creative Management), which was a large American corporation, and it took on the same name. The third group was Harold Davidson, who represented many of the stars he handled for personal appearances in European concert tours, including Frank Sinatra. He called his group Harold Davidson Associates.

EMI wanted to retain Bernie's services and at the age of fifty-eight, and after twenty-five years as his own boss, he was, he says, happy to become a salaried employee.

Two years later he was appointed Chairman and Chief Executive for EMI Films and Theatre Corporation, whose films and entertainment division, including theatres, cinemas, restaurants and hotels had a turnover of £100 million.

Some considerable time later, in 1973, Michael joined London Weekend Television, very soon becoming their Programme Controller. At the end of 1981 he went to America, where for three years he was President of Embassy Television. He is now Director of Programmes for the BBC. I feel very proud of him and I know Leslie, who always took a keen interest in Michael's progress, would have been tremendously thrilled with the status and position his son has achieved. But he did not live to see it happen. Sadly, Leslie died on 15 October 1979, having suffered two additional heart attacks, and the family miss him terribly. Even in the last years of his life he never let his condition rule him. He always had such a terrific zest for life and a wonderful sense of fun.

My mother was then living at Grosvenor House and, again, it was left to Kathie and Norah to break the tragic news to her. My mother's wonderful strength sustained her, and she bore up remarkably well with the help of all her family

Losing Leslie was like losing a vital part of myself. He was such a generous person, always wanting to share exciting experiences with friends. He had been so brilliant when we set out in business initially, and Bernie and I have always maintained that he was the brightest one in the family, and if it wasn't for his illness, he'd probably have left us well behind.

There were so many friends at his memorial service that the place was overflowing. I shall never forget the wonderfully moving tributes paid to him by friends and colleagues who felt such a great sense of loss at his passing.

*   *   *

Ever since I can remember, people have always been curious about how Bernie, Leslie and I got along with each other – whom we preferred, how much rivalry existed between us. As we were all in the same line of business, this curiosity is understandable.

I have never made any secret of the fact that Leslie was always my favourite brother. My concern for his well-being stretches back to his teens, when he was still my 'baby' brother, and, because we were part of the same company for so many years, I saw a great deal more of him that I saw of Bernie. This has always been the case, even when we were youngsters beginning to make our way in the world. The fact that I was totally unaware that Bernie had changed his name to Delfont, and was doing an act called The Delfont Boys gives some indication that we were never that close. For some reason a far greater sibling rivalry existed between the two of us than I ever felt with Leslie. No doubt the fact that we were both dancers had something to do with it; and that we were closer in age. It would never occur to me, for example, to ask Bernie to lend me money, and, apart from that one occasion in Paris when I was desperate for funds, and Bernie let me have £15, I have never approached him for help. Leslie, on the other hand, was a terrific support to me during the difficult, early years of ATV, when I was so financially strapped, and, just by the tone of my voice, he could always hear when I was in trouble. He never waited for me to ask for help, instinctively offering it unsolicited.

Which is not to say that Leslie and I didn't have our differences, and, as anyone who has worked for us will tell you, one of the main sounds coming out of our offices was the banging of fists on the table. Raised voices and flared tempers were not unusual between us – particularly from me. I've always maintained that even when I whisper I still shout. Leslie was much quieter, and where secretaries and other office staff were concerned, he rarely raised his voice. As a result, everybody adored him. He was a greatly loved man, and highly respected; for not only was he a thorough gentleman in all his business dealings, he was a brilliant entrepreneur. Watching him work was an eye-opener, and his handling of stars was quite magnificent. He was a tough negotiator to be sure, but he was always fair. In fact, all three of us had the same philosophy. Everybody you do business with is a partner. And how do you keep a partner happy? By doing a fair deal and making money for him, that's how. Though an agent only got 10 per cent of his client's takings, we still looked upon that client as a partner.

Leslie was also extremely kind. He was an open-hearted man who never put a ceiling on his favours. If you wanted tickets for the hottest show in town, or the Cup Final, or Wimbledon, you just had to ring Leslie and he'd get them. Furthermore, he paid for them himself, and refused reimbursement. I'm sorry to say that certain people took advantage of that – though I was never one of them.

Bernie was a generous man too, and extremely popular in the business. If Leslie was the great entrepreneur of the family, and I was the talent-spotter, Bernie came into his own as a producer. He had real flair, and one of the things he was proudest of was the Royal Variety Show which he arranged and presented. Of all his activities, this was the one that really pleased my mother most. It involved royalty, you see, which, next to her daughter marrying a doctor, gave her the most pride.

Since Leslie's death, Bernie and I have become much closer. We may not see each other regularly, but we're always in contact and less competitive now. We're still brothers, after all, and blood is thicker than water. Our wives are in constant touch and, with my sister Rita still very much a part of all our lives, we continue to be a united family. But then, in our own special way, we always were.

My wife Kathie spent a lot of time with my mother whenever I was away, which was often, and she grew to love Kathie like another daughter. One day she said to her, 'I'm very worried. Lew keeps going to America. Do you think he has a girlfriend there?' Kathie laughed and said, 'I hope he has the strength!' My mother was always very protective towards Kathie.

I always visited my mother regularly when I was in London and kept in constant touch by telephone. When she reached the age of ninety we decided to give her a special birthday party. We held it in a room at the Grosvenor House Hotel and all the family were there. It was a wonderfully happy occasion and in the midst of the celebrations my mother suddenly announced that she wanted to say a few words. She stood up and made a remarkable speech, saying how much she loved her family, how very proud she was of all her children and how thrilled she was at their achievements. I shall never forget how moved we were, listening to the words she spoke with such emotion. Although she was ninety years old that day, she spoke with the clarity and vigour of a young woman. I caught Bernie's eye as she finished, then looked at Leslie and Rita – we were all wiping tears from our eyes and bursting with pride for our wonderful mother.

It was a very sad day when, five years later, she fell and broke her wrist at Christmas. Her age made it necessary to get her into hospital as quickly as possible, but she soon recovered and returned home to her flat in Grosvenor House.

She was still a strong and powerful woman with a tremendously alert mind. In fact, it was impossible to believe that she was actually ninety-five years old. My sister Rita arranged for nurses to look after her round the clock, and Kathie and Norah were constantly with her.

She made a good recovery, and I felt it would be all right to go to Manila in January 1981 to open the new Manila Film Festival Theatre. I had to make a speech in President Marcos's Palace in response to the one he was making to the visiting dignitaries from all over the world. When I got back to my hotel room at 2.30 a.m. the telephone rang. It was Kathie with the heartrending news that my darling mother had peacefully passed away.

With the help of Madame Marcos I was able to catch a special plane to Hong Kong, in time to board the first connecting flight back to London.

Kathie comforted me by telling me the events that had led up to my mother's death. She and Norah had been with her until one o'clock in the morning, along with my sister Rita and the nurses, and they had then left to go home for some rest. No sooner had they walked into the front door than Rita telephoned and said, 'Please come back. Mother won't settle down without you.' So they rushed back and sat with my mother, each with an arm round her, holding her, and she talked happily about her life, how she had had all her dreams fulfilled. Her two oldest sons were peers, Leslie had made a great impact in the entertainment industry, her daughter had married a doctor . . . how lucky she had been. Then murmuring 'Oh! My lovely kinder . . .' she quietly went to sleep. In a strange way, although I had lost my precious mother, it eased my sorrow to know that her last moments were spent with such happy reminiscences, and to know that my dear sister Rita, Kathie and Norah were with her at the end. It was also a relief to me to know that Kathie and Norah were there to comfort Rita at a time of such grief.

*   *   *

But to return to 1973 and ATV.

After being appointed Chairman, I believe I'm correct in saying that I was one of the few people who never had to make an appointment with any specific network executive in New York. I'd just turn up and be shown into the offices of the vice president in charge of programmes, or if he was out of town, the president of the network himself. That, too, is relationship! As a result of the intimacy I enjoyed with all the top people at CBS, ABC and NBC, I made several unexpected deals.

For example, I was with Mort Werner, who was then Vice-President of Programmes at NBC, when he and some of his colleagues were talking about finding a summer replacement for the 'Dean Martin Show'. I said, 'What about putting in 'The

Saint' with Roger Moore? I can let you have forty-three episodes in colour.' We had previously failed to sell 'The Saint' series to the network because most of the episodes were in black and white and had already been out on syndication, playing approximately two hundred different TV stations.

They said, 'Lew, you're crazy. The series has been on syndication and we couldn't possibly do it.' 'We're only talking about twelve weeks,' I said, 'why don't you try it?' I persuaded them to take a chance. They did – and for the next five years we were the summer replacement for the 'Dean Martin Show'. Later on, when CBS were putting out one-hour adventure series after the news at 10.30 at night, I persuaded them to buy those 43 colour episodes as well.

That's relationship again!

One day in 1972, I received a telephone call from Sir Max Rayne (now Lord Rayne) who was Chairman of the National Theatre. He said that he and Laurence Olivier would like to discuss something with me. They came to my office and told me that the National Theatre was desperately in need of funds. They had a production of Eugene O'Neill's *Long Day's Journey into Night* on at the time, with Olivier, Constance Cummings and Denis Quilley, and wanted me to televise the production, then sell it worldwide. What they were really after was an advance and a share of the profits. I thought it a marvellous idea, agreed the terms of the deal and shook hands on it.

That evening I called Martin Starger, Vice-President of the ABC Network in New York, and said, 'Marty, I want you to buy *Long Day's Journey into Night* starring Laurence Olivier, which I'm producing for worldwide television. You may not get ratings,' I said, 'but think of the prestige, and that's what ABC needs right now.' At the time they had many Westerns in their schedules and a lot of action adventure series – but little quality stuff. He asked me how much I wanted. I told him, he agreed to my terms and closed the deal there and then. Through Cecil Clarke, who was our head of drama by then, we engaged the talented John Dexter to re-direct the play for TV, and had an extensive set built in order to open it out a bit.

We allowed four weeks for rehearsals. We were one week into rehearsals when Max Rayne and Laurence Olivier came to see me in my office. 'We've made a terrible mistake,' they said. 'We realize the only rights we have to *Long Day's Journey into Night* are for the National Theatre.'

'But this is ridiculous,' I said. 'We've already built this enormous set, engaged John Dexter and hired the cast. Even more important,' I said, 'I've sold the production to ABC and promised a delivery date.'

'Well, there's nothing we can do about it,' they said. 'Surely *somebody* has the rights,' I said. 'Yes,' they said. 'A man called Mr Golenbock. And for the last two weeks we've been ringing him constantly in New York but he never returns our calls. So we felt we had to come and explain the position to you.' They were clearly most embarrassed about the situation.

'Well, give me Mr Golenbock's telephone number,' I said, 'and I'll have a try.'

For one full week I must have called that number six or eight times a day, but to no avail. 'Mr Golenbock is out of town,' I'd be told, or, 'He's at a meeting. He'll call you . . . ' Every night, as soon as I got home from the office, the first thing I'd do was telephone Mr Golenbock. After a few days, my wife began to believe that this Golenbock was a figment of my imagination.

I had three separate telephone lines at home, and one evening, on about the eighth day, I was talking on one of them when the phone rang on another. My wife answered it. A voice at the other end asked, 'Is Sir Lew Grade there?' Kathie said I was, and asked who was calling. He said, 'Mr Golenbock, from New York.' She nearly fainted and handed me the phone.

I said, 'Hello,' and before I could say another word, the voice at the other end of the phone said, 'Hello, Lew. How are you? I've never forgotten what you did for me and Rosenburg.'

I was pretty sure I'd never met Mr Golenbock before, and had certainly never even heard of Mr Rosenburg.

However, he continued. 'You won't remember this, but we were in Paris and decided to come to London. We tried to get a hotel reservation but all the decent hotels were full. The William Morris Agency had told us, if you're ever in trouble, call Lew Grade. Well,' he went on, 'not only did you fix us up at the Savoy, but you also gave us seats for all your shows. So, what can *I* do for *you*?'

'I want the worldwide television rights for *Long Day's Journey into Night*,' I said. He answered, 'You've got 'em. Anything else?'

That's relationship! It also shows that if you do something helpful without having an ulterior motive in mind, it can pay off in the most unexpected ways.

I subsequently sold to the ABC Network in New York Trevor Nunn's remarkable production of the Royal Shakespeare Company's *Antony and Cleopatra*, starring Janet Suzman and Richard Johnson, as well as the National's *The Merchant of Venice*, directed by Jonathan Miller and starring Laurence Olivier, and a production of *Twelfth Night* with Alec Guinness, John Gielgud and Tommy Steele.

It was Sam Goldwyn, I think, who once said that every time he hears the word culture, he reaches for his chequebook. I know what he meant, for culture is expensive, and it doesn't always make money. But then money, as someone else once remarked, isn't everything . . .

And talking of culture, I'm once supposed to have said about a TV programme: 'It must be culture, because it certainly wasn't entertainment.'

Not true. I'm also quoted as saying: 'All of my shows are great. Some of them are bad. But all of them are great.' Again, not true.

Only *some* of them were great.

Here's the history of one of them – another 'cultural' event, as it turned out.

As I mentioned earlier, holidays were never part of my life. My idea of purgatory is sitting on a beach – in the South of France, or anywhere else for that matter – sunning myself, with nothing to do and no phone calls to make. Pure hell!

I realize that this was very selfish as far as Kathie and our son Paul were concerned. I'm sure they would have loved to go on regular family holidays, like most people, but it was not to be. Kathie was very long-suffering, but she never complained. I have always been a workaholic – which is better than being an alcoholic – and she accepted the fact with as good a grace as she could.

At the end of September 1963, I did, however, decide to take a break and Kathie, Paul and I went to Switzerland for a few days.

185

For starters, I thought it might be nice to re-establish contact with my old circus friends, the Knies.

We were travelling through one of the country's many breath-taking scenic passes, when I happened to glance at the English newspaper I'd bought and saw that Maria Callas and Tito Gobbi were about to appear in a new Zeffirelli production of *Tosca* at the Royal Opera House, Covent Garden.

'Wouldn't it be wonderful,' I said to Kathie, 'if we could get part of that production for television, and fill the rest with some other great classical items.' Kathie agreed, and no more was said about it.

But for the rest of the train journey my mind was ticking away like crazy, and as soon as we arrived in Zurich I found a phone and telephoned Sandor Gorlinsky, one of the leading impresarios of his day.

I told him my idea and said I thought the programme should be two hours in length, although we'd call it 'The Golden Hour'. Sandor thought it a great idea, and immediately came up with a line-up of classical talent for me. He also got permission for us to use the Royal Opera House on a Sunday, which was a terrific coup.

Needless to say, that was the end of our 'relaxing' holiday. I became so involved in this new project, I was never off the phone. Quite rightly, Kathie said I'd be far happier back in London, and we returned immediately.

Sir David Webster, who was then the General Director of the Royal Opera, agreed to be the host for the evening. The first half of the programme consisted of José Iturbi, the world-famous pianist and conductor who had appeared in many musicals at MGM throughout the 1940s, Rudolf Nureyev, who'd only just recently defected from the Kirov Ballet, and was the sensation of the West, Mischa Elman, one of the greatest violinists of his time, and the ballerina Nadia Nerina, who partnered Nureyev. The second half of the programme was to be Act Two of *Tosca*, with Callas, Gobbi and Renato Cioni. It lasted for forty-five minutes, and those who saw it at the time of its original trans-mission, and again on Channel 4 over Christmas, 1986, will agree that it is probably the greatest forty-five minutes of opera ever seen on TV. In his introduction, Sir David remarked that it was the kind of performance one would tell one's grandchildren about – and, twenty-three years after it was recorded, you can see how right he was.

Initially, however, when I announced that 'The Golden Hour' would, for that one night, replace 'Sunday Night at the London Palladium', the other television contractors across the country were reluctant to take it. It was back to Sam Goldwyn's remark about culture! They all felt the ratings wouldn't be high enough to generate the advertising revenue that was expected from this slot, and were extremely nervous about going ahead with it.

As it was very important to me that the show be networked throughout the country, I personally undertook to guarantee the advertising slots for the programme's two-hour duration. The first man I went to was the Chairman of Unilever, and I told him that although it was unlikely that the show would get very high ratings, I thought he should, nevertheless, take advertising space during such a prestigious programme. He agreed.

Next I went to see Henry Lazell, who was the Chairman of Beecham. He liked the whole format and idea of the show, and immediately instructed his advertising agency to take space. I then approached the chairmen of J. Walter Thompson, Young and Rubicam, and McCann Erickson, the three major advertising agencies, and was able to persuade them to convince their clients to take air time with us.

With all the available advertising slots filled, I now had no difficulty in convincing the network to take 'The Golden Hour' – and, in the end, they all did.

The big night arrived – 9 February 1964 – and the Opera House was packed with distinguished guests. The atmosphere was electric, and a buzz of expectation added to the general excitement of the occasion. A Callas performance was always something of an event, and that night was no exception.

Then, shortly before the transmission was due to begin, Sandor Gorlinsky came up to me ashen-faced. 'I don't think Maria Callas will be able to go on,' he said. 'She's got a tickle at the back of her throat and she's worried about it.' I was panic-stricken.

'There's worse to come,' said Gorlinsky. 'Tito Gobbi's also got a throat infection, he says, and thinks he may not be able to go on either.'

It was suddenly the end of the world. After all the trouble and effort it had taken to get the show assembled – and with that glittering audience assembled out front – I just couldn't believe what was happening. It was a nightmare!

Kathie, who had been a singer herself, of course, came up with a suggestion. With great presence of mind, she simply said, 'We'll get a throat specialist in. He'll spray their throats, and they'll be able to sing.'

We knew just the man, and he arrived at 8.00 p.m. By now the first half of the show had begun, so, as you can imagine, it was a real race against time. The suspense was unbelievable; not even the great Alfred Hitchcock could have improved on it!

Our throat specialist, I'm happy to say, proved to be a miracle-worker that night, and after spraying their throats and convincing them that no harm would be done to their voices, they finally agreed to go on.

And, as anyone who saw the recording knows, they were in absolutely glorious voice. Callas wore a deep garnet-red velvet dress and gave a performance of such extraordinary intensity that when she stabbed Scarpia (magnificently played and sung by Tito Gobbi), there was an audible gasp from the audience.

The whole evening was a spectacular success, and because of all the press coverage it received, and because there had been nothing quite like it on TV before, the ratings were excellent – proving, on this occasion, that Sam Goldwyn was wrong.

During my long career I have been responsible for many, many shows. But 'The Golden Hour' was an undoubted highlight.

Another cultural event I won't easily forget was the Eurogala which was also networked, and which took place on 20 May 1979 at the Theatre Royal Drury Lane.

This was a special Common Market and European Parliament birthday celebration and the guests of honour were the Earl Mountbatten of Burma, Edward Heath, Roy Jenkins, Lord and Lady Duncan-Sandys, Lord Gladwyn and several other leading political figures. We had a sparkling line-up of international talent, including Yehudi Menuhin, Mireille Mathieu, the Circus of Europe, the European Community Youth Orchestra, Katia

Ricciarelli, and the Royal Ballet Company, whose soloists that night were Lesley Collier and David Wall.

I had been warned, before the show began, that in the course of the evening a special award was to be presented, but I didn't know who the recipient was going to be.

Prior to the finale, Lord Thomson of Monifieth, Chairman of the European movement in Britain (who later became Chairman of the IBA), walked on to the stage and said: 'Ladies and gentlemen, it gives me great pleasure to present the Gold Cup of the Common Market to somebody who has done so much for the Common Market . . . '

In the royal box were Earl Mountbatten of Burma, Edward Heath and Roy Jenkins. Kathie and I were sitting in a small box adjacent to them.

When I heard Lord Thomson say this, I turned to Kathie and whispered, 'I bet it's for Edward Heath. He's worked so hard to get us into the Common Market.' 'No,' whispered back Kathie. 'It'll be for Roy Jenkins, who's President of the European Commission . . . '

Lord Thomson then announced the name of the recipient. I didn't hear who it was because Kathie and I were having our private little conversation.

He then repeated: 'Would Lord Grade kindly come on to the stage.'

I was tremendously surprised because I genuinely never expected such an honour. I made a short acceptance speech and can't remember what I said. All I know is that it was another exciting moment in a life full of such moments, and that the Gold Cup is one of my most treasured possessions.

One final 'cultural' story. In the early days of independent TV, I'd set my sights on Sir Kenneth Clark, then Chairman of the IBA, to do a series of programmes for us based on the history of art. I spoke to him about the possibility of such an idea becoming a reality, and he said he couldn't even discuss it with me as long as he was involved with the IBA.

Towards the end of 1957, on the last day of his term as Chairman, a big party was given for him, to which I and every other big-wig in the industry was invited. I kept my eye on him all through the evening, and, at exactly one minute past midnight, I went over to him. 'Kenneth,' I said, 'as of this moment, you're no longer Chairman of the IBA. Now, are you going to do those programmes for me, or aren't you?'

He said he would, and soon after made a highly successful series for us in which he so lucidly explained the works of the Old Masters to the general viewer. The programmes, it turned out, were the forerunners of his brilliant series, 'Civilization', which he made for the BBC several years later.

Once again, ATV had led the way.

15

In Full Stride

ALMOST FROM ITS INCEPTION, ATV became known for the outstanding quality of its drama series. I was particularly proud, for example, of 'Probation Officer', which the Trades Union Council called 'socially informative and entertaining'. A most unusual compliment from the TUC!

Bill Ward, our programme controller, was terrific. He was full of good ideas, and one day came to me with an idea for a series called 'The Plane Makers'. I saw the first few episodes, and couldn't help noticing that most of the action took place in the factory where the planes were being made. The noise of the machinery was deafening!

I spoke to Bill. 'Take it off the factory floor,' I said, 'and let's have it moving into the world of big-business and the boardroom.'

We did this, and it became an outstanding success, which we followed with 'The Power Game', starring Patrick Wymark, and which, as far as I'm concerned, was a forerunner of the present hit American series 'Dallas'.

When we acquired the Stoll Moss group of theatres, I thought we should become involved in the music business.

The big music company at that time, and even today, was Chappell's, which was owned by Louis Dreyfus and his late brother, whose share was owned by his widow. The Morgan Guaranty Trust were the executors of that portion of the estate. Louis Dreyfus and I got on remarkably well and in June 1966 he invited me to lunch at Claridges. He was then just over ninety-six years old. 'Lew,' he said, 'I know you want Chappell's. I give you my word that you'll have it by the Christmas after next.' That meant by Christmas 1967. He went on, 'You don't have to worry about the cost. I'll make it very reasonable. However, I first want you to do me a favour. I want you to put on *Fiddler on the Roof* at Her Majesty's Theatre and invest £25,000 in the production.' I said, 'OK,' (I didn't have the heart to say, 'you're over ninety-six years of age and who knows what can happen in nearly two years' time?') in spite of the fact that Prince Littler, who was Chairman of our theatre group, had seen the show in New York, as had Toby Rowland, his number two in the group. My brother Bernie had also considered it for one of his theatres, but they were all of the opinion that it was not suitable for London. I agreed with them. Broadway – yes; the West End – no. But, I'd given my word to Louis Dreyfus, and I never go back on my word.

I telephoned Prince and said, 'Prince, we're going to put *Fiddler on the Roof* into Her Majesty's, and we are going to invest £25,000 in the production.' 'But Lew,' he said, 'you yourself, as well as everybody else, said it wasn't suitable for London. I thought we all agreed on this.'

'Prince,' I said, 'I've given my word, and we're going to do it.' 'Okay,' he said. 'We'll do it.'

The show opened on 16 February 1967, and ran for five years. It made a star of its hitherto unknown leading man, an Israeli actor with extraordinary charisma called Topol (who, against terrific competition, was chosen to appear in the film version), and made a great deal of money for everyone involved. It was a wonderful show, brilliantly staged by Jerome Robbins, and with a superb score by Sheldon Harnick and Joseph Stein. It just shows how wrong the alleged experts – including myself – can be when it comes to the public's taste. It's easy after the event to say what a universally appealing show *Fiddler* is, and there is a true story I've heard that demonstrates this.

During the run of the successful Japanese production of the musical, its producer came up to Sheldon Harnick and expressed his surprise that the show had done so well on Broadway. 'Why are you so surprised?' Harnick asked. 'Because,' the man replied, 'it's so *Japanese*!'

Louis Dreyfus unfortunately died in October 1967 and we never did complete the deal for Chappell's. However, we did make an offer to Morgan Guaranty but were outbid by Philips.

A strong feeling persisted that we should buy a music company, and we began building up a stake in Northern Songs, which was owned by Dick James, and which then controlled the Beatles catalogue. We reached a stake of approximately 40 per cent and tried to acquire the rest. John Lennon decided to appoint a young American called Alan Klein to handle the negotiations. I don't think Paul McCartney was too keen on Klein, but he gave Lennon his support and went along with it. For the following two weeks I had meetings with Alan Klein for hours on end each day and didn't like the way it was going.

One morning I called Peter Donald, who by that time had acquired control of the Howard and Wyndham Theatres, as well as some theatres in Scotland. Peter Donald's company controlled 14 per cent of the Northern Songs shares. I had a strange feeling about Alan Klein because of all these unnecessary delays, so, when I called Peter Donald, I said, 'I want to buy your 14 per cent of Northern Songs. How much do you want for it?' We agreed a price and did the deal on the telephone. We now had well over 54 per cent of the company and therefore controlled Northern Songs. Alan Klein called me late that afternoon, and I must give him credit for what he said to me. 'Well,' he said, 'I have to admit it. You beat me to the punch. We're now ready to sell you the shares at the same price you paid Peter Donald.' He said he'd been considering doing the deal with Donald himself, but had obviously left it too late.

And that, my friends, is how we acquired the Beatles catalogue and got into the music business.

I have always been very interested in the World Wildlife Fund, and am in fact a member of their 1001 Club. The Fund was badly in need of money and in 1970 I had an idea to put on a major show at the Talk of the Town, which is now the Hippodrome. I spoke to my brother, Bernie, and he was happy for me to have the venue for the evening. I contacted all the stars who were eventually to appear on the show, and they all agreed to do it.

Rex Harrison was the compere and the cast was Bob Hope, Glen Campbell, Petula Clark, Engelbert Humperdinck, Rudolf Nureyev with Antoinette Sibley, Millicent Martin, George Kirby (an American comedian) and the Paddy Stone Dancers.

I had been assured by the World Wildlife Fund that for this great occasion they would ask all the members of the British royal family and all the crowned heads of Europe. We were fortunate in being highly honoured with the presence of Her Majesty The Queen, HRH Prince Philip, HRH Prince Charles, HRH Princess Anne, HRH Princess Alexandra, Queen Juliana and Prince Bernhard of the Netherlands, The King and Queen of Greece, The Grand Duke and Duchess of Luxembourg, Prince Juan Carlos of Spain (now King of Spain) and The Queen of Spain, The Crown Prince and Princess of Norway, Prince Henrik of Denmark, Princess Beatrix of the Netherlands, Prince Albert of Belgium – plus a host of other very distinguished guests, including, of course, Lord Mountbatten.

The entire show was staged by Robert Nesbitt, the well-known producer who staged the Royal Variety performances, and it was wonderful. The atmosphere in the theatre was like magic, and I was so thrilled. I was also convinced I'd be able to sell this show in America and make a substantial sum of money for the World Wildlife Fund. Feeling full of confidence, I went to visit the three networks. They all said they were interested, but that I was asking too much money. However, if I could get a sponsor, then, they said, they would definitely take it.

At that time I didn't have much contact with sponsors of television programmes in the United States, so I was feeling rather despondent about this. Then I had a brainwave. I knew that Cary Grant was a director of Fabergé – the perfume people – who sponsored many programmes on television. I telephoned him and said, 'Cary, I'd like to meet Mr George Barrie [Chairman and Chief Executive of Fabergé]. I want to sell him a project I'm setting up.' Cary said, 'Fine. I'll fly to New York tomorrow, we'll meet at the Fabergé offices, I'll introduce you to George Barrie and then it's up to you.' Cary was wonderful. He made a special point of flying to New York as arranged. I met him at the Fabergé offices where we waited for George Barrie to arrive. After a couple of moments, Barrie walked in, Cary introduced us, then left the room.

I told George Barrie all about the project and gave him a list of the stars who were appearing. He then said, 'How much do you want?' I gave him a figure and he said, 'You've got a deal.'

He then placed it with one of the networks and, of course, came over to London to the Talk of the Town where, on the evening of 18 November 1970, he sat next to Her Majesty The Queen.

That evening all the stars were waiting to be presented to the assembled royalty. I'd been given photographs of each of the visiting royalty, but was so nervous I kept them in my pocket and didn't look at them. Half of them I just didn't recognize, but fortunately, Earl Mountbatten of Burma – Lord Louis as his friends used to call him – came to my rescue and helped me identify them during the presentations. That was a memorable and very exciting time for me, and another highlight in my life.

My relationship with George Barrie continued for many years after this. In fact, I made a series of 26 half-hour shows called 'The Protectors', starring Robert Vaughn, which he sponsored, and eventually we did another 26 episodes of the same series.

*   *   *

Tom Moore left ABC late in 1967 and Elton Rule was appointed President of ABC Television Network. At that time Martin Starger was Vice-President in charge of programming.

This presented me with a problem. The head of our script department was Stella Richman, and she came to me with an idea for a series called 'Love Story'. I agreed to do this with her as Producer. The series was a popular success and I had no difficulty selling thirteen episodes to Tom Moore while he was still President of ABC. When Tom Moore left ABC, I pointed out to them that they had this commitment with me. Unfortunately, Elton Rule wasn't as keen on the idea as his predecessor and, as there was no written record of our deal, anywhere, I found myself stuck with the thirteen episodes.

Fortunately, however, we sold them on syndication throughout the States. It wasn't nearly as good a deal as it would have been had it first gone out on a network, but it helped.

I went to lunch with Leonard Goldenson, who had now become a great personal friend, Elton Rule and Martin Starger at ABC, and tried to persuade Elton to visit Europe in order for him to see what was happening in television on the other side of the Atlantic. Elton, however, was very hesitant about making such a visit. As Marty explained it to me: 'Elton is a bit worried about coming to Europe because he feels you'll badger him into buying something to compensate for the loss of the "Love Story" deal.' 'Marty,' I said, 'I can assure you I will not discuss any business at all with Elton Rule. This is merely an educational trip under my guidance.' Marty knew that I always kept my word and thus persuaded Elton to come over with him. I liked Elton Rule tremendously from the moment we met and was glad to have the opportunity to spend some time with him.

After his third day in London, we were chatting together one evening just before going to see a show. Elton had been watching television quite extensively during his stay in London (which was the whole purpose of his visit) and he suddenly turned to me and said, 'Haven't you got anything I can buy from you?' 'Elton,' I said firmly, 'we are not discussing any business on this trip.'

I then arranged for him to tour our studios and to see all our facilities and, like most visitors to Elstree, he was very impressed. After that we decided to go to Paris for three days.

Like clockwork, every evening before we went out, Elton kept saying to me, 'Lew, there must be *something* you want to sell me.' I repeated my remark – 'No business!' – even though I was dying to sell him some of the ideas I had in mind. But I'd given my word, and I believe Elton was actually quite impressed at my determination not to talk business. Instead, we went out on the town and had a lot of fun.

*   *   *

My relationship with RAI – Radiotelevisione Italiana, the Italian State Television Company – was exceptionally good, mainly through the efforts of Francesco De Crescenzo, who was running the Italian division of ITC. At the beginning of 1972 I had a meeting with Dr Fabiano Fabiani, who was then a director of the principal television channel in Italy. 'Lew,' he said, 'we've been offered a proposal to do a short mini-series on Moses by Vincenzo Labella. He thinks he can get Burt Lancaster to play Moses. Would you be interested in being partners with us in this venture and would you be prepared to control the production?'

I met with Labella and said that we'd be most interested, subject to getting a firm commitment from Burt Lancaster.

Labella then arranged for me to meet with Lancaster in California and he came along with me. I had met Lancaster previously with his former partner Ben Hecht. Our present meeting took place at Burt's home. He was very warm and enthusiastic and I received a firm commitment from him. I then flew back to New York, saw the President of CBS, Bob Wood, whom I had known for several years, and with whom I had done a considerable amount of business, and sold Moses to his network.

Dr Fabiani was thrilled, and we went ahead and made the series. It went out in Italy in April 1974 and was a spectacular success. Cinemas were half empty, because everybody seemed to stay at home to watch 'Moses, The Lawgiver', which is the title we finally gave it.

Immediately after the last episode of 'Moses' had been transmitted in Italy, I received a lunch invitation from the Italian Ambassador in London.

The Italian government was so thrilled with my production of 'Moses', they said that they wanted to arrange a private audience for me with Pope Paul VI, and wanted to know when would be most convenient for me.

I was quite flattered at the suggestion, but, of course, not being Catholic, it didn't seem anything extra special to me.

At that time I generally went to bed between 11.00 and 11.30 p.m. and Kathie would come to bed a little later – sometimes without putting on the light in order not to disturb me. Usually I'd still be awake, and I'd tell her to be careful and not to knock against anything in the dark. That's exactly what I said that night, so she knew I was still awake. 'Did anything special happen to you today?' she casually asked me. 'Nothing of any great importance,' I said. 'I had lunch with the Italian Ambassador and he suggested I have a private audience with Pope Paul.'

BANG! On came the bedside light. Kathie sat up. 'What did you say?' she said.

To Kathie, a Catholic, this was a momentous occasion. 'I said I'd let him have some dates.' She looked horrified. 'Kathie, don't worry,' I said reassuringly. 'I'll call him tomorrow and fix the date.'

Next day I called the Italian Ambassador, told him we would

be very happy to go to Rome the following week and a date was set.

Before we set off to the Vatican for our audience with the Pope, we were advised that Kathie should dress in black and wear gloves and that I must not shake the Pope's hand – just bow. All this didn't seem too important to me at the time.

In our hotel room, Kathie was in her long black dress and was just putting on her mantilla when suddenly she began to cry. I said, 'Whatever you do you must not cry in front of the Pope.' Then we went off to the Vatican and were ushered into a huge hall and sat on two chairs. Suddenly, we saw the centre doors open. We immediately stood up and Pope Paul entered with two of his personal aides. He glanced at us, then said something to one of the aides, who came over to Kathie. 'Madam,' he said, 'you may remove your gloves.' We were still standing. Pope Paul walked to the throne, they put on his mitre and he then held both his arms out and, with a smile, beckoned us towards him. I had been quite calm until now, but from that moment onwards I was gone! Kathie naturally kissed his ring and I bowed. He then held my hand for most of the twenty-five minutes of our audience, said how thrilled he was with our interpretation of 'Moses', and blessed the production. Kathie then said, 'May we tell the artistes and the press about this?' And he said, 'You may tell everybody.' After that, I was so moved I wasn't able to take in a word he said.

Once the audience was over, we went to dinner with Francesco De Crescenzo and Fabiano Fabiani and left for England the following morning. Two weeks later I returned to Rome. I was having dinner with Fabiano when he said, 'What shall we do next?'

To this day I don't know what made me say it, but without hesitation I said, 'Jesus of Nazareth'. He said, 'Wonderful!' We then discussed a possible director and I insisted that it should be Franco Zeffirelli. I had met Franco several times since the Callas-Tosca transmission, and knew that, as a devout Catholic, he'd be thrilled at the opportunity. Fabiani agreed with this, although he took a great deal of convincing! We discussed writers and settled on Anthony Burgess, the brilliant novelist and critic. He was later assisted by the Italian writer Suso Cecchi d'Amico.

I came back and told Kathie I was going to make a film of Jesus of Nazareth. Her face lit up with joy. 'I'm so glad,' she said. 'For the first time in your life, I thought you were going to break your word.' I asked her what on earth she was talking about. 'Well,' she said, 'at the end of our audience with Pope Paul he said to you, "I hope one day you will do the story of Jesus" and you replied that you would.' I had no recollection of this whatsoever.

After that I became a little anxious about the project, and felt I should first pre-sell the idea to a major American company. I called Tom Adams, Chairman and principal shareholder of Campbell Ewald, the house advertising agency of General Motors, who were located in the G.M. building in Detroit. We had a good working relationship, due, mainly to the number of variety specials we'd produced for them.

The date was 28 November 1973, and I asked him to arrange a meeting for me with Richard Gerstenberg, Chairman and Chief Executive of General Motors, for 4 December. 'Lew,' he said, 'you do mean *next* year, don't you?' 'No,' I said, 'I mean next week.' 'That's impossible,' he said. 'Even I can't get to see him.' Then he asked me what it was all about. 'Tom,' I said, 'you know me well enough to realize I wouldn't waste the time of the Chairman of General Motors unless I thought it was of major significance.' 'All the same . . . ' he said. 'Look,' I interrupted. 'If you don't fix the appointment, it's OK with me. I'll go and see Henry Ford.' Nor was this an idle statement. I had an extremely good relationship with Earl Mountbatten of Burma, who had once said to me, 'If you ever need anything from Henry Ford, just ask me and I'll arrange it for you.'

When I told Tom Adams that, he said he'd at least have a try. He called me back the next day. 'I managed to see Mr Gerstenberg,' he said, 'and he'll try and fit you in for ten minutes after lunch.' 'That's good enough for me,' I said, 'I'll take a chance and come to Detroit.'

I had lunch with Tom Adams and the heads of most of the divisions of General Motors and, naturally, they were all curious to find out why I wanted to see Mr Gerstenberg. But I refused to say a word.

At eighteen minutes past two, the message came to the dining room: 'Mr Gerstenberg is ready to see Sir Lew Grade.' I quickly threw away my cigar and went with Tom Adams to the top floor to meet the Chairman. I felt unbelievably nervous. I had so little time to sell such a big project, and – even worse – I wasn't smoking!

I entered the room, and gave a quick glance around it. Not a single ashtray anywhere! Mr Gerstenberg greeted me very warmly, 'Hello, Sir Lew. It's good to meet you. I read the article about you in *Forbes Magazine* and thought it was excellent.' 'Thank you, sir,' I said. 'And I read the article about *you* in *Forbes Magazine* and thought it was outstanding.' (I hadn't – but guessed there must have been an article about him at some point in *Forbes Magazine*!)

Then he said, 'What's the economic situation like in England?' This was a subject about which I knew very little – after all, I was in the television and entertainment business. I fluffed my way through something or other, then looked at my watch. Five minutes had gone and I hadn't even mentioned 'Jesus of Nazareth'!

He then said, 'Have you met Tom Murphy? He's Vice-Chairman and in eighteen months when I retire, he'll be taking over as Chairman. I think you really should meet him.'

He pressed a buzzer and in came Mr Tom Murphy. Again, 'How are you, Sir Lew? It's nice to meet you. What's the economic situation like in England?' By this time my ten minutes was up. I felt I'd blown it!

'Mr Gerstenberg,' I said, 'I know you have very little time and I'm rather nervous without my cigar. Would you mind if I smoked?' 'Not at all,' he said. 'I'll send for an ashtray.' I then pulled out of my pocket one of my biggest cigars – 9 inches long. 'Good heavens!' he exclaimed, 'What's that?' 'Something to bang you on the head with if you don't say yes!' That broke him up and he and Tom Murphy roared with laughter. Once again my cigars had come to the rescue!

I felt relatively at ease with them now, and spoke about 'Jesus of Nazareth', telling them I wanted $3 million for one transmission. I was explaining my concept of the production and finished up by saying: 'In the end a voice says, "I will be with you forever and a day".' Tom Murphy said, 'When does the voice say that?' Without flickering an eyelid I answered, 'After the Resurrection, of course.'

How that came into my mind I'll never know, because I didn't really know the answer.

Tom Murphy said, 'That's wonderful.'

Then Mr Gerstenberg said to me, 'When would you like a decision?' I replied, 'Yesterday will be fine.' 'I'm afraid we have passed the deadline,' he said, 'but you can have one now. Okay.'

At twenty minutes to five I left with a deal. It had been a wonderfully exhilarating experience.

Tom Adams said it would be networked by NBC, who were delighted with the idea of the programme, especially as it was sponsored by General Motors.

So everybody was happy.

16

'Jesus of Nazareth'

I THOUGHT A GREAT DEAL about the casting of 'Jesus of Nazareth'. I couldn't afford to make mistakes, as I had the feeling the project was going to be something very, very special.

I decided to have fifteen to twenty stars in it, realizing, of course, that it would end up costing far more money than I had originally anticipated.

I spoke to Franco Zeffirelli, and his casting director and associate producer, Dyson Lovell. 'I'm going to try to get Laurence Olivier for the cameo role of Nicodemus,' I said. 'Once we get him, all the other stars will follow.'

I then telephoned Laurence Evans, who was Olivier's agent, and told him I wanted Larry to play the role of Nicodemus in 'Jesus of Nazareth'. 'Larry doesn't play cameos,' he said. 'Just talk to him,' I said. 'Tell him I'd very much like him to do it. Just mention *Long Day's Journey into Night*, *The Merchant of Venice*, and remind him about the National Theatre's production of *Saturday, Sunday, Monday*, which I put on at the Lyric theatre, guaranteeing them all salaries, all the costs of the production, and then gave them an advance of £5000.'

Laurence Evans rang back a little while later and said Larry would be happy to do this for me, and to be a part of the production. After that, as I'd anticipated, Dyson Lovell had no difficulty in signing up stars such as Peter Ustinov, Ralph Richardson, James Earl Jones, Michael York, Christopher Plummer, Anne Bancroft, James Mason, Ian Bannen, Ian McShane, Ian Holm, Stacey Keach, Anthony Quinn, Rod Steiger and Ernest Borgnine. The list goes on and on . . . .

The main problem, of course, was to find the right actor to play the role of Jesus. We didn't want to cast an internationally known star, but a relative newcomer without an established personality or image to detract from the role. I had been discussing the problem with Kathie, and one day she said to me, 'Have you ever watched an actor called Robert Powell in the BBC series "Jude the Obscure"? He's got such wonderful blue eyes.' I said I hadn't, but would get a tape of it, which I did. As soon as I watched it, I knew I'd found our Jesus.

I immediately called Zeffirelli and told him I'd made a decision. He said, 'But I've got some other people in mind.' 'Franco,' I said, 'you'd better come to London.' But he said again, 'I've got some other possible choices.' He had never seen or heard of Robert Powell, which wasn't surprising. I assured him that once he saw Powell, he'd agree with me. All the same, he said, he'd have to test him.

'I don't care whether you test him or not,' I said. 'I honestly feel he's the only one for that role.' Franco did do the test and afterwards agreed that Robert would be perfect for the part.

Powell came in to see me two weeks before he was due to start principal photography on 'Jesus of Nazareth', to thank me for giving him the opportunity. I knew he had a lovely girlfriend called Babs, whom I had met on a couple of occasions, and I said to him, 'Are you taking Babs with you to Morocco?' (which is where we were starting to film). He said, 'Yes.' I then said, 'Don't you think it will look strange? Here you are playing such a vital role in this production and you're living with a girlfriend! Don't you think you should get married?' He said, 'It's strange you saying that. I was considering that too, and we had in fact decided that we would get married before we left.' And they did.

We decided we'd have a press conference, with the international press, in Rome in mid-July. Hundreds of them turned up. Somebody asked me why I was doing this particular film and I assured him it had nothing to do with the fact that I was born on 25 December!

That evening RAI hosted a dinner for all the press in a large villa on the outskirts of Rome, and the following day there was another dinner for the politicians and important dignitaries. Among those present were Herb Schlosser from NBC, his wife, representatives from General Motors, and many other distinguished guests.

I sat at the main table together with the Chairman and Director-General of RAI, and the American Ambassador to Rome and his wife. There were two other guests and one empty chair next to mine.

We had all been seated when in walked the person who was to be placed next to me. It was Adolfo Sarti, a minister in the Italian Government, who couldn't speak a word of English. We were just about to start eating when there was a great flurry of excitement. Cardinal Benelli, Secretary of State to the Vatican, had arrived to join us.

They moved the chairs around a little and put him to the right of me. He spoke English fluently.

During the course of the meal I began to tell him how I visualized the production of 'Jesus of Nazareth'. By the time I reached the part where Jesus is being baptized by John the Baptist, he was in tears.

Just before the coffee was served, Adolfo Sarti stood up and made a long speech in Italian. I had no idea what he was talking about, but I did manage to catch the words 'President of the Republic of Italy', and heard him mention my name twice. I was puzzled by this. At that point one of his aides stepped forward, handed him a box, which he opened, and then he conferred upon me the honour of Commendatore of the Order of Merit of the Republic of Italy.

This was totally unexpected, and, of course, I had to make a speech of acceptance. I did the best I could and finished up by saying, 'Without my wife I'd have only ever been known as the ex-World Champion Charleston Dancer.'

So the production got under way.

We shot 'Jesus of Nazareth' in many different parts of the Middle East, but the principal filming was done in Tunisia, where we had tremendous cooperation from the government.

Finally, we received a request to show part of the film to President Bourghiba, the President of Tunisia. Kathie and I, Franco Zeffirelli, Vincenzo Labella and Robert Powell were invited to attend the screening, to be followed by a special luncheon with the President and his wife. We saw two hours of the film and were gratified at the favourable reaction it received.

After lunch the President presented a special award to

Zeffirelli and to Labella, then gave me the Premier Order of Commander of the Order of Merit of Tunisia. Again, I was thrilled by the honour. As we were coming out of the palace, we walked on to a terrace with a huge stone staircase leading into the courtyard. An armed guard of honour was lined up all the way down the stairs, to where my car was waiting. The President and I were having a conversation, and he evidently knew a lot about my background, because he suddenly said, 'Do you still dance?' 'Of course I do,' I said, and was in such high spirits that I went into my charleston routine on the terrace. As soon as I started to move, the guards immediately lifted their rifles. They must have thought I was about to cause trouble. But when they saw me dancing, they all roared with laughter, including the President. Strange how I seem to dance the charleston at the slightest opportunity. Perhaps that's what keeps me fit and young.

We watched every aspect of the production extremely closely, and even had a panel of religious experts to act as advisers. Months later, after looking at thousands upon thousands of feet of film, we eventually had a final cut of seven and three-quarter hours – yet something was missing. Zeffirelli, in his anxiety to get down to the required length of the programme, missed out a vital scene. This was when Doubting Thomas had been following Jesus, but was not certain that he would join as one of the disciples. He then witnessed the miracle of Jesus bringing the little girl back to life. Zeffirelli had left out the Doubting Thomas scene, but subsequently, of course, it was put back in. It just goes to show how you can make mistakes when you are too close to a project.

My deal with General Motors and NBC was for six hours. I told Franco that as much as I loved every inch of the footage he'd shot, he'd have to edit quite drastically. He did the best he could, and reduced the length to six and a quarter hours. NBC agreed to overrun.

By this time, Franco and I had developed an excellent working relationship, but we did have a major argument about the ending. He wanted the door opening with just a hand visible and all the disciples kneeling. I wanted the ending to show Jesus after the Resurrection, saying those wonderful words: 'I'll be with you forever and a day.' In the end Franco agreed with me about this.

During the production there were frequent visits from representatives of NBC and General Motors, and together we looked at some of the outstanding film sequences.

Before filming was completed, however, I had a rather upsetting meeting with representatives of General Motors, who regretfully informed me that they felt they'd made a terrible mistake in sponsoring a religious project, and that, after due consideration, they'd decided it wasn't right for them. Still, they said, I'd receive the full $3 million, and NBC could transmit the programme as planned. NBC then got Procter & Gamble to sponsor it, the only cost to them being the air time.

'Jesus of Nazareth' was finally transmitted, and was one of the greatest TV successes of my career. The public adored it, and cables of congratulation poured in from all quarters, and from all the different religious denominations. Needless to say, Procter & Gamble were thrilled.

After the transmission of the last episode, NBC telephoned me and said they wanted to buy the rights for the United States for 'Jesus of Nazareth'. 'Fine,' I said. 'I'll arrive on Sunday. We'll have a meeting on Monday morning at 10.00 a.m. and I'll catch the 8.00 p.m. flight back to London.' So the meeting was set up.

On the Thursday morning, at 10.00 a.m. New York time (3.00 p.m. London time), I received a telephone call from Gene Accas of the Leo Burnett Advertising Agency, who represented Procter & Gamble.

He said, 'Lew, Procter & Gamble want to buy the rights for the United States for "Jesus of Nazareth".' I said, 'That's foolish. I have a meeting with NBC on Monday, and whatever happens, it has to air on NBC. After all, they supported me on this project, and I must now support them.' He said, 'Procter & Gamble have no objection to it going out on NBC, but they're particularly anxious to see you before you have your meeting with them. Is there any way you can get here for a meeting on Friday? They're prepared to come over from their headquarters in Cincinatti.' I said, 'OK. I'll get the first plane out on Friday morning, which arrives about 1.00 p.m., and I'll be glad to meet you at the Regency Hotel, New York, at 2.30 p.m.'

At 2.30 p.m. Gene Accas arrived with one of the most senior people from the Leo Burnett Agency and three representatives from Procter & Gamble. They were, they said, absolutely thrilled with the programme, very proud to have been associated with it, and wanted to buy the rights for future transmissions.

They then asked what kind of price I had in mind. I said, 'Coming over on the plane I had a vision. I saw a figure of twenty-five. Now I know it can't be twenty-five *thousand*. It must mean twenty-five *million*. That's what I want, *twenty-five million dollars*.'

To this day I have no idea how I plucked that figure out of the air.

They said that the figure was ridiculous because all they wanted were the rights to five different transmissions. I said, 'I don't care if you have ten or twelve transmissions over twelve years or even fifteen years. I had a vision. And that's the figure I want.' They said, 'When do you have to know by?' 'Any time before my meeting with NBC at 10.00 a.m. on Monday morning.' They said they understood and would call me before the close of business that day.

At five minutes to six that evening, Gene Accas telephoned me and said that Procter & Gamble had offered $11.5 million for five transmissions with $1 million for options for additional transmissions, making a total of $12.5 million.

'Sorry,' I said, 'I can't accept it. I had my vision of twenty-five and I'm sticking to it.'

I didn't sleep Friday night. I didn't sleep Saturday night, and, of course, I didn't sleep Sunday night, wondering whether I'd made a mistake in turning down their offer.

On Monday morning at 10.00 a.m. I went into my meeting with NBC with the President, Bob Howard, and his Head of Business Affairs, Al Rush, plus a couple of others. The first half hour was spent in small talk. 'How's Kathie? How are things in England?' 'How's your health . . . ' and all the time I was longing to get on with the business.

Eventually, I couldn't stand it anymore. 'Let's get down to it,' I said. And they said, 'You know we want to buy the rights of "Jesus of Nazareth". It was a remarkable programme and it did NBC a tremendous amount of good. How much do you want?'

I said, 'I had a vision. I saw *$25 million*.'

They said, 'Lew. You're crazy! We only want five runs.' After a lot of discussion they finally said, 'We'll give you $14.5 million for five transmissions and $1 million for an option on additional transmissions, making it a total of $15.5 million.'

'I'm afraid I'm going to have to think about it,' I said. 'You see, I'm concerned about that vision of *$25 million*.'

'So, when will you let us know?' they said.

'I'll call you at 4.00 p.m. today,' I said, 'but now I must leave because it's nearly 12.30 p.m. and I've a luncheon engagement with CBS.'

On my way to CBS I figured I could probably get another $1 million out of NBC. I then had my lunch with Robert Wussler, President of CBS, and Bob Daly, who was Vice-President in charge of all programmes. Lunch was served up, but I couldn't eat: I was too busy trying to sell them different products – Omar Sharif to star in six hours of 'The Moulin Rouge', a three-hour TV movie with Sophia Loren – but I seemed to be getting nowhere. I began to wonder what I'd done to upset them. My relationship with CBS had always been so good, and I was getting really worried. At about twenty minutes past two I said, 'I must go back to the hotel. I have to talk to NBC at 4.00 p.m., then I've got a plane to catch for London.'

As I got up to leave they said, 'What about "Jesus of Nazareth"?' 'You're being ridiculous,' I said. 'Whatever you bid, if NBC meet it, they must have it.' 'We understand that,' they said 'What are your terms?'

'I had a vision,' I said, '*$25 million*.' They said, 'When do you have to know?' 'I have to call NBC at 4.00 p.m. so any time up to then will be fine.'

I then went back to my hotel and waited for 4.00 p.m. to come round. All the time I kept wondering how much more I could get out of NBC.

At twenty minutes to four the telephone rang. It was Bob Wussler and Bob Daly on the line. They said, 'Lew, can you come over to CBS?' I said it wasn't possible. Bob Wussler said, 'I have an appointment in my office shortly. Can Bob Daly come over to you?' I said, 'Certainly.' So Bob Daly arrived at approximately two minutes to four and, as soon as I opened the door, he put out his hand and said, 'You have a deal at $25 million.' I said, 'Bob, I must call NBC first.' He said, 'I'll stay here with you for thirty minutes. This offer is only open until then.'

I immediately telephoned Al Rush at NBC and said, 'Al. It's $25 million – ten runs over a period of fifteen years and you have under thirty minutes in which to make a decision.' Al Rush said, 'I've got the message.' Seven or eight minutes later, Herb Schlosser, Chairman and Chief Executive of NBC, telephoned me. 'Lew,' he said, 'we've been friends for twenty-five years. How can you put us into this position? We need at least another forty-eight hours to consider this.' I answered simply, 'Herb, you have eighteen minutes left.' That finished the conversation.

Bob Daly said to me, 'I'm prepared to make you a higher offer now if you accept.' 'I don't do business that way, Bob,' I told him. 'If NBC come through by 4.30 then they have it. If they don't, you can have it for $25 million.'

Ten minutes later NBC telephoned and confirmed that they would pay the $25 million. I thanked Bob Daly, who took the news very well, and he left. To this day we remain extremely good friends.

So my vision was fulfilled. In the final accounting 'Jesus of Nazareth' took $45 million – and made a net profit of $30 million. Not bad for an idea that just happened to pop into my head on the spur of the moment.

It even received the approval of the Pope – who, of course, had inspired me to undertake the production in the first place. On the Sunday after the first episode had appeared on TV in Italy, he was making one of his usual appearances on the balcony overlooking St Peter's Square, addressing the assembled crowds. He told them that they should all go home and watch 'Jesus of Nazareth' on television that evening. Naturally, this made national press coverage as it was the first time such a public endorsement had been made in this fashion by any Pope.

17

*Wheeler-dealing
and Some Special
Occasions*

DURING 1968 BOB WOOD, the President of CBS, told me he'd
be going to the Television Festival in Cannes at the end of April
that year. Although at that time I had not yet entered the film
industry, I sometimes went to the TV festivals. I decided that
Kathie and I would both go on this occasion, and we met up with
Bob, his wife and two friends of theirs.

I arranged dinner one evening at the Bonne Auberge, probably the most famous restaurant in the South of France. We were
having a most enjoyable time when suddenly we noticed a tall,
slim, beautifully dressed lady going from one table to another,
carrying a large horoscope board and some tarot cards. I thought
it might be fun to get her to tell the fortunes of my four guests, so
I invited her over. She came and told them their fortunes, and
then looked at me very intently, and said, 'I would like to tell
your fortune.' I wouldn't hear of it, but was finally persuaded.
She looked at my hands and said, 'You have a remarkably long
lifeline.' I then gave her my date of birth, and she said I had a
great future ahead of me, that many remarkable things would
happen and that I'd have many unexpected highlights in my life.
I paid her and after we returned home, I said to Kathie, 'A joke,
that fortune teller. Here I am, a 62-year-old Managing Director
of ACC, which owns ATV and the biggest chain of theatres in
the country, *and* I have received the Queen's Award for Exports.
How much more can I do? What more can happen to me?'

In the latter part of November 1968 I was in the States. I had two assistants at that time, Pamela Grey and Marcia Stanton. Pamela called me in New York and said that an important-looking letter had arrived from Downing Street. She said that it was marked 'Private and Confidential' and 'Urgent'. I said, 'I'll leave tonight and be in the office tomorrow morning.'

I flew back to London, went straight to the office, and there was a letter from the Prime Minister, Harold Wilson, offering me a knighthood and asking me whether I wished to accept it.

With shaking hands, I wrote Harold Wilson a letter of acceptance and rushed home to tell Kathie the tremendous news. My knighthood was announced on 31 December 1968.

So, is there something in fortune-telling, or isn't there?

I remembered the earlier prediction about my name in lights and going overseas. Now, after such a full life, here was yet another turn of the wheel of fortune!

The day of the investiture came. I was nervous and, when my name was called, I walked forward very stiffly, knelt on the stool and Her Majesty tapped my shoulder with the sword. The Queen always spoke to each of the people being honoured for about thirty seconds, but when it came to me, she spoke for much longer. It seemed like an eternity, but it was probably only about two minutes. I then marched off and the press surrounded me. 'What were you talking about to the Queen?' they asked. I said that I couldn't remember a thing. I don't think they believed me. But it was true. Then I went back into the Great Hall and sat with Kathie and our son Paul. Kathie also asked me what we'd been talking about and I told her I simply couldn't remember. My mind had gone completely blank. I did, however, remark to Kathie that I was disappointed not to have seen James Callaghan, who was in Wilson's cabinet, and who had specifically told me we'd meet at the investiture.

'Look up there,' Kathie said. 'There he is. He's the one who called out your name!'

That shows how deeply affected by the occasion I was.

*   *   *

My relationship with Martin Starger and Elton Rule, who had become very great friends of mine, progressed tremendously. In 1967, on one of Marty's visits to London, I took him to the Talk of the Town to see Tom Jones, who had made several television appearances for us and was an enormous hit. Marty was so impressed with his magnetic performance that he gave me an order for twenty-four one-hour shows to be called 'The Tom Jones Show'. By that time Tom Jones's records were selling very well in America. I had set up a number of meetings with Gordon Mills, who was Tom Jones's manager and friend. Whenever Gordon came to see me, he brought Tom Jones with him. Tom liked to smoke a cigar and I used to offer him one of mine each time they visited me. Mills was a tough negotiator and the terms he was pushing were hard. Finally, at the third meeting, while Tom was sitting quietly on a couch in the corner smoking a cigar, I said, 'Gordon that's my final offer, and I tell you what else I'll do. I'll give Tom a box of cigars for every programme he does.' Then Tom, who'd always remained silent at these meetings spoke for the first time. 'You've got a deal!' he said.

We ran for two and a half seasons on ABC – sixty shows in all – and they were very successful. When Tom Jones finished I suggested to Marty Starger that we do a series with Englebert Humperdinck, who was also managed by Gordon Mills.

It was interesting how Engelbert Humperdinck became a star. The 'Sunday Night at the London Palladium' shows were going along nicely, when one Sunday, at 2.00 p.m., I received a telephone call from Alec Fyne, who was Head of Light Entertainment Casting at ATV. 'I've got a terrible problem,' he said. 'Tonight's star has missed his plane, and we've got to get a quick replacement. I'd like to suggest a young man called Englebert Humperdinck.' 'But I've never heard of him,' I said. 'Trust me,' said Alec, 'I assure you he'll do a good job. He's got a great singing voice, looks good, and the women go wild over him.' I had no alternative but to agree. Well, Englebert was such a success we put him on again the following Sunday. He became a huge star and eventually I persuaded Marty Starger to agree to launch him in America, which he did, but only for one season because his show was a little too similar to 'The Tom Jones Show'. All these shows, incidentally, were magnificently directed by Jon Scoffield, who was ATV's principal director for light entertainment.

'Sunday Night at the London Palladium' fast became the most

popular variety show on television and, over the years, artistes from all over the world, and in every sphere of music and comedy, appeared for us. Because of the number of shows we did, it was inevitable that, on occasion, we'd be let down by a last-minute cancellation of a headliner. This happened with the opera star Guiseppe di Stefano, who, because of illness, wasn't able to appear. Fortunately, we found a marvellous replacement – Luciano Pavarotti, then at the beginning of his career. His glorious voice made a tremendous impact at his Palladium début, and we all knew we were hearing someone destined for greatness. Today, of course, he is one of the most famous tenors in the world.

When, due to circumstances beyond our control, we were let down and unable to find a suitable replacement, I'd make a quick call to Bob Hope and ask him if he was tied up for the weekend. He invariably replied, 'Well, Lew, I thought I might get in a bit of golf . . . ' 'Bob,' I'd say, 'we've got some great golf courses in England and I need you to help us out on "Sunday Night at the Palladium".'

I did this on several occasions, and he always agreed. That's relationship!

In the early days of independent television I instituted a five-day-a-week lunch-time programme called 'Lunch Box' which was hosted by Noele Gordon, a well-known actress and singer. She had starred in *Call Me Madam* in London, and had also appeared at the London Hippodrome in the successful Broadway musical, *Brigadoon*.

We then decided to do a soap opera, called 'Crossroads', and felt that Noele would be perfect to play the part of Meg Richardson, the owner of the motel. It began in 1964 and became one of our most successful programmes – ever. We started doing it three days a week in the early evenings, but the IBA thought this was too much and eventually it was cut down to two. Despite Noele's death it still remains a highly popular programme.

*   *   *

As I grow older, the number of occasions which are memorable accumulates.

Lord Ted Willis, the novelist and creator of the BBC's popular series 'Dixon of Dock Green', and writer of several successful series including 'Mrs Thursday' and 'Sergeant Cork', invited me to join him for lunch at the House of Lords on 17 June 1967.

I was not all that keen to accept because I was so busy, but Ted persuaded me and I said okay. On that day, Robin Gill, my Deputy Managing Director, had evidently been given the task of making sure I got there on time.

I arrived to find places set for about two hundred people. Lord Willis greeted me and I was amazed to see the number of people gathered on the veranda of the House of Lords. All the big names from the television industry were there, and politicians from all parties, including Lord Goodman, one of the most brilliant and highly respected solicitors in Britain. I mingled with the guests for a while, then asked where I should sit. Ted Willis took me to the centre of the top table: he sat on my left and Lord Goodman sat on my right. I then looked at the menu and it said 'A Luncheon in honour of Lew Grade'. I was astounded and very moved.

Before the coffee was served, Lord Willis stood up and made a speech about me, then Bill Ward came forward with a huge chalice which was beautifully inscribed to mark my services to television. He, too, made a long speech, including a remark which has always been wrongly attributed to me.

He said that when he told me we had the rights to the Olympics, the world's greatest amateur sporting event, I replied, 'We don't want amateurs – get professionals!' I wish I *had* thought of that remark myself – but it's just one more apocryphal story which has become associated with me over the years.

After the presentation of the chalice (which became one of my most treasured possessions), I was so moved that I was unable to respond and I felt very badly about this. Lord Goodman and Ted Willis both consoled me and said they quite understood how such an occasion could affect a person who, most of the time, was never at a loss for words!

A similarly momentous event came six days later, on 23 June, which was my silver wedding anniversary. I had spent twenty-five life-enhancing years with Kathie – and looked forward to at least twenty-five more.

Wheeler-dealing and Some Special Occasions

*   *   *

Martin Starger and ABC were tremendously impressed with our facilities at Elstree Studios, and in 1973 it was suggested I do a deal with Gary Smith and Dwight Hemion to produce and direct a number of variety specials in London.

I met with them and their influential agent, Sam Cohn of ICM in New York, and we did a deal for a year. I subsequently became great friends with Sam, who now handles and manages some of the best-known directors, writers and actors in the motion picture industry. He is still with ICM in New York.

Gary Smith and Dwight Hemion were considered to be the best director/producer team in the United States, and just having them around was enough to secure orders from advertising sponsors, subject only to a star name.

They both loved London so much that they signed with us for another three years. Among the many specials they did for me were several starring Burt Bacharach, Steve Lawrence and Eydie Gorme, Glen Campbell, Ann-Margret, a special show with John Wayne and Glen Campbell, and an extra-special programme with Barbra Streisand which won the Golden Rose at Montreux in 1974. They also did a version of *Peter Pan* written by Antony Newley and Leslie Bricusse, starring Danny Kaye and Mia Farrow, and produced the first pantomime on ice at Wembley. Another big one they did for us was a Bing Crosby Christmas Show with David Bowie and Twiggy. We received a considerable number of Emmy Awards for these shows, the Emmy being the TV equivalent of the Hollywood Oscar.

In the meantime, our TV film-division had been extended and we found ourselves renting space in various film studios.

Hannah Weinstein, who had originally brought me her idea for the Robin Hood series, produced 'The Buccaneers' with a relatively unknown called Robert Shaw. We made 'The Baron' with Steve Forrest, 'Department "S"', 'Jason King' and 'Bird's-Eye View' with Millicent Martin. Craig Stevens, fresh from his success with an American series called 'Peter Gunn', came out to do 'Man of the World'; we made Paul Gallico's 'Zoo Gang' with Lili Palmer, John Mills, Brian Keith and Barry Morse, and a series about Sir Francis Drake.

215

We sold these programmes worldwide, including, of course Australia, where I found myself doing a great deal of business with Frank Packer, later Sir Frank Packer of Network 9.

Frank loved to bargain, and so did I. When I first offered him the Robin Hood series, I told him I wanted $4000 per episode, knowing that I'd accept $2000. He said he wouldn't offer more than $1500. There was a fair amount of toing and froing, and eventually we compromised at $2000 – the figure I'd always had in mind. It was all game-playing, of course. And we both knew it and loved it.

When Sir Frank Packer died, his son Kerry took over the business and I said to him: 'Do you want to do business the same way I did with your father, or do you want me to quote one price and that's it?' He said, 'Just quote a price and that's it!'

I remember a brilliant young anthropologist coming to see Bob Heller, the head of our documentary division, and me in 1967 with an idea for a documentary film. His name was Adrian Cowell and he said he would like to go on an expedition to the Upper Amazon to try to find a lost tribe of Indians in the rain forests of Brazil. He said it might take him years. I was so impressed that I said I didn't mind how long it took. It did indeed take him years, but that trip resulted in a programme called 'The Tribe that Hides from Man'. It was a triumph for ATV and won many international awards. He followed this with another major documentary called 'The Opium Trail'.

Lord Snowdon also produced award-winning documentaries for ATV and 'Born to be Small' – an extremely moving film about people of limited growth – was one of the best things he has ever done.

From the very inception of independent television there had been an understanding that we would not show theatrical films on television. I thought this ridiculous, but I went along with the general consensus of opinion as expressed by the other contractors.

One morning I received a telephone call from a man I'd never met. It was Sam Goldwyn. I was completely overawed. He said, 'Lew. Sam Goldwyn here. I want to sell you twenty pictures.' He gave me their titles and quoted a price of £1 million for the lot. I said, 'How long will I have the rights for?' and he said

'Seven years.' I said, 'You have a deal.' Thus we became the first commercial company to introduce theatrical movies on television in this country. When I did the deal, I thought seven years was a very long time. Little did I know that I should have got the rights for thirty years. These same films are *still* being shown on television today!

*   *   *

Throughout my life I have always felt that somebody up there likes me. I arrived for a meeting in New York one Sunday to be in good shape for a meeting with NBC at 9.00 a.m. on the Monday. I had a close friend at NBC – David Tebet – and he cautioned me that NBC were disappointed with one of the episodes of 'The Saint', and were going to tackle me about it at the meeting.

Now, I very seldom watch television on my first day of arrival in New York, but that night it just so happened that I did. I saw an episode of 'I Spy', which was a hit series at the time starring Bill Cosby and Robert Culp, and the whole one-hour film took place in just one room with just the two stars plus two subsidiary characters. I knew what had happened. They'd gone over budget on the series and had decided to economize by using only one set and as few actors as they could get away with.

When I arrived at NBC on the Monday morning, there were six people sitting at the table, plus Mort Werner, who was Vice-President in charge of programming. I had a cup of coffee, then I said, 'Mort – I can't understand *how* you get away with it! I saw "I Spy" last night – just one set! It's obvious to everyone that you're trying to save money on the budget.'

There was a dead silence. Nobody mentioned 'The Saint'. I then carried on discussing the rest of my business with them as if nothing had happened . . . .

There came a time when Roger Moore had worked for us for almost seven years on 'The Saint' and he now said to me, 'I'm never going to do another television series again. I'll appear in a TV special or anything else you want me to do, but I won't do another series.' At that time I believe he was getting £2000 per episode, as well as a share of the profits.

As I have said, my relationship with all three major American

217

networks was very strong, and one day, while visiting ABC, I heard Martin Starger and Elton Rule discussing the following year's schedules.

I said to them, 'What about a series starring Roger Moore about a couple of troubleshooters called "The Persuaders"?' 'No,' they said, 'Roger Moore's been around much too long in 'The Saint'. He's been overexposed.' 'Okay,' I said. 'What would you say if I could get Tony Curtis for the other role?' 'You'll have a firm order for 24 episodes,' they replied.

The next day I went straight to California and telephoned George Chasin, who was a partner in an agency called Citron Park Chasin. They were originally part of MCA before MCA disbanded their agency.

'George,' I said, 'I'd very much like to get Tony Curtis for a series I'm doing with Roger Moore.' 'Out of the question,' he said, 'Tony will never do television. Everybody's been trying to get him, but he just doesn't want to do it.' 'Well, at least talk to him,' I said. He did, and called me back the next day. 'Tony doesn't want to do it,' he said. 'He appreciates your offer very much but he just doesn't want to do television.' I said, 'Any chance of my talking to him personally?' 'Sure,' he said, 'but I know it'll be a waste of time.' A while later he telephoned me to say that Tony Curtis was on his way to see me at the Beverly Hills Hotel.

There was a ring at my doorbell and I opened the door. Tony Curtis shook hands with me and said, 'What do I call you?' (I was Sir Lew Grade at the time.) I said, 'I don't care what you call me as long as you do the television series.' After about one and a half hours of discussion, during which I once again proved my powers as a salesman, he agreed to do the series. Later George Chasin came over with a one-page letter of agreement which we all signed.

So I'd got Tony Curtis. Now I had to face an even bigger problem – Roger Moore.

I telephoned Roger on Saturday to say I had to see him on Sunday morning at eleven at my office in London. 'Lew,' he said, 'it's not about a television series, is it?' 'Roger,' I said, 'it's important that I see you at 11.00 a.m.' I flew back to London, arriving at Heathrow at 6.40 a.m., went home, had a quick bath and shave and got to my office at about 10.00 a.m. Roger arrived promptly at 11.00 a.m. I gave him a cigar – he liked cigars – which I knew would put him at ease.

I said, 'Roger, I have a problem. I've sold a series to ABC called "The Persuaders" starring you and Tony Curtis.' 'But Lew,' he said, 'I've told you I'm never going to do a television series again.'

'Now just a moment, Roger,' I said, and went to my desk. I opened the drawer and took out a cheque which I'd already written out for a substantial sum of money. I went back to Roger, who was sitting on the couch. 'Roger, old boy,' I said, 'this is to be getting on with . . . ' Roger looked at the cheque. 'When do we start?' he said.

And that's how we got 'The Persuaders' together.

Unfortunately, we only did one season of 24 episodes. Roger and Tony Curtis didn't hit it off all that well. Apart from an understandable rivalry – they were both extremely handsome, extremely popular male sex symbols – Roger was annoyed at Tony's insistence that work should cease on the dot of 5.00 p.m. Roger was always willing to work late so as to finish filming a sequence; but Tony had just got married, and wanted to spend as much time as possible with his new bride. He couldn't wait to get home each day. A pity, as the series was always well-received wherever it was shown.

After I had completed the deal with Tony Curtis for 'The Persuaders', I thought I'd like to get Shirley MacLaine to do a television series based on the situations a roving female photographer might find herself in. I had several meetings with her and her agent, Herman Citron, but she refused to give a firm commitment. Eventually, Herman and I worked out a deal, subject to Shirley agreeing to do the series. She was 'half' interested, she said, but couldn't make up her mind.

At Herman's suggestion, I telephoned Shirley and was invited to lunch at her home in California. Shirley had a great sense of humour, so, before I arrived, I took one arm out of my jacket sleeve, put it behind my back, and then rang her doorbell. When she came to the door I said, 'Look. I've just been with Herman Citron. He's worked out a deal and it's cost me my arm.' She roared with laughter and said, 'OK, Lew, I'll do the series.'

Then I joined her for lunch. She had four other guests, including Professor Salk and his wife. 'Tell them the story about your mother and the Queen Mother,' Shirley said. So I told them the story.

What had actually happened was that my brother, Bernie, who at that time was responsible for all the Royal Variety Performances, had had continuous calls from my mother saying that every member of the Grade family had met royalty except her. Even her grandchildren had had the privilege, having presented flowers on a couple of occasions. 'So, what's wrong with me?' she said. 'Why can't I meet the Queen Mother?'

Bernie telephoned me and said, 'Mum is driving me crazy. She wants to present the flowers at the next Royal Variety Performance.' 'So why not?' I said. 'If she promises not to say a single word, let her do it.'

Well, the great evening duly came along. My mother, who was then well over eighty, curtsied to the Queen Mother and handed over the flowers. The Queen Mother then said, 'Mrs Winogradsky, you must be very proud of your children.' And my mother replied, 'And Ma'am, you must be very proud of yours!' The next day the press were full of photographs and the quotes. My mother was walking on air for days after that!

Long before Shirley signed for me we had become good friends. I told her I was trying hard to get major stars to appear in some of my television series, and she arranged for me to meet Sidney Poitier at the Beverly Hills Hotel at 4.00 p.m. that day. At 3.00 p.m., just as I was about to leave, she said, 'You can't go yet. I want you to meet somebody special who is just arriving any minute.' Her guest finally arrived and she introduced me to a charming man whose name I did not catch. She told him I had to leave almost immediately, but persuaded me to stay and have coffee with them. Then she said, 'Tell him the story about the Queen Mother and your mother.' So I had to go through the whole routine again. At 3.45 p.m. I said I really had to go, and I made my way to the Beverly Hills Hotel.

Sidney Poitier was a delightful man, but he really wasn't interested in doing television. The fact that I didn't have a specific project in mind didn't help matters either. At around 6.00 p.m. Shirley called me. 'I can't understand why you didn't stay,' she

Two glittering Royal occasions: The Royal Show in aid of the World Wildlife Fund, with the Queen, Prince Philip and Rex Harrison; and (below) the Royal première of 'Moses the Lawgiver' (1976), with Burt Lancaster (right).

Momentous occasions: a private audience with Pope Paul VI, who said how thrilled he was with their interpretation of 'Moses the Lawgiver', and blessed the production; and with Pope John Paul II, who said he thought 'Jesus of Nazareth' was wonderful.

Yes, Minister!
Lew and Kathie with
Harold Wilson.

Lew with James
Callaghan on the
Fiftieth Anniversary
of Votes for Women . . .

. . . and in deep
conversation with
Margaret Thatcher.

SEEING STARS:

1 Lew with John Wayne and son
Michael Wayne.

2 Lew and partner Martin Starger
with Dave Goelz (second left),
Jim Henson and Frank Oz of the
fabulously successful 'Muppet Show'.

3 Lew and Kathie with Shirley
MacLaine.

4 Kathie and song-and-dance man
Gene Kelly.

5 . . . with Kirk Douglas . . .
and cigar . . .

6 At the National Academy of
Television Arts and Sciences's
'Salute to Sir Lew' dinner in
1975. The guest of honour was
Earl Mountbatten of Burma.

7 Lew dances the charleston with
his close friend Jerry Perenchio
at a dinner in the South of France.

8 . . . with the incomparably suave
Cary Grant.

9 Chatting to comedian Bob Hope
at a special Royal Variety Show
in celebration of the Twenty-fifth
Anniversary of the Coronation of
Queen Elizabeth II.

10 Roger Moore – 'extremely
handsome, extremely popular' –
and his wife Luisa.

11 Two showbiz giants embrace:
Lew and the mighty Orson Welles.

A cultural landmark. Opera superstars Maria Callas and Tito Gobbi brought distinction to ATV's 'The Golden Hour' in their legendary performance of Act II of Puccini's *Tosca*, directed by Franco Zeffirelli. 'A Callas performance was always something of an event, and that night was no exception.'

Lew, Julie Andrews and the Emmy Award she won for 'The Julie Andrews Hour' in 1973.

Lew's greatest TV triumph 'Jesus of Nazareth' with Robert Powell as Jesus and Rod Steiger as Pontius Pilate. 'We watched every aspect of the production

xtremely closely, and
ven had a panel of
eligious experts to act as
dvisers. The show took
45 million, and made a
et profit of $30 million.'

Laurence Olivier and Joan Plowright in *The Merchant of Venice*
directed by Jonathan Miller. 'Culture is expensive and it doesn't
always make money. But then money isn't everything . . .'

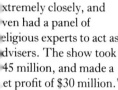

1uppet superstars Miss
iggy with the man in
er life, Kermit the Frog.

On Golden Pond The only teaming of Henry and his daughter
Jane Fonda; and of Henry Fonda and Katharine Hepburn. 'I
just had a hunch that with these three stars, and the chemistry
they'd generate, the film would be successful.' It was
nominated for ten Oscars and won three.

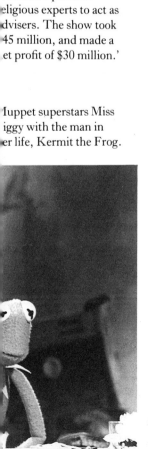

'The Julie Andrews Hour': a few extra arms would have been useful!

Another great honour – a peerage on 23 June 1976. 'One of life's great coincidences: it was the date of Kathie's birthday, *and* the date of our wedding anniversary.'

said. 'Sidney could have waited. After all, it's not every day you get to meet Henry Kissinger, is it?' That was the one and only time I met Mr Kissinger and I didn't even realize who he was!

A few weeks later, shortly before we were due to start production on the series, which we had decided to call 'Shirley's World', Shirley telephoned me to say that she was with Frank Gilroy, an outstanding director and writer who had given her a screenplay called *Desperate Characters*. She was prepared to do the script for next to nothing, she said, 'just for a share of the profits'. It would only take four weeks to shoot and would cost $250,000. I had great confidence in Shirley MacLaine. I thought she was one of the most talented actresses in America, and, of course, she was also a wonderful dancer and singer. So I agreed, because I knew I was safe in getting that kind of money back on the film. This was in 1971.

As soon as she finished filming the sixteen episodes of 'Shirley's World', she was given a script called *The Possession of Joel Delaney*. She sent it to me, I liked it, and we decided to make it. Once again, Shirley took a very low fee and the picture came in at $1.5 million.

They were both good films. Of *Desperate Characters* the New York critic Rex Reed said: '. . . The most blistering indictment of New York City since *Midnight Cowboy*.'

The Possession of Joel Delaney, directed by Waris Hussein, was a fine picture, and one of the first films to deal with the occult before the subject became the trend with *The Exorcist*.

Both films were distributed by Frank Yablans, who, at that time, was President of Paramount Pictures. For me, it was a foretaste of things to come.

I sold 'Shirley's World' to ABC, but it wasn't a success. The problem was that the producer, Sheldon Leonard, was too much in awe of Shirley and allowed the production to slip away from him. And when a producer or executive director allows that to happen, it usually means trouble. Shirley was given too much rope – and she took advantage of it, making most of the decisions, several of which weren't good for the show. She's a wonderful actress, but she's not a producer, and was therefore only able to see what would work for her, rather than for the series as a whole.

221

What was really lacking was Shirley's effervescent personality. It just didn't come through. Maybe her mind was on other things. At any rate, she subsequently appeared for me on 'Sunday Night at the London Palladium', on a special Royal Variety Show in celebration of the 25th Anniversary of the Coronation of Queen Elizabeth II. It was a Silver Jubilee gala, and, apart from Shirley, the line-up included Bob Hope, Harry Belafonte, Cleo Laine and Johnny Dankworth, and Rudolf Nureyev.

It was a wonderful night, followed by a dinner party at Claridges attended by Prince Charles and Lord Mountbatten, and I was particularly grateful to Shirley, who'd cancelled a special event she was meant to be attending in Houston, Texas, in order to take part in our celebrations.

That's relationship . . . .

*   *   *

I had lunch one day at CBS with William Paley and his second-in-command, Dr Frank Stanton. During the lunch they asked me if I had any fresh series ideas. I told him I had a project called 'The Prisoner' with Patrick McGoohan, and showed them a portfolio of pictures of the village of Portmeirion, which was the location we intended to use. 'At the moment though, Patrick only wants to make 17 episodes,' I said. 'How much money do you want?' they asked. I told them the terms, and they said we had a deal.

Generally, I negotiated with the Vice-President in Charge of Programming, who at that time was Michael Dann. They then asked me what else I had. I now had to think very quickly. 'I've got a wonderful idea for a series called "The Skull",' I said. 'What's it about?' they asked, not unreasonably. 'Well,' I said, 'I'd like you to visualize a monastery and you see a figure creeping up to it and leaving a box there. A few seconds later the monastery door slowly opens and a nun comes out, sees the box, opens it and discovers it is full of money. On top of the money is the drawing of a skull.' 'That sounds wonderful,' they said. 'We love it!'

For weeks on end I racked my brains to see if I could come up with a format. I failed, so 'The Skull' was never made.

After four or five episodes of 'The Prisoner' had been made, Michael Dann visited London, looked at them and said to me, 'I really can't understand what it's all about.' So I said, 'Why don't I fix up a meeting with Patrick McGoohan. He'll explain everything to you.' I arranged the meeting. Michael Dann came back the next day and said he still didn't understand the series. Furthermore, he added, 'I really don't understand how you can get on with Patrick.' 'I have no problems with him,' I said. 'He's very easy to get along with. I just agree to all his requests.'

'The Prisoner', which was first shown in 1967, is still highly popular and continues to fascinate audiences all over the world.

*   *   *

Billy Marsh and Michael Grade had been pushing me to try to sell Morecambe and Wise in America. Once again, an opportunity arose for me at ABC. The network was talking about replacement series which they ran throughout the summer, and I managed to sell them Morecambe and Wise. They gave me an order for sixteen episodes. ATV had started Morecambe and Wise on their TV careers in 1970. From the very beginning they were a talented duo. But as time went on they improved out of all recognition and became great stars. I was so excited about getting this order and also imagined how thrilled Billy Marsh and Michael would be as well. I called Billy and asked him to meet me with Ernie Wise (who was the businessman of the team) at my office on Sunday, lunch-time, as soon as I arrived back from New York. I expected them to go down on their knees and thank me for having achieved what seemed an impossible task. Instead, I got some unexpected resistance from Ernie Wise who would not agree to do sixteen shows, only twelve. I had to accept some tough terms. Eventually we did a deal, and I then asked Eric and Ernie to slow down their pace a little because I felt they were a bit too fast for American audiences to understand. They refused to do this. The result is that although they were well received in America, they didn't get high ratings. I believe if they'd taken my advice and slowed down just a little, they'd have been much more popular in the States, because they were certainly an extraordinarily talented team.

As they were only prepared to do twelve shows, ABC allowed

me to complete my commitment by presenting four programmes starring singer Val Doonican, whom I have always admired.

In time Michael Grade took Morecambe and Wise away from ATV and sold them to the BBC. Whenever I had to deal with either of the agencies with whom I had once been associated – Lew & Leslie Grade and The Grade Organisation – they were relentlessly tough on terms, and negotiating for any of their stars was always a struggle.

ATV regularly presented the Royal Variety Performance – usually from the London Palladium. When my brother Bernie became President of the Variety Artistes' Benevolent Fund, he felt it was only fair that we should alternate the Royal Variety Show with the BBC. I fought as hard as I could to retain the exclusivity of these shows, but in the end I had no alternative but to agree. To this day the Royal Variety Show is shared between the BBC and the commercial network.

Towards the end of the 1960s I met up with Larry Gelbart, the brilliant writer of 'M*A*S*H'. He was living in London at the time, and presented me with the idea of doing a half-hour comedy series with Marty Feldman. Because of Gelbart's reputation, I had no problem in selling thirteen episodes to ABC as a summer replacement. I completed the contract with Gelbart and Marty Feldman for thirteen half-hour episodes, with an option for another thirteen. But after seven episodes, Larry came to me and said he was being driven crazy by Marty, who kept extending the sketches. He was so unhappy, he said, that he wanted to get out of his contract. 'Larry,' I said, 'we have a commitment for thirteen and we're going to make thirteen.' We did, and the series was only a moderate success. I'm sure Larry was right; had the sketches been a little shorter, Marty Feldman would have run a little longer. Over the years Larry and I discussed several possible projects together, and it was a running joke between us that whenever I found his terms too heavy I'd say, 'Larry, I'll take up the option on the other Marty Feldman shows!' Thereafter we always came to an amicable agreement.

*   *   *

Early in 1972, Elton Rule and Marty Starger were trying to get Julie Andrews to commit to a series, but had had no success.

I told them I'd known Julie and her family since she was a little girl, and explained my relationship with her agent Arthur Park of Citron Park Chasin Agency. They said it would be wonderful if I'd go with them to California to see what could be done. By that time, of course, Julie Andrews had become a superstar. She had been a tremendous hit on Broadway in the stage production of *My Fair Lady* and had also won an Oscar for *Mary Poppins* – not to mention her triumph in the film version of *The Sound of Music*. As you can imagine, it would have been quite an achievement for all concerned if we could get her.

So we went to California and had our meeting. It went on for ages. I reminded Arthur Park of my earlier association with Julie, told him that our facilities in London were magnificent and that the producer/director would be Nick Vanoff, who had a wonderful track record. Finally, he said he'd consult with his client and that we'd meet again the following morning.

We duly met the next morning and, after a great deal of discussion and negotiation, he came up with a proposal that she would do the 24 episodes if I committed myself to making two feature films which Blake Edwards (her husband) would direct. I knew that Blake was a great director, and had been particularly impressed with his work on the hit TV series 'Peter Gunn'. I asked how much Julie wanted for the films and they said $250,000 and $200,000 for Blake. I thought that was very reasonable. Then he threw in something to which I agreed, but knew nothing about, and frankly didn't understand. It was that Julie's fee was against 10 per cent of the gross and Blake's was against 5 per cent of the gross. I was so anxious to conclude the deal that I agreed, without trying to find out what this clause meant first.

Well, what it meant was that she would get 10 per cent of all the film rentals, i.e., 10 per cent of what the film's distributor makes, which usually works out at 40–45 per cent of the box-office takings. We then proceeded to set up the series.

ABC believed this to be such an important project for them that they decided to hold a press conference, followed by a dinner, in Malibu, California. I agreed to be present but my plane was delayed and when I arrived the press conference had already started. Julie and Nick Vanoff were both seated on a small dais and there were about 150 journalists in front of them.

They were asking Julie the most controversial questions I have ever heard in my life.

She had recently made a film called *Darling Lili*, directed by her husband. It had gone way over budget and lost millions for Paramount Pictures. The press were demanding to know whether she felt she was all washed up as a movie star and had agreed to go into TV only because no major studio would employ her.

She'd also made a picture at 20th Century-Fox called *Star!* in which she played Gertrude Lawrence. That film was another box-office flop – and the reporters that night were really rubbing her nose in it. Julie, who's a tough lady in all circumstances, did her best to answer these questions as respectfully and politely as she could, but I sensed she was hurt by them. The press then went on about her saccharin Mary Poppins image, and that didn't go down well either.

I was so angry on Julie's behalf, I had to be restrained from running on to the dais and telling them all what I thought of them.

In the end, I calmed down a bit, and we all went to dinner at a nearby restaurant. I sat at a special table with Julie and Blake, Leonard Goldenson (Chairman of ABC), Elton Rule (President of ABC) and Marty Starger.

As we started our dinner, I looked round at the press. They all had such long and gloomy faces, you'd have thought they were at a funeral. I couldn't take any more. 'Elton,' I said, 'would you please stand up and introduce me to the press? I want to say a few words.'

Elton stood up and said, 'Ladies and gentlemen. Sir Lew Grade, who is responsible for "The Julie Andrews Show", would like to say a few words to you.'

Then I stood up. 'Ladies and gentlemen,' I said. 'If the press conference you have just held had been in London and you had asked the same questions you asked tonight, each and every one of you would have been sent to the Tower and had your heads chopped off.

'However, to prove to you that I have every confidence that "The Julie Andrews Show" will be an outstanding quality production, and will show off Julie Andrews's unique talents to the best advantage, I now formally invite all of you to visit London at the end of October 1972, as my guests, and while you're over there I hope you'll get some first-hand knowledge of the quality of British television.'

Although nobody really believed me, suddenly it was as if 150 people had left the restaurant and 150 new people had walked in. Their faces lit up, they were all laughing and chatting and it was an entirely different atmosphere.

I kept my promise and brought them all to London. In 1973 'The Julie Andrews Show' received seven Emmy Awards, so my hunches were right . . . .

Julie only wanted to do 24 shows, and as soon as they were completed, Blake and I discussed the first feature film he was going to make under the terms of our agreement. He came up with a film called *The Tamarind Seed*, which starred Julie and Omar Sharif. It was a good film and did fairly well, although ATV couldn't possibly make much money out of it because of the gross percentage due to Julie and Blake.

Incidentally, I pre-sold the two films to ABC TV. They took a chance, of course, as they had no idea whether the films were going to be any good or not, and that's when I realized what a good opportunity there was to pre-sell feature films to television, even though at that time I had no intention of going into film production. I just wanted to honour my commitment.

Then Blake came up with the second feature film proposal for Julie. It was called *Rachel and the Stranger* and was set in the snow-covered mountains of Canada. I disliked the idea intensely.

I had a meeting with Blake in London and told him I didn't want to make *Rachel and the Stranger*, and that I'd buy off the remainder of his contract. I said I'd pay the full amounts due to him and Julie plus a little extra to account for the percentage of the gross. He said, 'Fine.'

Later that day, however, he called me back. 'Lew, I've been thinking it over,' he said, 'and I'm afraid I have to go back on my word.' 'But, Blake, you can't do that,' I told him. 'You know, when I say we have a deal, we have a deal and that's that.' 'I understand that, Lew,' he said, 'but my whole future is at stake. People will automatically think I went heavily over-budget on *The Tamarind Seed* and it'll affect my career.' (After *Darling*

Lili, he clearly didn't want that to happen again.)

Then I had a brainwave. 'Blake,' I said, 'you own the rights to the *Pink Panther* films. So why don't we make a film called *The Return of the Pink Panther*?' 'Because you'll never get Peter Sellers,' he replied. 'He and I don't get on very well and he has absolutely refused to do any more Pink Panther films.' 'What happens if I get him?' I asked. 'Then we'll do it,' he said.

I telephoned Peter Sellers, with whom I had been closely associated for many years, and asked him to come and see me. Two hours later I'd persuaded him to do *The Return of the Pink Panther* with Blake Edwards directing. We got a short letter of agreement typed out and he signed it.

I then telephoned Blake and said, 'Blake, you'll be pleased to hear we've got Peter Sellers for *The Return of the Pink Panther*. It's all signed.'

'Lew,' he said, 'I'm afraid we've got a little problem. United Artists own half the rights to the *Pink Panther* films and any sequels.' 'Don't worry about it,' I said, 'I'll call Eric Pleskow [the President of United Artists] and I'll do a deal with him.'

So I telephoned Eric Pleskow in New York and asked whether he'd like to be partners with me in this film, adding that I'd already pre-sold it for television to ABC. He said that he wouldn't touch it with a bargepole. He thought it would be a total disaster, and, as far as he was concerned, I could go ahead and make it with his blessing.

I said, 'Eric, I don't know anything abut theatrical distribution. Will you please distribute it for me?' 'Certainly,' he said, 'I'll do that for you, but I'm telling you now – it'll be a failure.' 'All the same,' I said, 'I've got a commitment and you know I honour every commitment once I've made it.'

Blake made the film. It opened in the States and was a runaway hit. The box-office figures were incredible and there were queues wherever it was shown. But I still hadn't seen it. I was so busy with ATV business, I'd never found the time.

One day in 1976 I was on an aeroplane on my way back from New York and noticed it was the in-flight movie. In those days the sound equipment on aeroplanes was pretty primitive, and as I watched the film I thought it was one of the worst things I'd ever seen. I simply couldn't imagine how something so bad could have taken so much money.

A couple of days later, United Artists decided they'd have a *Return of the Pink Panther* press reception in Gstaad, Switzerland, for the world's press, and naturally the invitations were all sent out in my name. They told me that Kathie and I would have to come to Gstaad.

So we went and I was very relaxed. After all, Gstaad is a beautiful place, and I thought I'd have a couple of days' rest. At about 5.30 p.m. there was a knock on the door. It was the Head of Publicity of United Artists. 'We're all waiting for you downstairs,' he said. 'What for?' I asked. 'There's a big cocktail reception, then we're all going to a cinema for a screening of the film.' 'I'll come down to the reception,' I said, 'but I won't go anywhere near the film.' Kathie then interjected, 'We'll have to go,' she said. 'After all, the invitations are in your name, and if you don't go there'll be a lot of questions asked.' 'But Kathie,' I said, 'the film is terrible!' In the end she managed to persuade me to go. We went downstairs to the party, mingled with all the guests, and then we went on to the cinema.

The film duly began and it was like seeing an entirely different movie. The press shrieked with laughter – and so did I! It taught me a lesson: never watch films on planes, even though the sound and projection equipment are much better than they used to be.

And that is how, accidentally, through television, I had my first real taste of the film business.

18

Business As Usual and a Peerage

AFTER THE SUCCESS of *The Return of the Pink Panther*, United Artists, predictably, demanded their rights to a half interest in any other Pink Panther projects and, of course, we agreed, and together made the highly successful *The Pink Panther Strikes Again*.

Meanwhile, Cecil Clarke was producing a series of thirteen one-hour episodes on tape at our Elstree Studios, and on location, called 'Edward the Seventh'. It was a beautiful, costly production, which Leslie Halliwell, the well-known film historian, described as 'a superb piece of historical re-creation and one of the milestones of TV dramas, with research, writing, production and acting alike impeccable . . . '

The series starred Timothy West, Annette Crosbie (as Queen Victoria), Robert Hardy and John Gielgud. It was the life story of Edward VII – Queen Victoria's heir – and we were fortunate enough to have the royal family's cooperation in the use of the actual locations.

When the series opened in England the public loved it and the press went overboard.

I had not made 'Edward the Seventh' with the intention of selling it to America, but I realized that this was a mini-series that could go well in the States. I showed it to Herb Schlosser, President of NBC. He looked at the thirteen one-hour episodes and liked them a lot. But he felt that he couldn't air them at prime-time, which was from 8.00 to 11.00 p.m. He was, he said, prepared to give me a Sunday afternoon slot but wouldn't pay me the sort of money I was hoping for.

I then saw Robert Wood and Fred Silverman of CBS. Silverman was Vice-President in charge of Programming. I left the cassettes with them and said I'd return in two weeks' time to see whether or not they were interested.

They were interested, and sent Bob Daly, Head of Finance for Programming, to negotiate terms. As Wood and Silverman were leaving the room, Bob said to Fred, 'You know, it might be a good idea if we put two one-hours together and ran them in the movie slot as a two-hour programme.' Fred agreed.

I absorbed that remark and, while waiting for Bob Daly, realized CBS could pay a great deal more if they put it in their movie slot. When Daly came in he asked me how much I had in mind, and I said $200,000 per hour. (Initially I was only going to ask half of that.) He said, 'Okay. Relax and I'll be back with you in a moment.' Five minues later he returned. 'You've got a deal,' he said. So it just shows what a chance remark can do, and how on the ball you always have to be in business.

Later on, after Fred Silverman left CBS and Daly became Vice-President in charge of Programming, Daly was a little nervous about putting 'Edward the Seventh' in the movie slot.

Meanwhile, at about this time, Herb Schmertz of the Mobil Oil Corporation had been trying hard to buy the rights from me, and, when we met, I told him he was too late, and that I'd sold them to CBS. Eventually, however, CBS sold Mobil the rights and it went out in America under the title 'Edward the King' so that there wouldn't be any confusion in anyone's minds with the story of Edward and Mrs Simpson.

Herb Schmertz had it transmitted on independent broadcasting stations throughout America, and, once again, it was a phenomenal success. Mobil received tremendous acclaim and CBS a great deal of flak for letting it go. Well, that's show business.

I subsequently sold Mobil a trio of mini-series on Disraeli, Nelson and William Shakespeare. I believe I'm correct in claiming that ATV were the pioneers of the mini-series, a form of TV entertainment which, today, is a staple of every major TV network's programme schedules.

*   *   *

In 1975 the National Academy of Television Arts and Sciences honoured me with a special dinner they called 'Salute to Sir Lew'. This was the first time such an honour had been given to a non-American and I was asked to arrange a special stage performance which ABC were going to record for transmission at a later date.

Kathie, who hadn't been back to America since her first trip twenty-seven years earlier, agreed to accompany me, with our son Paul, on this auspicious occasion. Several of the Directors of ACC and ATV came too.

The dinner took place at the New York Hilton on 18 April and the performers taking part in the show were Tom Jones, Julie Andrews, John Lennon, Peter Sellers, Dave Allen and the Second Generation Dancers. A modest little line-up!

I had approached John Lennon, who hadn't performed in public or made personal appearances for some time, and asked him if he would appear at this Salute. He readily agreed to do so and had the full support of Yoko Ono.

The guest of honour was Lord Mountbatten. Just before the finale, he appeared on the stage to pay me a very great tribute. This was followed by a speech from the President of the Society, who then asked me to come on to the stage – which I did, holding my customary cigar. I made a speech thanking everybody for the effort that had been put into the dinner and was presented with a huge plaque. Just as I was walking off the stage, the orchestra started to play the charleston. A host of celebrities from every conceivable branch of show business – actors, actresses, producers, people from the three television networks and from all the major film companies – were in the audience. They all stood up and shouted, 'Come on Lew, do the charleston.' I then had to make a tremendous decision. Should I do my dance carrying the plaque or smoking the cigar? There was no way I could do it with both. I decided to keep the cigar and put the plaque down on the stage.

What a fantastic ovation they gave me. I later discovered that Julie Andrews had planned the whole thing, as she knew that I wouldn't be able to resist that music.

The Salute was commemorated by a most wonderful brochure, which describes through pictures and letters the different phases of my career. It was only when I returned to England that I discovered that my assistant Marcia had for weeks been quietly collating all the relevant material for this brochure. And I hadn't known a thing about it.

At this point, I must say a word or two about my attractive assistant, Marcia Stanton. In short, Marcia is amazing and does not know the meaning of the word 'impossible', and her efficiency is matched only by her loyalty. Over the years she has shared our joys and sorrows, and she and Kathie are really close friends. In fact, Marcia has become one of the family.

She joined me in 1960, and when I left ACC in June 1982 she left with me, and we both joined Embassy the very next day.

She is now a co-Director in The Grade Company and, as I am often away on extensive business trips, she really runs everything more efficiently than I would.

Two days before the Salute, Herb Schlosser gave a dinner party for me and my family at his apartment in New York. Incidentally, this was Paul's first trip to America and he was just over twenty. Herb took me up to a young lady and said, 'Lew, you know Barbara Walters, don't you?' She threw her arms around me and said, 'Hello, Uncle Lew.' I was astonished. I certainly had no recollection of having met her before. I knew the name. After all, she was the most famous woman interviewer on television in America – and the highest paid – but I didn't know her personally. She could see my look of bewilderment. 'I can see you don't remember me?' she said. 'I'm Lou Walters's daughter. You and Auntie Kathie looked after me many years ago when I came to London.' Kathie, of course, remembered her, but isn't it amazing the coincidences that crop up in one's life?

Among the many guest stars featured on 'The Julie Andrews Show' was Jim Henson's Muppets. I was tremendously taken with both Jim and his fabulous puppets, and suggested to Abe Mandell, the President of ITC Inc., that he might try and place a series of 24 half-hour Muppet episodes with CBS's five owned and operated stations. In addition, I was confident that we could sell the series to the rest of the United States as well.

CBS loved the idea, and we went ahead and made the programmes at Elstree. Each segment featured a prominent guest

233

star, and so popular did the Muppets prove that we had stars from all over the world clamouring to appear on the show. As soon as I heard that CBS wanted a further 24 programmes, I called all the staff at Elstree Studios for a meeting.

They were all very nervous, wondering what I wanted to talk to them about. 'Boys and girls,' I said, 'I want you to know that we've got an order for another 24 episodes of "The Muppets".' They cheered at this. 'However,' I went on, 'because we'll always be on a very tight schedule, you must promise me that whatever happens you will never strike on "The Muppets".' They all shouted out, 'We promise.'

Half way through the second series I got a call on a Bank Holiday Monday to say that Elstree Studios was about to strike and that we weren't going to be able to proceed with 'The Muppets'. Catastrophe! We *had* to work every day in order to get 'The Muppets' completed on time – Bank Holiday or not. I quickly jumped into my car and Kathie and I drove out to Elstree Studios. I called the senior shop stewards together and said, 'Do you remember the meeting I had? I promised you another series and you promised me that you would never strike on "The Muppets". I've kept my promise, now I expect you to keep yours.' And sure enough they did. That was the strength of my relationship with the unions.

And, while on the subject of relationships with the unions, at one stage a statutory law was passed which said that people working in London were entitled to an increase of £6.40 per week to make up for their travelling expenses. ATV's advertising revenue was a little low at that time and we were not going all that well. Consequently, I refused to pay Elstree personnel the London Weighting Allowance because I simply couldn't afford it. I therefore called a meeting at ATV House of the two chief shop stewards of each of the four unions. No one else was present, not even my head of labour relations. I sent the union people into a small conference room and then walked in smoking a tiny cheroot. Now, everybody knew I always smoked big cigars. 'Boys,' I said, 'you can see for yourself how bad things are.' They had to laugh, and I then lit my usual cigar. 'I've called you to this special meeting,' I said, 'at the particular request of my wife. She wants you to do her a personal favour. As you know, she does all the Easter parties for the children of the Elstree staff, and she also does big Christmas parties for them. She does it all on her own initiative and pays for it herself. This is the favour she is asking – she wants you all to go out on strike for four weeks so that at long last she can have a holiday with me, because I'm not going to pay you the London Weighting Allowance. However, I promise to pay you when things get better, and you know I never break my word.' They agreed to accept this undertaking from me, but Kathie lost her holiday, and a couple of years later, when advertising sales were back on track, I made good my promise.

On another occasion, we had a disastrous six months' Actors' Equity strike, and it was eventually settled by a negotiating committee led by Paul Adorian, who was then Managing Director of Rediffusion. They settled everything but foreign residual payments, which Equity was claiming. None of the companies was really concerned because hardly any of them were selling product overseas. We then reached a point where sales were going remarkably well and I felt it was time to settle this problem. All our technicians were so talented and competent that people from overseas were always more than happy to work with them.

I called Gerald Croasdell, who was the General Secretary of Equity, and said, 'We must have a meeting to settle foreign residual rights.' He agreed, and came the following day to a meeting at 4.00 p.m. in Paul Adorian's office at Television House in Kingsway. I arrived there a few minutes before he did and said to Paul Adorian, 'Just say hello, and let me handle all the negotiation.'

In thirty minutes we had settled the residual fees for foreign transmissions and, as Gerald Croasdell and I were leaving, he turned to me and said, 'I wish the Actors' Equity strike had been handled in the same manner. It could have been settled just as quickly and would have cost the companies much less money.'

The important thing to bear in mind about negotiations, I have learned, is: one to one, or two to two – but never more. When too many people gather around a negotiating table, everyone of them is anxious to have his say, but they tend to lose sight of their main purpose, which is to settle the dispute.

As 'The Muppets' went into its third year, word got around that Jim Henson wanted to make a Muppet movie. I invited him to have lunch with me and, at the end of the meal, I said, 'I understand you want to make a Muppet movie.' He replied that he did. 'Jim,' I said, 'here's my hand. You have a deal not for one Muppet movie, but for two.'

'The Muppet Show' ran for five years. In all, we made 120 programmes, and, working with the show's production team – Jim Henson, Frank Oz and Dave Lazer – was one of the most pleasurable experiences of my life. It was a happy show, and, in turn, generated a great deal of pleasure. The guest artists we used included such stars as Julie Andrews, Beverley Sills, Rudolf Nureyev, Bob Hope, Liza Minnelli and Carol Burnett – to name but a mere handful. After five years we went out on syndication in the United States and Canada, and our sales, for the 120 episodes, totalled a mammoth $104 million – and that was just for syndication in the USA and Canada.

*　　*　　*

In March 1976 I received a call from the private secretary at No. 10 Downing Street to say that the Prime Minister, Harold Wilson, would like to see me at 11.00 a.m. the following day. 'I'm sorry,' I said, 'it's impossible. I've got some very important visitors from overseas and I'm taking them to lunch, and I'm afraid I can't change the plans.' He asked when I would be free and I said at 3.00 p.m. 'Fine,' he said. 'He'll see you then.'

When I arrived, I sat down with the Prime Minister. 'Lew,' he said, 'I would like to offer you a peerage. Will you accept it?'

I said I'd be tremendously honoured, and then asked, 'Is that what you wanted to see me about at 11.00 a.m.? If I'd known I'd have cancelled *any* appointment!' I was immensely grateful for this magnificent honour.

In fact, Harold Wilson – now Lord Wilson of Rievaulx – was always a great supporter of mine. NBC once told me that when he was in New York and visiting their headquarters, in the course of conversation he had said, 'I hope you're buying programmes from Lew Grade!'

In due course I had to go to the House of Lords with two sponsors of my choice. I selected a couple of friends of many years' standing. One was Lord Gibson, of the Pearson Longman Group, and the second was Baroness Burton of Coventry, whom I had known for many years since her early days as a member of the Independent Broadcasting Authority.

The date that was selected for me to present myself for introduction into the House of Lords was 23 June 1976 – another of life's great coincidences since, as you now know, that is the date of Kathie's birthday and the date of our wedding anniversary!

In 1978 I put on a show at the London Palladium, to celebrate the fiftieth anniversary of women receiving the vote in this country, with an all-star woman cast. At the entrance to the theatre I met the Lord Chancellor, Lord Elwyn Jones, who said, 'We don't see much of you in the House of Lords, do we, Lew?'

I said, 'You're the Lord Chancellor. You're also an eminent QC. You make the decision. Either I go to the House of Lords regularly, or I continue with what I'm doing now in my own little way – building a relationship between Great Britain and the rest of the world through the medium of films and television.'

He laughed and said, 'Lew, carry on, and don't come to the House.' So I had clearance from the Lord Chancellor!

In 1976 Lord Mountbatten came to the first party I gave at the House of Lords to celebrate my being made a peer. We had a terrific number of guests from all over the world, including all the chairmen and senior executives from the three American television networks. Lord Mountbatten came and brought as his guest Barbara Cartland, which was the first time I'd met her. In 1978, he was to bring her to another party I gave at my flat to celebrate Kathie's birthday and our wedding anniversary. It was on this occasion that he presented me with the No. 1 issue of a special, limited edition plaque which Wedgwood had made of his portrait.

For many years I have been involved with, and have supported, The Duke of Edinburgh Award Scheme. Just before Christmas each year, the principal supporters are invited by the Duke for cocktails at Buckingham Palace, which is his way of expressing his thanks for the support given to him by everyone present. For several years I used to meet a man there, whose name I could never remember because he spoke with such a difficult foreign accent. One day I said to him, 'Do you know, I never know how to spell your name.' He gave me his card and I saw his name was Edgar Ivens. I asked what business he was in and he said he owned a company called Ansaphone, and there, in Buckingham Palace, I said, 'How much profit do you make each year?' He told me and I said, 'I'm interested in buying your company.'

He said he didn't want to sell it, so I said, 'Well, I'll ring you in a couple of weeks' time and let's have lunch to discuss it.' He said, 'OK, you ring me.'

I telephoned him a few weeks later and invited him to lunch. 'Can I bring my finance director?' he asked. I knew then that he had taken me seriously.

We had the meeting, I bought Ansaphone, and it did very well for many years until it was sold. I should point out that while we were having our first discussion at Buckingham Palace, Prince Philip came up to us and said, 'What are you two hatching?' I said, 'We're doing a deal, Sir,' and he laughed.

One day I asked the Duke of Edinburgh if he would be gracious enough to visit our Birmingham Studios. There was terrific rivalry between the Elstree and Birmingham Studios, and Birmingham always felt they were neglected. I thought if Prince Philip visited them it would give them a tremendous boost. HRH visited Birmingham and we had an afternoon programme which was called 'Market Fair', where all different crafts were on display.

While I was showing Prince Philip round, we got separated, and a little later I heard him call from the other end of the studio, 'Lew. You must come over here.' I went over to join him at a silversmith's exhibition and he pointed to a beautifully worked silver cigar box. 'You've got to have that,' he said. 'It's perfect for your cigars.' I said, 'Fine. I'll take it.' Later on, when I received the bill, I had quite a shock! But it's a splendid bit of craftmanship and enjoys a pride of place in my cigar box collection.

*   *   *

Although I have never been an active participant in sports, I have always been a keen follower, and was actually the first person to sell televised English football matches throughout the world.

I am also a life member of the Royal Windsor Polo Club. This came about because I was interested in polo and realized its potential as a TV sport. Being the first person to do so, I was able to buy the television rights for a reasonably low fee. One day I was watching a match at Windsor Park, when Prince Philip said to me, 'Have you any idea how much these polo balls cost? They're very expensive, you know.' I said, 'What you are really saying, Sir, is that you'd like an increase in the fee I pay for the television rights.' He just smiled at me, but I took the hint – and raised the fees.

The Royal Windsor Horse Show, which I thought an interesting and important sporting event, was also first televised by me. In fact, when Lord Hill left as Chairman of the Independent Broadcasting Authority to become Chairman of the BBC in 1967, I had a meeting with him, and he said, 'I look to you to see that independent television builds its sporting image. I'd like you to remain Chairman of the Network Committee for another year and I'll rely on you to do this.' Of course I agreed, and we subsequently established the programme 'World of Sport' for ITV.

Another programme I initiated was 'Police Five' with my good friend Shaw Taylor. This programme has been going on for over twenty-five years now and I am very proud to have been associated with it.

*   *   *

In 1977, when I was seventy years of age, I had to give up my chairmanship of ATV, which was a wholly-owned subsidiary of ACC (Associated Communications Corporation). It was the mandatory rule of the Independent Broadcasting Authority that nobody was allowed to retain the chairmanship or be a director of a contracting company after the age of seventy. With the full approval of the IBA and of my board, I appointed Jack Gill, my deputy, as Chairman of ATV. Lord Windlesham, who had been the Leader of the House of Lords and had a great deal of television experience originally with Rediffusion, became Managing Director.

Also in 1977 I was asked to do a segment in one of the most

popular programmes in America called 'Sixty Minutes'. Mike Wallace was one of the main presenters and they generally had three items in a one-hour programme. Everybody had warned me not to do it because of the controversial nature of the programme. But I had no worries on this score because my philosophy has been always to tell the truth. For several weeks I was followed round by camera crews in London, and they even came with me all the way to Tokyo. Finally, I got to doing the interview with Mike Wallace.

I was naturally smoking one of my big cigars at the time. He had already interviewed Bob Hope and Shirley MacLaine, thinking he might get something abrasive from Shirley because of the failure of 'Shirley's World' – but without any success. In the end he had what he thought was a great idea. He'd heard that Telly Savalas's show 'Kojak' had, after a run of several years, been cancelled, and that Telly was upset about this. He also knew that Telly had been involved in some of my films and, as he was in the process of shooting the final episode of 'Kojak', thought this would be the right moment to catch him in a vulnerable and rather irritable frame of mind. So he called Telly's agent, Jack Gilardi, and asked if he could have a meeting with Telly because they were doing a 'Sixty Minutes' on me.

Jack Gilardi arranged the meeting at the studios and Mike was convinced he'd get something controversial. What he got from Telly was this, and I quote: 'Lew is the greatest showman there is. He's Barnum and Bailey and all the movie tycoons put together.'

Finally, Mike Wallace had to admit defeat and said the programme, which was to go out in October 1978, would be a 'Valentine' to me. Indeed it was. As a result of that programme I was instantly recognized in America by people who were not in the industry. For example, Kathie and I went into Gucci's on 5th Avenue to buy some shoes. I, of course, was smoking my cigar. The assistant said to me, 'No smoking is allowed here.' I then took the cigar out of my mouth and put it in my hand. 'I'm not smoking, I'm just holding it,' I said. Suddenly the manager of the store came rushing up to me and, with great excitement, said: 'You're Lew Grade aren't you? I saw you on "Sixty Minutes" the other day!' I said, 'Well, I understand I'm not allowed to smoke my cigar here.' He said, 'You certainly are!'

Shortly after the 'Sixty Minutes' programme I received a letter from a man in Idaho who said he had watched it and would love to have one of my cigars. I wrote back saying that if he made a charitable donation, and sent me the receipt, I'd send him a cigar. In due course he sent me the receipt for a very considerable contribution he had made to a charity and I sent him a whole box of cigars.

In the 'Sixty Minutes' programme, I made predictions that certain films would be blockbusters, and that others would be duds. Well, several of my so-called 'duds' became runaway hits, and some of my 'certainties' were flops. That, as they say, is show business. And it is the sheer unpredictability of show business that makes it so stimulating and so exhilarating. Fortunately, throughout my career as an agent, and later as head of ATV, most of the certainties I put my money on came through for me. As I said, somebody up there likes me!

*   *   *

At the beginning of January 1979 I had a telephone call from Rome to say that they wanted to fix up a private audience for Kathie and myself with Pope John Paul II, and the date was set for 17 January.

As I had already had an audience with Pope Paul, I was not so nervous on this occasion. His Holiness was wonderfully kind, warm and very friendly. He spoke faultless English and I presented him with cassettes of our 'Moses' series which I discovered he had not seen. I asked him if he had seen 'Jesus of Nazareth' and he said he thought it was wonderful and looked at it constantly.

At the end of this twenty-minute audience, he spoke to one of his monsignors, who went away and came back with a red box. Then His Holiness made me a Knight Commander of the Order of St Silvestre with an additional Order of a Star. This was quite a unique occasion, as I believe I was the first Jew to have been presented with this great honour. I was overcome with emotion and shall never forget it. Kathie too, was overwhelmed at my receiving this tremendous honour.

Later on in 1979 Kathie and I were at the annual British Academy Film and Television Awards Dinner, quietly enjoying ourselves with a host of old friends in the industry. At the end of the evening, Lord Olivier went up on stage and began a eulogistic speech, and then announced that I was being made a Fellow of the British Academy of Film and Television Arts – a very great honour indeed. I was absolutely dumbfounded. As Larry went on to give details about my career, clips of some of the films and television programmes I'd been responsible for were projected on to a big screen. I was so moved and so proud at being recognized like this by my associates in the entertainment industry I found it very difficult to make a speech of acceptance, but managed to say my 'thank yous'. Yet another wonderful moment for Kathie and me.

*   *   *

By the end of the 1970s, I felt I'd gone about as far as I could in TV and had met most of the challenges the medium had thrown at me. It was time to take some different risks – and what is riskier in this business than the film industry: the Big Time?

PART III

19

The Big Time

THE FILM INDUSTRY is very different now from what it was ten years ago. In those days, if a movie wasn't a hit, you could kiss goodbye to most of your investment. Nowadays, however, films that fail to make it at the box office, can, unless their initial costs are astronomical, continue to bring in revenue through TV and videocassette sales. Cable TV is another lucrative outlet, and it is only a matter of time before we have worldwide satellite broadcasting to add to the 'shelf life' of a film – regardless of its age.

In the movie business blockbuster mega-hits are the exception rather than the rule. Having one is like winning the jackpot.

You buy a book which reads excitingly well, but somehow the screenplay doesn't have the same pace. And, even if it does, you have to be sure you've picked the right director for the project. Even that's no guarantee for success. You might have a good script and a good director, but the chemistry between the leading actors doesn't gell. And, even with a terrific script, a great director and a brilliant cast, the public have been known to stay away in droves.

For a film to become a blockbuster in the *E.T.* mould, it has to capture the public's imagination, and no writer or director can possibly know whether his project has the necessary ingredients to do that. The ingredients may all be there on paper, but in the movie business that's not enough.

When I did *The Return of the Pink Panther* I never imagined for one moment it would be the smash it was. I did it simply to extricate myself from a commitment and was confident I couldn't lose on the deal. I'd pre-sold the picture to the three networks in America, and this was my safeguard against losses.

If a film becomes a hit, you build in 'escalators', meaning that the money you receive for its TV transmission is based on the rentals it earns.

Apart from the four films I'd made so far, my energies hadn't been specifically directed towards the cinema. But I was thinking about it.

One day the producer Elliot Kastner came to me and said he had a small production in Canada called *Dogpound Shuffle* starring David Soul (who later went on to become a big TV star in 'Starsky and Hutch') and Ron Moody.

Kastner explained the idea to me, and I agreed to put up the money because I felt it had TV series possibilities. I never followed up this aspect, but, because of the modest budget involved, there was no way ATV could lose money.

A year later, in 1975, Kastner brought me *Farewell My Lovely*, a remake of the famous Raymond Chandler thriller, which Robert Mitchum and Charlotte Rampling had agreed to do. Again, the budget was reasonable and we went ahead with it, knowing that it, too, would be pre-sold to TV. It was well reviewed, but was only a moderate success.

We then did another Chandler remake – *The Big Sleep* – with Mitchum and Sarah Miles in 1977. Predictably, the critics compared us unfavourably with the famous Humphrey Bogart version, and again, we only did moderate business. Incidentally, I'd been told that Mitchum was a difficult man, but I found him thoroughly professional and always cooperative; a really terrific guy.

By this time I was really beginning to become more and more involved in movies. In fact I was, as they say, hooked!

Carlo Ponti, whom I'd known for several years, came to me in 1975 with a project called *The Cassandra Crossing*, starring his wife Sophia Loren, Burt Lancaster, Richard Harris, Martin Sheen and O. J. Simpson. It was about an American commander (Lancaster) who develops a secret chemical device for possible germ-warfare, and I thought it a pretty gripping story. Unfortunately, the American public disagreed, and I was convinced we were going to be in trouble on this one – even though I had pre-sold it to NBC television – until it became a massive hit in Japan, where we recouped almost the entire cost of the film. That's what I mean about the unpredictability of the business.

One day I had a meeting in California with Bob Shapiro and Peter Hyams. Bob Shapiro was a producer, and Peter Hyams was an outstanding writer/director. The project they wanted me to look at was called *Capricorn One*. I took the script back to London with me, read it, and liked it very much. I telephoned them and said I'd be in New York the following week and would like to meet with them. They flew in specially from California and the first thing I asked them was what budget they had for the picture. They told me. I then asked whom they had in mind for the cast, and they said James Brolin, Sam Waterston and O. J. Simpson. They were with me for fifteen minutes. I gave them the go-ahead and apologized for bringing them all the way from California for a fifteen-minute meeting.

Of course, they went away delighted. The film, an adventure thriller about a reporter who discovers that the first manned space-flight to Mars is a hoax, was a tremendous success everywhere. By that time I had formed a separate division to deal with sales of theatrical films throughout the world, excluding the United States and Canada, and I'd pre-sold *Capricorn One* on guaranteed percentage to The Toho-Towa Company of Japan. I was invited to the opening in Tokyo and found the Japanese wonderful people to deal with. They were always honourable in their business commitments and exceptionally warm and hospitable. First of all, we had a press conference with a truly great interpreter, and I began by saying something I had said on many such occasions: 'Ladies and gentlemen,' I said, 'if you ask any embarrassing questions I always say, "Shut up." And who can you say "shut up" to but to your family and your friends?' They always ask the same question: what's the budget? Sure enough, one of the reporters there asked this very question and I told him to shut up, adding, 'Of course, this means you are now a friend of mine.'

The conference went extremely well. Then came the première. I arrived at the cinema, and there, on a special rostrum in front of the theatre, was an orchestra playing English tunes. Outside the theatre was a big banner saying 'Welcome to Lord Lew Grade and *Capricorn One*'. I was told that I would have to make a short speech to the audience, and that I would have an interpreter by my side.

I walked on to the stage to find that the entire theatre had been decked with British flags on each side. Then the orchestra played the British National Anthem, and the whole audience stood up – a very moving gesture.

I then went on to Australia for the première of *Capricorn One* and, once again, we hosted the usual press conference. I told the press how delighted I was to be back in Australia after such a short lapse of time. The last time I was there, I said, was in December 1947 – and here I was again, exactly thirty years later!

At the beginning of 1977 I felt I needed somebody of stature and creative ability to look after the production side of things and I thought I'd try to get Marty Starger to look after the films we produced in the United States, or on those that I needed advice. Marty had left ABC in 1975 to start his own company, and at that time was exclusively contracted to ABC for all television production. I had tremendous regard for his creative ability. After all, regardless of the claims that had been made about certain programmes that were transmitted by ABC, Marty Starger was responsible for that remarkable series 'Roots', as well as 'Rich Man, Poor Man' and many others. He had two excellent people working under him: Michael Eisner, who is now Chairman and Chief Executive of the Disney Company, and Barry Diller, who was in charge of Movies for Television but is now Chairman of 20th Century-Fox, having been Chairman of Paramount for many years. After many long and difficult discussions, I persuaded him to join us, and, together with Jack Gill and Ellis Birk, a lawyer who dealt with a lot of our company's business, we finally agreed the terms. But it was a real tough battle.

In 1978 I read the novel *The Boys from Brazil* and I thought it would make a marvellous film. I had a screenplay prepared and engaged one of the top directors – Franklin Shaffner. The problem was, however, that the director had the final cut. This means that his word is law, and if he refuses to make changes, there's nothing you can do about it. In other words, he has the final say. When we saw the film we were not happy with the ending, which we thought too gory, but Franklin Shaffner insisted that his version was to be the definitive one. The film did respectable business but was nowhere near the blockbuster I'd anticipated.

We had two magnificent actors in it – Laurence Olivier as the Nazi head-hunter Simon Wiesenthal, and Gregory Peck as Mengele – and they both gave brilliant performances. I honestly believed we were on to an absolute winner with this one, but it was just one more example of a film not living up to the high expectation of the book.

Sir John Woolf – the noted film producer of such hits as *Oliver!* and *Day of the Jackal* – came to me with a book he had read and which he thought would make a great film. It was called *The Stone Leopard* and I liked it very much. A script was written, which we both liked, and I thought Warren Beatty would be perfect for it. Warren liked the script, I negotiated with his agent Stan Kamen of the William Morris Agency, and we virtually had a deal, although nothing had been signed.

Soon afterwards, when I was in California, *en route* for Australia, Stan Kamen phoned me and said that unfortunately Warren Beatty had decided to do a film called *Heaven Can Wait* instead. He expressed deep concern about this new project because Warren, it appeared, wanted to write, direct, produce *and* star in it himself. A real one-man band. Stan was worried that this would be too much for him. Then he said that Warren had expressed a wish to come and see me personally to apologize for letting me down.

I said fine, and Warren duly arrived at my suite in the Beverly Hills Hotel. He said he was very keen to make *Heaven Can Wait* and regretted any inconvenience he had caused me. I liked him tremendously and graciously accepted his excuse. Then, for the next hour or so, I ranted on at him. 'Warren,' I said, 'you must be out of your mind to take on such a tremendous responsibility. At least get a co-director to assist you so you don't get tied up with a load of back-breaking chores.' He listened very carefully to everything I had to say and said, 'Lew, I think you're right.' I then had to leave for the airport. Warren walked to my car with me, and, as he helped me put my luggage into the boot, he suddenly said: 'Lew, I want you to play a part in *Heaven Can Wait*. How about it?' 'Warren,' I said, 'thanks a lot – but no thanks!'

Perhaps if I *had* taken him up on that offer I might have been an international movie star by now.

Somehow, though, I don't think so . . . .

*   *   *

When I left Australia I decided I would stop by to see Sir Run Run Shaw in Hong Kong. I had never been to Hong Kong before and, as it was on my way home, I thought it would be an excellent opportunity to see an old friend and a new city.

I called Run Run in advance and was met at the airport by the largest Rolls Royce I have ever seen – and I have a Phantom VI. The car was at my disposal all the time. I was shown around the city and loved it. I had dinner with Run Run several times and, a couple of days before I was due to leave, he gave a party in my honour at his home – one of the most beautiful I have ever seen. Run Run's guests included Lord Shawcross, one of the most eminent legal men in Britain, and the evening was a delight. Before the evening began, Run Run asked me whether I'd mind picking up two of his guests. Of course, I agreed, and imagine my surprise when they turned out to be John Kinge, who owned Metromedia, and his lovely wife Patricia, who were great friends of mine.

One day, Jack Wiener and David Niven, Jr, came to me with Jack Higgins's book *The Eagle Has Landed*. I enjoyed it immensely, and decided to make it with a cast that included Michael Caine, Robert Duvall, Larry Hagman, Jean Marsh, Anthony Quayle, Donald Sutherland, Donald Pleasance and Jenny Agutter. Our director was John Sturges. The film did well – so Messrs Niven, Jr, and Wiener approached me with two more projects: *Escape to Athena* and *Green Ice*. *Escape to Athena* was to be shot in Rhodes with a starry cast, including Roger Moore, Telly Savalas, Stephanie Powers, Claudia Cardinale, Elliott Gould and David Niven in the leading roles. George Cosmatos, who directed *The Cassandra Crossing*, was hired to do this film as well. I knew he'd make a great action movie, and as 'action' was the vogue at that time I was confident that we were on to a winner. Again, the film did not live up to the expectations of the script. It turned out to be a broad comedy with action-adventure sequences, and the combination just didn't work. The first eighty minutes were a failure because of these different ingredients, but the last forty, action-packed minutes were wonderful. If only the emphasis had been on action throughout, the film would have been a hit. Unfortunately, it wasn't. Still, with the pre-sales I'd made, we didn't lose nearly as much as we might have. Then came *Green Ice*, starring Ryan O'Neal, Anne Archer and Omar Sharif. I found Ryan charming and helpful and cannot understand all the criticism that has been levelled at him. We did, however, have a problem with the director, who had to leave the locations in Mexico and was replaced by Ernest Day. *Green Ice* made no one green with envy. It was quite a nice little film, but, in the end, too much like a TV movie.

By this time I had done a deal with Martin Starger, who came to me with a proposal to make a film written by Larry Gelbart called *Movie Movie* to be directed by Stanley Donen and starring George C. Scott, with Trish Van Devere, Red Buttons, Eli Wallach, Barry Bostwick, Art Carney and Barbara Harris.

It was to be a film in two parts with two entirely different pastiches of 1930s film. The first part was a Busby Berkeley-type musical; the second, a Warner Bros. boxing melodrama. When I saw the finished film, I was thrilled with it. In fact, I thought it was so good I commissioned Larry Gelbart to write a sequel, which he did.

The film opened over Christmas 1978 to wonderful critical reviews and I thought we were home and dry. However, Warner Bros., who were distributing the film, had some important Christmas releases of their own and didn't give *Movie Movie* their best shot.

It was then that I made a fatal mistake. I knew that EMI, which was headed by Barry Spikings, were also dissatisfied with the way the majors distributed their films, so we got together and formed our own distribution company – Associated Film Distributors. I knew that we had the first Muppet movie available for the new company and felt confident it would be a huge hit.

We also had several other major films in development, and so had EMI.

We owned 60 per cent of the company and EMI owned 40 per cent. However, on the advice of Jack Gill and others, it was felt that $9 million would be sufficient to capitalize the film distribution company together with a credit line from The First National

Bank of Boston. In retrospect, I realize how ridiculous it was to go into distribution with only $9 million. But, as I was not *au fait* with this particular aspect of the business, I took the advice of the financial experts.

Some time later I realized what a mistake I'd made. What I *should* have done, of course, was to make a deal with one of the major film companies to distribute all our films. That way I'd have none of the problems of bearing the massive overheads that go into theatrical distribution, such as the prints and advertising costs.

The first film we released was *The Muppet Movie*, which, fortunately, was a huge success worldwide, and we thought we were well on the way to establishing ourselves as a major distribution company in America.

The next film, from EMI, was *Can't Stop the Music* starring a pop group called Village People. It was a financial calamity. By 1980 there'd been such a spate of youth-oriented musicals that we'd missed the boat. Our timing was wrong, and in this business timing is everything. If *Star Wars* had come along at any other time, who knows whether it would have been the smash it was?

EMI lost a fortune on *Can't Stop the Music*, and so did AFD, who'd put up all the money for prints and advertising.

Next came an updated version of *The Jazz Singer*, starring Neil Diamond and Laurence Olivier. Once again, the results were disappointing and we weren't able to recoup our prints and advertising costs. EMI, however, didn't do too badly with it as I'd sold it on their behalf to American TV for $4 million. At least that helped a bit with their recoupment. The album 'The Jazz Singer', however, was an enormous success and, ironically, made a lot more money than the film itself.

Meanwhile, sometime prior to this in 1977, through William Thompson, head of the entertainment division of the First National Bank of Boston, I was given the chance to purchase 20 per cent of Columbia Pictures for a maximum sum of $30 million.

The loan would have been for eight years, unsecured, with the Columbia shares as the only security. This was well before I had started our own distribution company. Naturally, I thought it a tremendous opportunity for us. It would mean that Columbia Pictures would distribute all our films – as well as EMI's. So I asked Jack Gill to talk to the board about it.

Gill, however, wasn't all that enthusiastic, and didn't present the case forcefully enough. This was long before cable had been introduced into the market, and just before the boom in video-cassettes, and he clearly didn't believe it was worth the money.

In 1981 Columbia Pictures was bought by Coca-Cola for $790 million.

How I missed Lord Renwick, C. O. Stanley and Sir Max Aitken! These were men of tremendous vision and drive, and while I was Lord Renwick's deputy chairman, I constantly relied on his support and guidance.

Most of my board knew virtually nothing about the film industry and, of course, were apprehensive about embarking on what they saw as a highly speculative venture.

If we had bought Columbia with our 20 per cent, we would have stood to make a profit in the region of $130 million. Today, Columbia's stock has to be calculated in billions! The studio's impressive catalogue of films alone (and the numerous outlets for them) has to be worth a fortune.

But there you are – it was not to be.

20

Lose Some . . . Win Some

Every year, during the last week of October, there is a National Association of Theatre Owners' convention, and in 1979 we were asked if we could give the last night party to the exhibitors and talk about all our productions. This was to take place on 31 October and accordingly we made all the arrangements for the dinner.

I flew to Los Angeles on the 30th and arrived in the evening to find an invitation to a black-tie Motion Pictures Pioneers' Award Dinner in honour of Henry Plitt, who owned a large circuit of cinemas.

I was told that I'd be sitting on the dais next to Henry Plitt and Lew Wasserman. Although I was pretty exhausted and jet-lagged after my long trip, I decided to attend. I quickly bathed and changed and went straight to the dinner, which was due to start at 7.00 p.m. At seven on the dot we were led to the dais, where I sat until 11.00 p.m. (7.00 a.m. London time!) listening to a lot of speeches extolling Henry Plitt's virtues. The food wasn't very good, and, given my prominent position on the dais, it wasn't possible for me to slip away unnoticed.

I knew I had an important evening ahead of me – the NATO Convention Dinner – so when I got back to my hotel I took two sleeping pills and went straight to bed.

I always know what time it is when I open my eyes because I have an illuminated clock at my bedside. At exactly twenty minutes past one I woke up. I wanted to go to the bathroom, but was so dizzy because of the sleeping pills that I let my pyjamas slip, and as soon as I walked into the marble bathroom I tripped over them and fell backwards on to the side of the marble wash-basin. I gashed myself from halfway down my forehead to the back of my head and there was blood all over the place. It was a miracle that I didn't lose consciousness. I wasn't able to stand up because I kept slipping on the blood. I managed to crawl to a telephone and pressed the number of David Tebet, who was staying in the same hotel. I said, 'David, I'm in trouble. I need medical help.' By now the floor looked like the Red Sea. My pyjamas were soaked through with blood and, to stem the flow, I put a towel round my head.

Within two to three minutes David Tebet was in my room with the manager of the hotel. In the meantime he had telephoned the hospital and arranged for them to send an ambulance and two paramedics.

David was shocked when he saw what state I was in, but, being practical, helped the paramedics, who undressed me, washed me down, put a big bathrobe round me, and wrapped some towels around my head. Then one of them took my blood pressure. He turned to his colleague and said, 'You'd better take it again.' 'What's wrong,' I asked anxiously, and he said, 'I can't understand how it can be so normal.' I said, 'Don't worry. My blood pressure is generally very good.' They shook their heads, put me on the collapsible stretcher and rushed me to the hospital.

Apparently most of the hospital staff had seen me on 'Sixty Minutes', so they knew who I was. When I arrived, there were four nurses, two male doctors and a special lady surgeon they'd managed to get hold of in a hurry. I was X-rayed, and because my forehead needed a lot of stitching, they said they'd have to inject me. I told them I didn't want any injections, but allowed them to give me an anti-tetanus shot in each of my arms. They then put me on a raised steel operating table and when they were through with me I was absolutely fine.

I had arrived at the hospital at 1.40 a.m. After half an hour I asked how much longer they were going to be. I was laying very still and very quiet and had no pain whatsoever. Another twenty minutes went by. It seemed like hours. I again asked how much longer it was going to take and they said it would be another twenty minutes. The surgeon finished sewing me up just after 3.30 a.m. Not only did I have extensive stitches on my head and forehead, but also some six or eight stitches above my eye. The side of my face was blood red because the skin had come off it, and I had a black eye which stretched almost down to my lips. One side of my head was swollen like a football.

As I was lying on the table I heard the surgeon say, 'We've found a room for him, but he can only have it for two weeks, then we'll have to move him. Still, we have a TV set, telephones and we'll get a telex in there tomorrow.' As soon as I heard this conversation, I said, 'Get me off this table and bandage my head. I have a NATO dinner for about two thousand people tonight and I intend to be there.' 'But that's impossible,' they said. 'You mustn't move.'

I said, 'Get me off this table and put on whatever bandages you think necessary. But I'm going to be there.'

They still thought I was crazy, so I said, 'I'll tell you what I'll do. I'll take the four of you disco dancing' – and I did a disco movement – 'or I'll take two of you back to the hotel.' They laughed and, at my insistence, bandaged me up fully. In fact they put so many bandages on my head, it looked like I was wearing a huge turban. They also bandaged my eye, then drove me back to the hotel. The surgeon who had done my stitches had done them so beautifully, and so minutely, that when I returned to London, my doctor was only able to remove them with the aid of a magnifying glass.

Whenever I'm away from home I ring my wife first thing every morning. I knew I had to ring her otherwise she'd worry, so, as heavily bandaged as I was, I rang her and told her all about the Henry Plitt dinner, but not about the fall. My head was throbbing slightly, but otherwise I felt no pain at all. When I finished my call I sat down, but couldn't sleep, and at two that afternoon I went to the doctor's private clinic for another X-ray. David Tebet stayed with me all the time and was a tremendous comfort.

Finally, the time came to dress and go to the Bonaventure Hotel in downtown Los Angeles where we were having our dinner. I went through a side entrance straight to a special room and was greeted by several of the stars who had appeared in films for me and were going to appear in future films. As we started to walk into the hall, there were around forty to fifty reporters and photographers waiting for us. As soon as they caught sight of this apparition – me! – walking towards the entrance of the ballroom, bang! The cameras started clicking and everybody rushed forward. I asked the stars to go ahead of me, and told them I wanted to speak to the press on my own.

I went up to them and said, 'Ladies and gentlemen, I left London yesterday. I had this terrible fall last night and you can see for yourself what I look like. If my wife reads about this or sees any photographs of me, she'll have the most almighty shock of her life and fly over immediately, and it will be an absolute catastrophe. I would consider it a personal favour, therefore, if there was no story about this incident and no photographs published at all. I know it would be a scoop for you, but I'm asking you to help me in these extra special circumstances.' One of the reporters turned round, looked at the others – and they all nodded their heads. 'Sir Lew,' he said – the press always called me Sir Lew – 'we understand what you're saying and we give you our assurance that nothing will be published about this incident and there'll be no photographs at all.' And there weren't. That's what I call relationship with the press.

The evening went on. David Tebet had arranged for Johnny Carson to be the host and Carson made a speech saying, 'Before I introduce Lord Grade, you can see he has had a meeting with Billy Martin.' Billy Martin was a well-known American baseball manager who was always in the news after having had a punch-up with somebody or other. As you can imagine, Johnny's introduction got a huge laugh. I then went on to talk to the cinema owners, after which they presented me with the NATO special award.

I stayed in California for another seven days because I didn't want to return to London looking so frightening. I asked David Tebet to call my wife one hour before he knew she would be leaving to meet me at the airport. Kathie always sees me off and always meets me from any of my trips abroad, and David warned her that I had had a little fall but that there was nothing to worry about.

During my stay in California I'd spoken to Kathie daily and she was totally unaware of what had happened to me. It really thrilled me that, despite all the things people say about the press, they had kept their word to me. As David Tebet had warned

Kathie in advance, she managed to contain her horror when she saw me, knowing how worried I'd be if I thought I'd upset her. So she put on a brave face even though I think she was ready to faint when she saw me.

The exhibitors who were present at that NATO evening were all enthusiastic about our planned production schedule, which included *Raise the Titanic* and *The Legend of the Lone Ranger*.

Jack Wrather and his wife Bonita were very close friends of President Reagan and his wife Nancy, and they arranged for a special charity première of *The Lone Ranger* to take place at the Kennedy Center, Washington, in mid-May 1981. The date was set and a special list of VIP guests was drawn up.

Kathie does not like flying on the same plane with me, unless it's absolutely essential, so she went on to Washington two days ahead of me. I had a number of board meetings in London and had booked to go on the evening Concorde to Washington. At about 2.00 a.m. in the morning (London time) of the day I was planning to leave, I received a telephone call from Kathie telling me to bring one of her evening dresses, with all the appropriate accessories, and my dinner suit. 'What for?' I asked. 'I really don't know,' she said. 'All I've been told is that we have to be ready at 7.00 p.m. sharp. I don't have any other details. It's all very secret.'

I had already sent one of Kathie's evening dresses and my tuxedo ahead to New York in preparation for a dinner that was being given there the following weekend in honour of Burt Reynolds, and at which I was to make a little speech. Fortunately, I had another dinner suit at home. I was worried about Kathie, though, and asked her which dress I should bring. She said, 'I leave it to you to pick one out for me,' because she was confident I'd select the right one for her.

I arrived in Washington at 5.00 p.m., rushed to the hotel, changed, and we were ready by 7.00 p.m. All the guests were assembled and we boarded the special double-decker London bus waiting for us.

I couldn't understand why we had special police motor-cycle escorts. We arrived at a private restaurant, but still had no idea what was happening. Jack Wrather had assured us it would be a surprise, and, as we went upstairs to the dining room, there was the President of the United States, with his wife Nancy, greeting the guests. He automatically kissed each lady on the cheek, and, when Kathie walked in with me, he kissed her on the cheek too before Jack had had a chance to introduce us. The President looked at Kathie and said, 'Do I know you?' and she said, 'You do now!' And while everybody laughed, the introductions were made.

After the dinner, Jack presented the President with the silver buckle of the Lone Ranger's belt. The President stood up and said, 'Jack, Lord Grade, thank you for this lovely gift.' Then he continued, 'Jack did ask me to play the part of the Lone Ranger, you know, but I think I've got a better job now.'

It was a most exciting evening. Only 54 of the President's friends were there, and we were so thrilled to be among them.

When the President and his wife had left, I felt it was time for Kathie and me to go back to our hotel, but we didn't have a car. I happened to be speaking to the Attorney-General at the time and he said, 'Wait, Lew. The President has just gone off in my car, but as soon as it returns, I'd be happy if you'd go back in that.'

The première was held the next day, the film itself being preceded by a specially filmed message from the President, and, based on the reaction from the audience, we all thought we had a tremendous hit.

Unfortunately, it did not turn out that way, and the film only did fair business. Luckily, though, I'd managed to sell it to TV for $7\frac{1}{2}$ million. I also sold it to Home Box Office for cable transmission, and, as an added bonus, made a deal for the cassette rights.

What had happened with this film was that Jack had insisted on doing the *entire* legend of the Lone Ranger. It took an hour and ten minutes before he put on his mask – and it was only at that point that the audience started cheering. But this left a mere forty minutes for the action sequences, which were absolutely terrific. The mistake was not dispensing with the legend in ten minutes and getting going with the action much earlier on.

But that's the movie business – it's always so easy to know where you've gone wrong – *after* the event . . . .

*   *   *

The history of *Raise the Titanic* is one of strange coincidences and unforeseen circumstances – something which all too often occurs in the making of films.

I had originally been offered the manuscript of *Raise the Titanic* by an agent working with the William Morris Agency and said I had no interest in making a picture about the *Titanic*. The subject had been done to death.

Some little time after this, ACC formed a partnership (which only lasted for a short while) with Richard Smith – the Chairman and Chief Executive of the biggest circuit of cinemas in America, The General Cinema Corporation. On a visit to London early in 1978, Richard Smith handed me a box. He said, 'It's a manuscript and I'd like you to read it.' I said, 'Fine. I'll read it.' He left London and, two nights later, I thought I'd better read it in order to give him a reaction. I didn't even know what the box contained. I opened it and there was the title – *Raise the Titanic*. I thought, 'Oh! Not again!' I began reading it at ten o'clock at night and I couldn't put it down until I'd finished it – four hours later.

After reading the script, which was by Clive Cussler, I realized that here was a potential series along the lines of the James Bond films. I telephoned Cussler's agent the next morning and arranged to meet with him in New York. When I arrived, I discovered that it had already been submitted to Stanley Kramer, the well known Oscar-winning director. I knew Stanley well and so did Martin Starger. He had previously made a film for us called *The Domino Principle* on a fairly medium budget – and we asked him not to bid against us. We said we'd buy the book and he could be producer/director on it with Martin as executive producer. He agreed to this, we purchased the property for a reasonable figure, and while the model of the ship was being built, Stanley went to work.

Unfortunately, the model was at least two to three times as large as it should have been. We had various artistic differences with Stanley, and finally reached an amicable settlement whereby he would no longer be involved in the production.

We went to work on a draft script and this took a considerable time. Then we discovered that there wasn't a tank in the world large enough to accommodate our 'model' and to photograph it from underwater. We therefore asked Bernard Kingham, who was head of production for ITC in England, to look for a suitable location, together with Dick O'Connor, who was Production Supervisor for our production company in Los Angeles. By then we were called Marble Arch Productions (and had been since 1977). Martin Starger was President, and I was Chairman.

They finally found a tank in Malta which was suitable for certain model work, but it wasn't large enough to hold our 'miniature *Titanic*' and the numerous submersibles that would have to be built.

There was some land adjoining this tank in Malta, and the Maltese Government agreed that we could enclose the tank to the size we wanted, which was 300 ft by 250 ft, and 30 ft deep. We had been promised a completion date which came and went without the tank having been finished. Meanwhile the crew and cast were all standing by on full salary. When work on the tank was finally completed we discovered that the pressure of the water crushed the submersibles. So we had to keep on making more submersibles, with the result that the film overran its shooting schedule by a disastrous four months.

The final print of the film was not delivered to us until three days before the première. We had committed ourselves to dates throughout the United States, and therefore had no alternative but to show the film without the luxury of 'sneak previews' prior to doing a final edit on it.

I personally thought the movie was quite good. Two scenes in particular were worth the price of admission. One was the actual raising of the *Titanic* itself; the other, the sequence in which the hero Dirk Pitt walks into the wrecked ballroom, then on to the masthead and places the ensign on the flagpole.

I really believe that the failure of the film was inadvertently, and ironically, due to my brother Bernie. He was the Managing Director of EMI's Entertainment Division and had a production company based in America that was making movies and mini-series for television. One of these projects was a four-hour version of *SOS Titanic* – a story about the sinking of the *Titanic*. It was shown on television and was a real flop.

In order to recoup some of their money, they decided to edit the TV version for theatrical release, and, because EMI were strong on foreign distribution, they sold it to all the territories, including Japan.

The Japanese people, Toho-Towa, are really brilliant. They bought the film *SOS Titanic* for very little money, put it on the shelf, and never showed it, because they had already given me a $1 million advance plus a percentage for our film, *Raise the Titanic*. As a result of *SOS Titanic* not being shown in Japan, *Raise the Titanic* was one of the biggest box office successes in that country that year. So, as I have to blame somebody, I'm blaming my brother. To be fair to him, he did try to stop the production of *SOS Titanic*, but his head of production in America had already made the commitment and Bernie didn't want to override him. I believe the final outcome of *Raise the Titanic* would have had an altogether different complexion had the film been completed three or four months earlier, and had *SOS Titanic* not been made. But that, as they say, is show business . . . .

The première of *Raise the Titanic* was held in Boston. Kathie and I went over, and were invited to attend a reception at the Governor's mansion. Initially, we thought it was just another formal gathering. When we arrived, however, there were British flags everywhere and the occasion was stage-managed to resemble a British historical military event. All the soldiers were in period uniforms and they saluted us as we walked up the staircase to the main reception hall, which was filled with some of the most distinguished people in Boston.

The Governor, Edward J. King, made a speech in which he presented me with a special citation for my outstanding contribution to the entertainment industry worldwide. He then beckoned me to accept a unique plaque commemorating this event. I was so overcome that I broke down completely. The assembled guests applauded, and somehow or other I managed to thank them from the bottom of my heart.

The *Titanic* took about $8 million at the box office in the United States. (Some films don't even take $1 million!) Our share of the $8 million was 45 per cent – i.e., $3.6 million. However, we had spent well over $8 million on printing and advertising, and AFD had to suffer yet another loss. As I have often said – it would have been cheaper to lower the Atlantic!

Lose Some . . . Win Some

*   *   *

In 1980 Martin Starger telephoned me and said he'd been offered the film rights of *On Golden Pond* starring Katharine Hepburn, Henry Fonda and Jane Fonda. He'd already seen Ernest Thompson's play on Broadway, and loved it. 'But I want you to know,' he said, 'that most of the major studios have already turned it down.'

I said, 'How much is it going to cost?' 'About $7.5 million,' he said. I just had a hunch that, with those three stars, and the chemistry they'd generate, the film would be successful. I asked if he had a director in mind and he said they were talking about Mark Rydell. 'Go ahead,' I said. 'Make it.'

We were at the Cannes Film Festival at the beginning of May 1980 when Marty received a telephone call from Stan Kamen, Mark Rydell's agent, telling us that the lowest terms he would accept were $750,000, plus $2500 per week living expenses, and a car and driver twenty-four hours a day. Marty took the call while we were at lunch, and he asked Stan Kamen to hold on while he discussed the matter with me. I said, 'No. It's too much money. I understand about the weekly expenses, and it's probably OK about the car, but I don't want to give him more than $600,000 and that's final.' He went back, passed on my feelings to Stan Kamen and that was it.

We had just finished lunch when another call came through for Marty. He took it, then came back to me and said, 'Mark Rydell's just telephoned me and he's made us a proposal. He doesn't want any salary. He doesn't want any profit participation [which incidentally he would have been getting out of Jane Fonda's share], he doesn't want any living expenses, or a car. All he wants is $500,000 for every Oscar-nomination and $1 million for every Oscar.' 'That's great Marty,' I said. 'We'll save a million dollars because now the picture will only cost us $6.5 million instead of $7.5 million.' 'Wait a minute, Lew,' Marty said. 'Henry Fonda is getting on. Katharine Hepburn is getting on. Jane Fonda has never worked with her father before. They're bound to get two or three nominations and possibly even an Oscar. It could cost us millions!' 'You're right,' I said. 'If Mark Rydell is that confident about it, give him the money he's asking for.'

263

And that's how we settled the deal for *On Golden Pond*.

There was due to be a 'wrap' party to celebrate the completion of the film on 24 August. Around this time we had a call from Dick O'Connor, our production supervisor, telling us that Mark Rydell needed another ten days. 'No way,' we said. 'We finish shooting on 24 August whether the film is completed or not.' It was indeed finished on 24 August, which just goes to prove that it is possible to complete a film on time if you really have to. Incidentally, the film won three Oscars and was nominated for a further seven. So Mark Rydell's instincts were absolutely spot on!

*   *   *

Through Paul Kohner, the celebrated Hollywood agent, we purchased in 1978 the exclusive American rights to Ingmar Bergman's film *Autumn Sonata*, starring Ingrid Bergman and Liv Ullman. This was something of an event, for it was the first time that Ingrid Bergman and Ingmar Bergman, the distinguished Swedish director, had worked together. It was a beautiful film, superbly acted – and, happily, a box-office success.

I was so thrilled with Ingrid's performance in *Autumn Sonata* that I optioned one of Robert Ludlum's books – *The Scarlatti Inheritance* – because I thought it would be perfect for her. We discussed the project together but unfortunately it entailed a very lengthy and strenuous production schedule, which she didn't feel like undertaking at that time, so I decided not to pursue it any further. A pity, as she would have been wonderful in it.

We made several important television movies with Norman Rosemont for CBS and other networks, including 'The Count of Monte Cristo' (Richard Chamberlain, Tony Curtis, Trevor Howard, Louis Jourdan, Donald Pleasance, Kate Nelligan and Dominic Guard), 'The Man in the Iron Mask' (Richard Chamberlain, Patrick McGoohan, Louis Jourdan, Jenny Agutter, Ian Holm, Ralph Richardson and Vivien Merchant) and 'All Quiet on the Western Front', which was also sold theatrically in several countries. Most of these TV movies were sponsored by Hallmark – the American greeting card company.

At the beginning of 1981 there were many stories in the press about ACC's shortage of money. *On Golden Pond* was in production, *The Great Muppet Caper* – the second movie that Jim Henson made for us – had been completed, and he was at work on a big-budget fantasy called *The Dark Crystal*.

While all this publicity was going on, I received a telephone call from Michael Fuchs, of Home Box Office Cable TV, who said to me, 'Lew, we read all these reports in the press. Please remember that both Steve Scheffer and I and everyone at HBO are your friends. If there's anything at all that we can do to help, don't hesitate to call us.'

Early in March, I telephoned Michael and Steve and told them I wanted to sell them some product. So I flew to New York and the following morning Steve Scheffer arrived at my apartment at nine o'clock, together with four other people from his legal department. We went through a list of eight films, several of which hadn't even been made yet. Some of these films were sold on an exclusive basis, and others non-exclusively, which meant I could also sell them to other cable systems. Among the exclusive films were *On Golden Pond* and *The Lone Ranger*. *The Dark Crystal* wasn't on the list.

By about 11.15 a.m. we had completed our negotiations and the figure we arrived at was $10,900,000. 'I'd really appreciate it', I said, 'if I could have the cheque today so that I can leave for London tonight.' Steve Scheffer said he'd see what he could do. He suggested that I join him and Michael Fuchs for lunch at 12.30, so that I could sign some papers. He hoped, he said, to deliver the cheque to me by 4.00 p.m. As he was at the door, I suddenly said, 'Steve, you know it's getting very difficult for me to remember odd numbers. $10,900,000 is very hard for me to remember. Now $11 million is a round number and I'm sure I won't forget it.' He smiled and left. Thirty minutes later, Michael Fuchs called me. 'Lew,' he said, 'you're quite right. $10,900,000 *is* a hard number to remember. You've got the $11 million.'

In addition to this fixed sum of $11 million, I actually received escalators based on film rentals for the films that were exclusive to them.

I went out, had lunch, signed the papers and left at 4.00 p.m. with the cheque. That's relationship!

I was particularly disappointed with the box office results for a movie I made called *Voyage of the Damned* which had a formidable list of stars: Faye Dunaway, Max Von Sydow, Oskar Werner, Malcolm McDowell, James Mason, Orson Welles, Katherine Ross, Ben Gazzara, Lee Grant, Sam Wanamaker, Julie Harris (who was nominated for an Oscar), Maria Schell, José Ferrer, Denholm Elliott, and Lynn Fredericks.

Stuart Rosenburg directed it and I thought it was one of the most moving and important films I'd seen for a long time. I just couldn't understand why it failed to become a success. It was the story of a boat-load of Jewish people leaving Hamburg for Cuba just before the outbreak of the Second World War. When they reached Havana they were refused entry and were subsequently turned away by every other country in the world. It was a heart-breaking story. Finally, Holland allowed them in, though most of them were to die during the days of German occupation of that country.

Strangely enough, it did outstanding business in Japan!

*   *   *

By 31 March 1981, AFD had to repay its line of credit to the bank, so I decided I'd try and do a deal with Lew Wasserman on the bank loan and on the distribution of our future pictures, some of which I knew were very good.

On Golden Pond was in production, and *Sophie's Choice* was due to start shooting in 1982. It was to be directed by Alan Pakula, who was highly regarded in the industry, and would star Meryl Streep and Kevin Kline. We had already completed production on the second Muppet movie, *The Great Muppet Caper*, and had *The Lone Ranger* waiting in the wings. Jim Henson's *The Dark Crystal* was also in production at that time.

Several meetings took place with Lew Wasserman and Sid Sheinberg of MCA – the parent company of Universal Pictures. With me at these meetings were Marty Starger, our legal people in America, and Barry Spikings and his legal representatives. We were all trying to work out a deal whereby we could repay the bank loan and arrange for Universal to distribute our pictures.

Meanwhile, I kept Jack Gill informed at all times of the discussions that were going on with Universal. One thing that remains fresh in my mind is how, on the last day, negotiations were stuck because Lew Wasserman was refusing to budge on one point. The whole thing hinged on this particular point – and we'd reached a stalemate.

I suddenly said to Lew Wasserman, 'Lew, would you please come into the bedroom with me. I want to have a word with you privately.'

He followed me into the next room. 'Lew,' I said, 'I *need* this deal.' And he said, 'If you need it, we'll forget about that point and we'll go ahead.'

That was relationship working for me once again. Of course, it worked out tremendously well for Universal. *On Golden Pond* took $64 million in film rentals, i.e., approximately $150 million at the box office, *Sophie's Choice* did well, *The Dark Crystal* did well and *The Great Muppet Caper* did well, so all round everybody was happy.

One day Stanley Donen presented to Martin Starger and myself a project called *Saturn III*. I read it and felt it had possibilities. I asked him if he could shoot it in England (I always wanted to promote work for British studios and technicians), and he said he could. I then started to think about casting it.

I flew back to London from California with the script in my briefcase, and on the plane I met Jay Bernstein, who was a well-known publicist in America. 'I'm travelling to London with Farrah Fawcett,' he told me. 'As a matter of fact, she's sitting next to me.' It occurred to me that if I could get her for *Saturn III* it would be something of a coup because she'd just finished making the highly successful TV series 'Charlie's Angels', and was a very 'hot' property indeed. Jay, who was her manager, asked me to come over and meet her and I took the script with me. We chatted for a while and then I said, 'I'd very much like you to read this script for a film I'm planning to make in England.' She laughed and said it would help pass the time away. After about two and a half hours, Jay Bernstein came up to me, returned the script and said, 'Farrah likes it very much and would love to do it.' I then did the deal with him for Farrah Fawcett to star in *Saturn III*. I engaged Kirk Douglas and Harvey Keitel to co-star with her, then set the production wheels in motion.

Two weeks later I went to New York to pre-sell the property to NBC. The film was budgeted at approximately $7.5 million, so when I had a meeting with Mike Weinblatt, who was then Head of Business Affairs at NBC, I offered him *Saturn III* for $4 million. 'I want to think about it and we'll let you know,' he said. That meant a possible negotiation! He then said, 'Come and say hello to Bob Mulholland,' who, at that time, was President of NBC. Bob greeted me warmly, then he turned to Mike and said, 'Have we got Farrah Fawcett or not?' Mike replied, 'Yes, we have.' I knew then that my $4 million was in the bag.

The film was made in 1980, the effects and performances were fine, but once again the finished product parted company with my original expectations. However, because of my deal with NBC, plus a few other sales, it didn't do too badly.

21

Back at the Board

FOR MANY YEARS I had watched Jack Gill's progress in the corporation, and I was very impressed with his business ability. He was the accountant for the ATV Network, then Group Accountant, and eventually I put him on the Board and he became Finance Director. When I became Managing Director, I made him Deputy Managing Director of the ATV/ACC Group with the Board's approval. I felt a tremendous warmth towards Jack and thought he felt the same towards me. I relied upon him completely for all financial matters pertaining to the Group. Then I made him Deputy Chief Executive and eventually got him appointed as Managing Director.

I felt this would leave me free to concentrate on the more creative areas of the corporation, with the secure knowledge that the financial aspects were in safe hands.

Unfortunately, he began to feel restricted in this role, and, misguidedly, he wanted to involve himself in the creative side of show business. In short, he wanted to become an impresario. He'd been bitten by the bug, and was seduced by what he considered to be the more exciting side of the business. Unfortunately, he did not have the ability to do so. You cannot teach people how to be creative if basically they aren't – and Jack's talents lay elsewhere: in the boardroom rather than on the studio floor. He was a superb businessman and financier, clever at organization and administration, and, had he carried on in this capacity he would most likely have become Chairman and Chief Executive of the company, a position he desperately wanted.

He chose, instead, to form a company within the Group called Black Lion Films in the hope of producing films both for TV and theatrical distribution.

This was a ridiculous move, for the last thing the company needed was another film division.

I did my best to dissuade him from this course, but he was adamant.

And so was I. I did not approve of Jack's impresario ambitions, and felt that if he insisted on pursuing this new departure, he would no longer be the right man to run the company – although I did not say so publicly.

It all came to a head when I returned from the United States in August 1981 and found that he had formed three different entertainment groups in the USA without consulting me. When I challenged him about this, he said he had only done it to protect the name of a subsidiary company. Which is nonsense.

I realized now that Jack would have to go as he was not devoting sufficient time to the financial affairs of ACC in his official capacity as Managing Director. I had to have someone on whom I could depend, and I felt that Jack, regrettably, was no longer that person.

It was a tough moment for me because, over the years, I had become very fond of Jack Gill. But, in the end, I cared more about the company than I did about him, and, at a board meeting, he was asked to leave.

To this day many people in the business believe that Jack received a settlement of £560,000, which was the balance due to him under the remaining contract. He was not, in fact, paid anything. The Board felt he was asking too much compensation, as a result of which Gill sued the five members he held responsible for the balance of the contract: myself, Louis Benjamin, Bill Michaels, Leo Pliatsky and Norman Collins.

As the case was about to go to court, Jack withdrew his claim for the £560,000, and my belief is that he was suffering some remorse. In spite of our differences, I believe he still had some warm feelings towards me and didn't want to face the prospect of a much-publicized and expensive court hearing.

We agreed to pay a small portion of his legal fees, although we were advised that we did not have to do this. By this time Norman Collins had died, and we were not going to ask his widow to contribute. Leo Pliatsky was a non-executive director, who wasn't really involved, so we didn't ask him either. This left myself, Louis Benjamin and Bill Michaels to pay the costs, which we did.

Jack Gill had always been friendly with Louis Benjamin, who was then Managing Director of Pye Records – the company that we had acquired from C. O. Stanley. They had risen through the ranks of the corporation along similar levels and worked well together. However, it seemed as if each of them considered himself my heir apparent and, instead of consolidating their relationship and working in unison for the good of the Group, they each became increasingly ambitious and were continuously complaining to me about each other. This friction led to a total breakdown of their relationship as each pursued his own course.

Meanwhile, the record industry was going through a bad patch. In such a mercurial business you have to have one or two major hits at regular intervals to maintain profits. And you had to be far-seeing and perceptive enough to take a gamble on something you felt might be the in-coming vogue.

My nephew Philip Black and my son Paul had been at Mill-field School with Richard McPhail, who became manager of the group Genesis (which Phil Collins later joined). Philip and Paul came to me one day and said, 'Listen to the group – they're wonderful. Why don't you let Pye Records have a tape of theirs?' I did arrange for the group to see the powers-that-be at Pye. Unfortunately, those powers didn't care for them – which simply proved that Pye were out of touch with the tastes of the contemporary record-buying public, because Genesis with Peter Gabriel and Phil Collins went on to become bestseller material, and remain so to this day. However, I did arrange for our records contract department to advise the Genesis group on the contract that they were offered by another company. I still hold a letter from Peter Gabriel, signed by all the group, thanking me profusely for the help I had given him at the very beginning of his career.

It's always easy to speak with the benefit of hindsight, but I do feel that perhaps if Pye *had* taken on Genesis, other modern groups might have been attracted to the company – to everyone's benefit.

Louis Benjamin was appointed Managing Director of the Moss Empire Theatre Group, which included the London Palladium, Victoria Palace and numerous provincial theatres – most of which were subsequently sold off. When Prince Littler died, I made Toby Rowland responsible for the theatres that made up the Stoll part of the group, namely: Drury Lane, Her Majesty's, Queens, Apollo, Lyric and The Globe. And when Toby Rowland retired, I, as chairman, appointed Louis Benjamin to run the whole Stoll/Moss group of theatres.

*   *   *

There have been a lot of stories in the press about all the luxury yachts and fleets of Rolls Royces owned by my company. Allow me to put the record straight. During one of the better periods in the record business, Louis Benjamin always wanted a Rolls Royce. We said that the first year he made £1 million profit for Pye Records he could have his wish. He reached that figure and we kept our promise. After all, he was meeting important people and we felt that a man in his position warranted it, quite apart from the fact that in the entertainment industry a Rolls Royce is an important status symbol.

Louis then remarked that each time he went to the Record Industry Fair, which is held twice a year in the South of France, all the other major record companies entertained prospective foreign buyers on their own yachts. We should have one too, he said. We listened to his views on the matter and said that the first year he made £2 million profit for Pye Records the company would buy a yacht. He eventually reached this figure and we bought a yacht for £40,000, which was moored in the South of France.

There was a lot of talk in the press about a second yacht. In fact, the advertising sales department of ATV Network had an £18,000 boat which they moored on the Thames, and which they used for entertaining prospective clients. There was nothing extravagant about that. Many other TV companies did the same thing. Selling advertising space on TV is a tough competitive business, and if entertaining clients in congenial surroundings helps drum up business, it is money well spent.

Now to the matter of the third yacht.

I had an idea for a film called *The French Villa* which was to be directed by Stanley Donen and shot in the South of France. We found that we would have to hire a boat for twenty weeks at £10,000 per week. Jack Gill was consulted about this and suggested it would make better business sense to buy one and, when it wasn't in use, charter it out, which we did.

Unfortunately, after several attempts to get the screenplay right had failed, we abandoned the idea.

So we now had the yacht which, considering its size, we had paid a reasonable price for. It was moored at Cannes and chartered out regularly. I, personally, only set foot on it on three occasions. Once for a press conference during the Cannes Film Festival, once for a meeting with some German investors, and once for a board meeting with our American distribution company during the Cannes Festival. On each occasion the boat was only within the perimeter of the harbour, as I am no great sailor.

So much for our fleet of yachts!

As far as the Rolls Royces are concerned, it was said in the press that we had ten Rolls in all. These are the facts: I had one – LG 10 – which was my own. I have had a Rolls Royce since 1948 – long before Independent Television was started – and always with the number plate LG 10. When I won the third Queen's Award for Export in 1971, Lord Renwick – then Chairman – was so thrilled that, with the support of the Board, he offered to buy me a second and newer Rolls Royce. I said I already had one, but they were most insistent. A Phantom VI became available which a foreign buyer had decided not to take. The buyer put an initial deposit on it, which he forfeited, so we were able to purchase it at a reasonable price, and I gave my own Rolls in part exchange. So, here I am in 1987, still using the same Rolls I acquired fifteen years ago!

Jack Gill also had a Rolls Royce. He was, after all, Deputy Chief Executive and then Managing Director of ACC, so this was thought to be justifiable. Prince Littler had always had a Rolls Royce prior to our buying his company, and when he died his car belonged to ATV and we kept it in our garage.

So much for our own fleet of Rolls Royces!

22

Courting Disaster

I FIRST HEARD of Robert Holmes à Court from reading in the press that he had acquired approximately 25 per cent of ACC's non-voting shares.

He attended the ACC annual general meeting in September 1981 and I spoke to him briefly afterwards. I found him quite affable, and suggested that he and I should have lunch together, which we did.

At the time I was very excited about the film *On Golden Pond* and I had just received the first print in London. Kathie was keen to see it, so I thought it was an opportunity to show the film to Robert and his wife too, before going out to dinner afterwards at the Ritz Hotel. They loved the film and over dinner the conversation revolved around it, but none of us dreamt that it would be such an amazing success. I took to Robert and his wife instantly and both Kathie and I found them pleasant company.

After this, Robert would come in to see me at the office regularly and sit with me while I conducted various business negotiations. He appeared to be fascinated with the way I operated and, just by being in the same room with me, he was, he said, learning so much about the entertainment industry.

In October 1981 Robert told me that he was going to Los Angeles with his wife and I said I would try to use my contacts there to see that they both had a really interesting time. I fixed them up at the Beverly Hills Hotel and arranged for Marty Starger to show them around. I explained to Marty that Robert was an important investor and that I'd really appreciate it if he took special care of him, and talk to him about the different facets of the entertainment industry.

I subsequently flew out to Los Angeles and Robert spent a

great deal of time with me in my suite at the hotel, listening to me negotiate with Sid Sheinberg of MCA for the foreign distribution rights of *On Golden Pond*, *Sophie's Choice*, and *The Dark Crystal*. I finally did a deal whereby we had a substantial advance on each of the three films, payable immediately. Robert heard me discussing all these details on the telephone while he was in my suite and he congratulated me, because he thought it was a great deal. As we spent more and more time in each other's company and talked a lot about our respective lives, I grew to like him immensely.

One day I asked him if he'd ever been to Las Vegas. He said he and his wife hadn't, but that they'd love to go. I told him I hadn't been there for years myself, and suggested that we should all go together. I also asked Marty Starger and a friend of his to join us. I was able to arrange hotel reservations at the MGM Grand Hotel through a good friend of mine, Bernie Rothkopf, who was the general director of the Hotel on behalf of Kirk Kerkorian.

When we arrived in Vegas, we had a huge two-bedroom suite, with masses of fruit and flowers spread around. Marty Starger and his friend had rooms in another part of the hotel. Bernie Rothkopf arranged for us to see the hotel's spectacular show, 'Hallelujah Hollywood!' as well as various other shows in other hotels. Wherever we went we had the best seats in the house and were given fabulous attention – and there were no bills to pay because we were the guests of Bernie Rothkopf and the MGM Grand. Sammy Davis, Jr, was the star of one of the shows and Robert and his wife were so overwhelmed by his performance that they said how wonderful it would be if I could persuade Davis to appear on their annual TV charity Telethon in Perth. I told them that Sammy had appeared for me at the Palladium and on many TV specials, and, as he and I were such good friends, I'd ask him to do it for me.

After the show we went backstage and Sammy greeted me enthusiastically and said he was delighted to meet Robert and his wife. I then asked him if he would do a Telethon in Perth in the latter part of 1982 and he said, 'Lew, if you really want me to do it, I certainly will.' So that was arranged, and I thanked him very much.

In June 1982, after I had left ACC, Sammy Davis telephoned

me and said, 'Now that you're no longer with ACC, do I still have to do that Telethon in Perth?' 'Sammy,' I said, 'I gave a promise and you did too, and, as you know, I never break my word. And I know you won't either.' Sammy Davis, Jr, went to Perth and was a fantastic success.

During this period, I spent a lot of time with Robert and his wife because we shared a two-bedroom suite. Robert talked a great deal about his past financial successes and he told me how anxious he was to achieve the same sort of success in the entertainment industry.

I had been without a finance director for a couple of months and found it easy to talk over certain matters with him because he had obviously done a great deal of research into the company background. I was encouraged to do so because he was constantly declaring his growing respect and affection for me, as well as wanting to be involved in show business. He also struck me as being extremely perceptive.

Early in December 1981, Robert had acquired 51 per cent of the ordinary voting shares of ACC. As he was now our principal shareholder, I suggested to him and to the Board that he should be appointed a Member of the Board, and should also acquire 1000 of the voting shares, because each member of the Board had some voting shares. This acquisition required the approval of the Independent Broadcasting Authority, and I went to see Lord Thomson, the Chairman of the IBA, to ask for it. I told Lord Thomson that I felt Robert was a man of great integrity and one in whom I had complete faith and confidence. The Authority gave their approval and Robert was duly appointed to the Board of ACC on 17 December 1981.

Robert told me he was spending Christmas in London with his family, and as I was planning to go to New York on 3 January 1982, I suggested that he might like to accompany me in order to see our New York operation. We travelled to New York together, staying at the ACC apartment in the Galleria, which was just above our offices. We spent the next three days in close proximity, and naturally talked frankly about our personal lives and problems. I told him we were looking for a finance director to take over Jack Gill's responsibilities, and generally took him into my confidence.

We returned to London on the night plane on 6 January, and, in the car travelling to the airport, Robert said to me, 'Lew, I think I'll make a bid for ACC.' I asked if he was serious about this, and he said he was and that we would talk more about it on the plane.

On the plane he said he had been thinking about it for a while and that he was going to make a full offer for the entire company provided I gave him my support and sold him my voting shares. I was so impressed with him that I agreed to this. I assured him of my full support and my voting shares and we shook hands on it.

We continued talking throughout the flight and he said to me, 'You're not an accountant, Lew, and I really believe you should be left alone to do what you know best in the business while I handle the other aspects.' Then he kept repeating that he felt I was ACC's greatest asset and that we would make a great team together. On reflection, perhaps he was just saying these things to impress me and to make sure I didn't change my mind. He obviously didn't realize that once I gave my word – that was it! Nothing would make me take it back.

We arrived in London early in the morning of 7 January, and Robert insisted that we stop off at my flat as he wanted to talk things over with Kathie. By this time he knew what a tremendous influence Kathie had on any career decisions I made.

So he spent quite a long while talking to Kathie alone, evidently singing my praises, telling her what a marvellous job I'd done for ACC, which was precisely why he was proposing to take over the company.

We had a board meeting on 8 January 1982 and I informed the Board of the decision I had taken to support Robert and sell him my voting shares. They were surprised, but eventually agreed. Robert was then appointed Chairman and Chief Executive and prepared his bid.

Then, individual members of the Board tried to dissuade me from the course I had taken, but I just said that once I had given my word I would never go back on a commitment, and I truly felt that Robert Holmes à Court would be good for the future of the Corporation.

We had several board meetings to discuss this takeover and, of course, Robert was in the chair. We also received bids from another company, as well as several individuals. But I told everybody who called that I'd given my support to Robert Holmes à Court.

Robert then asked if I would help him with a special charity appeal he was organizing in Perth, Australia, and for this purpose, requested a special gala showing of *On Golden Pond*. This presented me with something of a problem because I now had to get permission from Terry Jackman, Managing Director of Hoyts Cinema Group, to allow the première of this important film to be held in Perth. Generally, major films opened in Sydney or Melbourne, but he finally agreed to allow this special screening for one night only.

Robert knew that I was going to be at the Manila Film Festival in the middle of January, and arranged things so that I could fly from there to Perth to help promote the charity evening. Once we had fixed the date, he invited my wife Kathie and her sister Norah to be his guests in Perth. I went on radio and television and held many press interviews to help promote the event.

It was an exciting and spectacular evening, attended by all the important political figures and top businessmen. After the première, the opening part of which was televised, Robert gave a small supper party for about ten people in the hotel where we were staying.

The next day he arranged a dinner party in the dining room on the top floor of his office building, at which twenty people were present. They included prominent politicians, some of his directors, as well as Terry Jackman, and Sir Larry and Lady Lamb. At the end of the dinner he stood up and made a speech, thanking me for my support and saying that I would be with the company until the year 2000, after which I would join them in Perth! Then he asked everybody to drink a toast to me.

After dinner we had a short meeting with Terry Jackman to discuss the possibility of buying the Hoyts Cinema chain, but Jackman said it wasn't possible at that time.

We then returned to London. In view of the other bids that had been made, Robert had to revise his offer and it was not until the beginning of April that it was finally accepted.

Robert mentioned the year 2000 because I had always said I would never retire until the year 2000, but it didn't necessarily mean that I would stay with ACC until then.

Meanwhile, ATV Network had become Central Television, of which ACC owned 51 per cent. I was at home one evening when I had a call from the Independent Broadcasting Authority asking me to come and see them. As my flat is close to the IBA's headquarters, I was there in about five minutes.

I had to reassure the IBA again that I had every confidence in Robert Holmes à Court and that, if necessary, I was sure he would put his 51 per cent of the voting shares into the hands of a nominated trustee. They accepted my assurances and agreed to the proposal.

After the deal was completed, I received proposals from all sorts of unexpected quarters. People seemed to sense far quicker than I myself did that I would not be happy in the new circumstances. Much to my surprise, one of these approaches came from Gerald Ronson, who owns the Heron Corporation, and whom I had only met twice before at board meetings when he was making representations to bid for the company. He asked to see me and said he had a feeling I wouldn't want to stay with the company now that it had changed hands, and he put an extraordinary proposal to me. He said he would be willing to put up £10 million for an entertainment division within his group, of which I would own 50 per cent. I was very appreciative of his generous offer and said I'd let him have my decision shortly.

By this time I'd begun to realize that there was a decidedly different atmosphere in the company and that Mr Robert Holmes à Court wasn't the warm-hearted Mr Nice Guy I'd thought he was. As soon as he took control of the company, he started firing people who'd been there a long time and were part of the ACC 'family', so to speak. For example, he got rid of Katie the tea lady, who'd been with us for years. Whenever I had visitors in the office, I'd ring through to Katie, and she'd arrive with a tray of tea or coffee or, even, on occasion, with a cold lunch for me. Holmes à Court gave her notice and bought coffee percolators for his principal executives. From now on, if I wanted to offer a guest a beverage, my assistant Marcia had to make it.

279

I was very depressed about all this and realized, with a certain degree of shock, there was no future for me with the man. His attitude changed completely once he was in the chair, and he became hard and ruthless. I was told that my official position with ACC at this point would be Executive Deputy Chairman of the Entertainment Division – a position I was happy to take up, and wanted to announce to the press, who were obviously eager to know what my role was to be.

I kept asking Holmes à Court to hold a press conference and he kept promising me that he would. It was always 'sometime next week' or 'the day after tomorrow'. He procrastinated for weeks, and no press conference ever took place. It was then, of course, that I suspected his intention was to keep me well in the background. Perhaps it niggled him that although he now had official control of ACC, it was still known as my company – and, within our offices, I was still 'the Guv'nor'.

Since he refused to make any official announcement about me, I found that I had very little authority. I had assumed I would continue as Executive Deputy Chairman, being, in his own words, 'ACC's greatest asset'. It was as simple as that. But, in addition, I was no longer on the Board, which both surprised and upset me. I'd founded the company, and built it up to what it was.

Adding injury to insult is the fact that Holmes à Court bought the company at a bargain price – having bought 51 per cent of the non-voting shares at a very low price. What had happened was that, in the year ending 5 April 1981, Jack Gill had written off £35 million from our film stockpile because of the failure of one or two of our films. He had the approval of the Board to do this. If I'd had men like Robert Renwick, C. O. Stanley and Max Aitken around at the time, this wouldn't have happened. They would have known the true value of our film library, and, with their business acumen, would have realized that we were sitting on a potential fortune. Videocassettes and cable TV were just beginning to come into their own, a fact which was never taken into account by the then Board. So, as I say, our stockpile was undervalued and Holmes à Court got himself a bargain.

In retrospect I realize that Holmes à Court was a much more persuasive man than I had given him credit for. He was obviously well aware of the company's potential from the very beginning. Certainly more so than our own Board of Directors. But he played it so cool that he never revealed his hand.

An incident occurred that made it only too obvious to me that my days at ACC were numbered.

Before the takeover I'd given the okay on *Sophie's Choice*. Martin Starger was the executive producer, and Alan Pakula the director. Three or four days before principal photography was due to commence, Holmes à Court, now Chairman and Chief Executive, came into my office and said that unless Pakula put up half the completion guarantee money, which was $600,000 in total, he was going to cancel the production.

I was appalled and extremely distressed. I told him that such behaviour was unheard of. But he was adamant. Unless Pakula came up with the money, he insisted, no production. For me, personally, this was a catastrophic blow. The completion guarantee had not been part of my deal with Pakula and, for the first time in my life, I was being forced to go back on a deal. In desperation I offered to put up the money myself. I had enough assets to do so, and raising the cash wouldn't be a problem.

No, he said. It had to come from Pakula.

Deeply humiliated, I had to call Martin Starger in California and tell him what had happened. Starger, in turn, contacted Pakula, who agreed to put up half the amount because he loved the project. As it happened, the film came in under budget, so the money was returned.

To this day I cannot understand why Holmes à Court insisted on Pakula's personal involvement with the completion guarantee. One possible explanation could be that it was a safeguard against the film going over budget, but, as several people involved in the picture – including Meryl Streep – accepted lower salaries because of their belief in it – the film turned out to be over-budgeted. Another explanation is that Holmes à Court realized that such unheard-of behaviour would undermine my reputation – for it was well known in the industry that *Sophie's Choice* had, from the outset, been a project of mine.

After this there was no way I could continue to work for him, and I made up my mind to leave. I discussed this with him and he agreed that I could leave the company.

Still Dancing

*   *   *

Whenever I went to the Cannes Film Festival I always stayed at
the Hotel du Cap where I often met Jerry Perenchio. Everybody
told me of his high standing and integrity in the entertainment
industry, and I also knew that he had started one of the very first
cable TV systems called On TV. He had gone into partnership
with Norman Lear, the man credited with changing the face of
television in America. Jerry and Norman owned a company
called Tandem Productions, Embassy Television and Embassy
Communications, and had recently acquired a film production/
distribution company which had been called Avco Embassy, and
whose name they changed to Embassy Pictures.

Jerry and I became very friendly, and on a trip I made to
California on 1 May 1982 I thought I'd call in and say hello to
him. He welcomed me, and, to my surprise, said, 'Why don't
you come and work with Norman and me?' He went on, 'I know
you can't be happy with the situation at ACC and I'm sure it's
only a question of time before you leave there.'

I told him I appreciated his suggestion a great deal, but that I
was still toying with the proposal I'd had from Gerald Ronson.
'Well, think about it,' Jerry said, 'I'm sure you'll be very happy
with us,' and he made me an outstanding offer which, in effect,
meant my becoming Chairman and Chief Executive of Embassy
Communications International, which would be headquartered
in London, and that I'd only be responsible to Norman and to
him.

I was a little shaken by this proposal and knew I had to make a
decision quickly. I said I'd think it over and get back to him as
soon as possible.

I telephoned Kathie and told her what had happened. She had
met Jerry Perenchio once or twice and liked him. We discussed
the possibilities, and she pointed out that, as far as Ronson was
concerned, I should seriously consider the fact that he wasn't in
the entertainment business and I'd have to start from scratch.

Jerry Perenchio and Norman Lear, on the other hand, were
showbusiness people and spoke the same language as I did.

I felt exactly the same way and immediately called Jerry. 'I've
spoken to Kathie,' I told him, 'and thought it over. And I just

want to say that I very much look forward to joining you.'

I flew back to London, telephoned Gerald Ronson and asked whether I could come and see him. I explained the situation fully, and he said: 'Whatever you think is right for you, Lew, is fine for me.'

I went to Cannes on 17 May and met with Jerry and Norman. They asked me when I wanted to start with the company and I said 23 June because that's my lucky date.

When I returned to London I saw Robert Holmes à Court and told him I wanted to leave ACC on 22 June.

I still had two years to run on my original English contract and three on my American contract with ACC and ITC. As it was my decision to leave, I received no financial compensation, nor did I want any. All I took away with me was my Rolls Royce and my pension.

Before I left, however, I told Holmes à Court that I expected to keep my presentation credit on *Sophie's Choice*, just as I'd had on *On Golden Pond*.

'Absolutely,' he said. 'You'll have it.'

And that was that.

On 23 June, before we had even acquired premises, we held a press conference at the Inn on the Park in London at which Jerry, Norman and Alan Horn – the President and Chief Operating Officer of their group – were present.

That night we had a party at the Ivy Restaurant to celebrate two special events – Kathie's and my ruby wedding anniversary, and the day I joined Jerry Perenchio and Norman Lear. Jerry, Norman, our son Paul, and many close relatives and friends of Kathie and me joined us on this memorable occasion – another wonderful highlight in my life.

Then I had to look for offices. Jerry and Norman gave me *carte blanche* to find whatever I felt suitable. I found premises at 3 Audley Square, which Kathie and Marcia then had completely renovated, and that is where I am to this day.

In September 1982, Robert Holmes à Court telephoned me at my office in Audley Square and invited himself round for coffee.

He was extremely charming, affable, said all the right things, and not for an instant would you have believed there had been any trouble between us.

I'm not a man to bear grudges, and three months had passed since my last dealings with him. I was in business on my own, no longer had the responsibilities of a major company, and, one way and another, was in a pretty good frame of mind. We chatted about all sorts of things, in the course of which he mentioned he'd be interested in investing money in anything I wanted him to. I thanked him politely, though nothing in this world would make me take him up on his offer.

We had some coffee and I then repeated to him my concern over my credit on *Sophie's Choice*. It was to read 'Lord Grade presents . . . ' and, again, he said there'd be no problems. Shortly after that, he left.

Sophie's Choice opened in December in New York and in Perth – and my name was *not* on the credits. Naturally, I was upset, because I had considered it one of my special projects, but not as upset as Martin Starger and Alan Pakula, who had no idea my credit had been dropped until the film premièred in the USA. All the versions they'd seen prior to the official opening had contained my credit, and they saw no reason why it shouldn't remain so. Quite apart from which, the film belonged to ACC, and Starger and Pakula had no authority whatsoever to interfere.

There was nothing I could do either, and I put the whole thing out of my mind.

In April 1983 I received another call from Robert Holmes à Court.

He wanted to come round for a general chat, he said. I said fine, and he did. I offered him coffee. Again he expressed his willingness to invest in any future projects I may have had in mind, and, again, I thanked him politely. Then I said, 'Robert, I have to ask you why you went back on your word about my credit for *Sophie's Choice*.' And he said, 'Lew, I knew absolutely nothing about it. The first time I saw that your name wasn't on the screen was in Perth, at the première.'

Martin Starger sued Robert Holmes à Court for certain non-payments of money on *Sophie's Choice* and also on *On Golden Pond*. Holmes à Court claimed that he wasn't entitled to any as I'd done a 'sweetheart' deal with him, and inferred that I was getting a 'kickback'. That was his defence.

So Martin duly went to court, and I was to be called as a witness because my integrity had been compromised. But the lengthy case was settled the day before I was due to appear on the stand. Holmes à Court dropped all the 'sweetheart' and other allegations, and Marty Starger was financially compensated to a degree that was high even by American film standards.

So much for Robert Holmes à Court – a major miscalculation in my life. To this day I cannot understand why he felt the way he did and why he behaved the way he did.

23

On the Brighter Side

AT THE BEGINNING OF AUGUST 1982, I went to Los Angeles where Jerry and Norman threw a special dinner party to introduce me to all the principal executives of their group of companies.

Later that same week, Jerry hosted a huge party for me at Chasens Restaurant, to which he had invited some of his principal executives, plus distinguished guests from all the other major film and television companies. It was a remarkable occasion and I was deeply touched by Jerry's generosity.

Jerry has several houses in Malibu Colony and I stayed in one of them. To this day, whenever I visit Los Angeles, he insists that I should be his guest in one of them.

I had now met all my colleagues at Embassy and felt very happy to be part of that new family circle. I returned to London, full of enthusiasm and, at the age of seventy-five, ready to begin another career.

My next trip to the States was arranged for 4 November, and this time Jerry asked Kathie to come over with me to join us for a huge dinner party and concert he was giving to celebrate twenty-five years of Andy Williams being in show business. It was to be held in the Beverly Hilton Hotel on 6 November.

It was a fabulous party and Kathie and I were among over a thousand guests. Of course, Andy Williams sang, and he was followed by a surprise appearance by Luciano Pavarotti, who had flown in after his performance at the Metropolitan Opera House in New York especially to be present at this tribute.

Pavarotti sang and received a standing ovation. He then made a speech, saying that he had flown from New York only because of his friendship with Jerry. Afterwards, Jerry took Kathie and me to see Pavarotti in his suite and we reminisced about the time, many years ago, when he had appeared for me on the 'Sunday Night at the London Palladium' show, replacing Guiseppe di Stefano.

Several weeks before this, I had suggested to Jerry that, since he now had a film distribution and production company, he really ought to go abroad to meet the principal foreign film distributors and theatre owners.

So we set up a comprehensive trip to take in the Far East and Australia.

Kathie returned to London and Jerry and I set off for Japan on 10 November. During a five-day visit there, we met all the distributors, went to several special dinner parties, including one given by my very good friends Toho-Towa, at which the President, Mr Shirasu, was the host, and we met Mr Matsuoka, the owner of Towo-Toha and many other huge business conglomerates in Japan.

The Japanese were, as usual, tremendously warm and hospitable and Jerry and I felt we were laying the foundations for great future business transactions with them.

On 16 November we went to Hong Kong, where we were greeted enthusiastically by Sir Run Run Shaw, who again proved to be the perfect host.

We went on to Bangkok (my first visit there), where we were met by the owners of the biggest circuit of cinemas in Thailand, and taken to dinner that evening. The next day they took us on a tour of Bangkok, followed by dinner at a special restaurant where there was a fascinating Thai dance cabaret. On the third day, we were the guests of the Thai TV Colour Co. We were driven to their studios, and, as we arrived, saw a huge sign outside welcoming Jerry Perenchio and Lord Grade to Bangkok. They had arranged a special cabaret performance with all their leading artistes – singers, dancers, musicians – in our honour, and it was absolutely beautiful.

On 22 November we left for Singapore, where we met Harold Shaw and some of his colleagues. At that time Harold Shaw, the son of Run Run Shaw, was in charge of an important chain of cinemas in Singapore, as well as being responsible for a considerable part of the Shaw empire which included hotels and property. Again, we were introduced to important businessmen and were royally entertained.

On 25 November we went to Sydney, Australia.

Before leaving London, I met a literary agent, who suggested I make a film based on a book written about Bob Champion, the famous jockey. Champion had contracted cancer, conquered the disease, and in 1981 won the Grand National on Aldaniti, a horse who'd broken a leg and was considered finished. Together, man and horse, each fought their disabilities and it was out of Bob's determination to win the Grand National on that horse that he regained his will to live.

It was an inspiring story, full of hope and courage, which I felt would give great encouragement to cancer sufferers all over the world.

The producer who had the rights to this book was Peter Shaw. We had several meetings and discussions about the possibility of making a film of it, and came up with the title *Champions*. John Hurt had expressed great interest in playing the part of Bob Champion, and the director we had in mind was John Irvin. We also heard that it would be possible for Aldaniti to appear in the film as well. By the time I was ready to set out on my Far East trip, the script had been completed. I read it, and liked it immensely, and told Peter Shaw I'd give him my decision by the time I returned to England.

I actually had the script in my briefcase, but had not yet discussed it with Jerry.

*   *   *

Kerry Packer was a great host to us. At that time he had formed his own film and videocassette company, although he is now no longer involved in it.

We had a wonderful stay in Australia, and several enjoyable meals with Kerry, and Terry Jackman, who was Managing Director of the Hoyts Cinema Chain. We also met the people from the Greater Union Cinema Chain, the other major circuit.

We then decided to break our journey to California by stopping off in Honolulu for a couple of days' rest.

On the plane from Sydney to Honolulu, I told Jerry I'd like him to read the script of *Champions*. He read it and said to me,

'You really like it, don't you?' I said, 'Yes, I do, but what do you think about it?' He said, 'It brought tears to my eyes. Make it.'

When we arrived in Honolulu I telephoned Peter Shaw and told him that, subject to his signing John Hurt, we would go ahead and make the film.

We then arrived in Los Angeles after what had been a strenuous but exhilarating trip.

After a few days in Los Angeles, I flew back to London and, on Monday, 6 December, had a meeting with Peter Shaw and John Irvin. Hurt had agreed to be in the film – and the other major role, that of the trainer Josh Gifford, went to Edward Woodward, who gave such a fine performance in the successful Australian film *Breaker Morant*.

We were able to assemble a wonderful cast of fine actors in cameo roles, because they all believed in the film and were anxious to appear in it. The young lady we chose for the role of Jo, Bob Champion's girlfriend, who later became his wife, was Jan Francis.

By 14 March 1983 we were ready to start production. A few days before this, I decided to see what I could do about making some pre-sales deals.

I called Steve Scheffer of Home Box Office in New York at his home on Friday night. It was 8.00 p.m. New York time, so it was 1.00 a.m. London time. 'Steve,' I said, 'I'm making my first film for Embassy and I want you to buy it. It's called *Champions*.' He asked me what the story was about and when I told him he said it sounded exciting. Then he asked how much I wanted, and I told him. 'I'll get back to you in a couple of weeks,' he said. 'Steve,' I said, 'I want to know by Monday.' 'But I've got to speak to Michael Fuchs,' he said. 'Steve, I'm going to tell you about a wonderful invention, but you must promise me you'll keep it a secret. It's called "a telephone".' He said, 'I understand.'

On Sunday night he telephoned me at home. After a brief discussion about the fee he gave me the OK.

On the Monday morning I received a telex confirming the deal, and on Tuesday, by special courier, a cheque arrived for half the amount. The rest was to follow.

That's relationship.

Next, I called Kerry Packer. I told him I was making a film and wanted to sell him all the Australian rights in perpetuity, and I told him how much I wanted for them. I outlined the story to him and he said, 'What's the Grand National?' which is a good example of his sense of humour, because every year he transmits the Grand National on his television network. In fact, he actually transmitted the Grand National in 1981 in which Bob Champion had ridden to victory on Aldaniti. 'How much do you want?' he said. I quoted a figure. 'Call me tomorrow. I want to discuss it with my people.' And he hung up.

I telephoned him the following day. He told me his people didn't think it was worth my asking price and he quoted a much smaller amount to me. 'You must be joking!' I said. 'How can they possibly tell when I haven't even started the film yet?' 'I'll tell you what I'll do,' I said. 'If you run the opening night as a charity première, I'll fly out to Australia especially for it.' 'OK, OK,' he said. 'Anything to get you off the phone!'

The next day a telex arrived confirming the deal and saying that, in view of the terms he was paying, I ought to make him a director of the company!

I also sold *Champions* to Hong Kong for a guaranteed sum and, again, undertook to go if they had a charity première. I did a similar deal in Israel – so I had three commitments for charity premières, all of which I fully intended to keep.

Rolf Mittweg, Head of International Sales for Embassy, and Massimo Grasiosi, his associate based in Rome, sold the film in all the other territories.

We started production on 14 March 1983, and Bob Champion was the adviser. John Hurt and Edward Woodward were wonderful in their roles, and John Hurt was a sufficiently experienced rider to do a large amount of the riding in the film himself.

The world première of *Champions* was held in the presence of Her Majesty the Queen Mother and HRH Princess Anne on 1 March 1984 at the Odeon, Leicester Square, and it was in aid of the Bob Champion Cancer Trust.

I found the film an extremely moving experience. It didn't make a killing on the box office, but no one who bought the film complained. They all thought it an inspiring human drama which carried an uplifting message of hope. Because it was made on a reasonable budget, and because of all the pre-sales I'd negotiated, it made money for Embassy.

*   *   *

I had known William Forman ('Bill' to his friends) for many years. He was the owner of a huge chain of cinemas in the United States and was a close friend of Jerry Perenchio.

In 1981 when there were all the press reports about ACC's financial problems, I was at the Beverly Hills Hotel. I'd always let Bill know when I was going to be in town, and he called and said he wanted to come over and see me. I knew he hadn't been too well, so I offered to drive to his place.

He insisted, however, on coming to me. We talked about this and that for a while, and then he said, 'I want you to telephone William Thompson of the First National Bank of Boston.' 'What for?' I said. 'Never mind "what for" – I want you to call him now.' So I telephoned Bill Thompson. 'I'm here with Bill Forman and he's asked me to call you,' I said. 'What's it about?' Bill Thompson said to me, 'Bill Forman has £10 million in England and it's yours to help you out with ACC's financial problems. Use it any way you want.'

There was no mention about interest charges or securities – just simply that £10 million was available to me.

I was very touched at this and thanked Bill Thompson, saying I was going to thank Bill Forman and tell him that I wouldn't dream of accepting his gracious and generous offer to me.

Bill Forman died some months later, and I subsequently saw his son Michael and told him now deeply sad I felt for him at his terrible loss. I then mentioned the wonderful offer his father had made to me and was happy to tell him it was one of the greatest expressions of friendship I'd ever received. It is also one I will never forget.

*   *   *

I always enjoy dealing with people who are considered to be tough, hard-headed businessmen. Once you manage to establish a relationship with such a person, it usually lasts. Leo Kirsch, the owner of Beta Film and Taurus Films (the largest producers of German TV in the world), has this kind of a reputation.

I had met him a couple of times, and he once came to the annual luncheon I used to host each year for foreign film distributors at the Hotel du Cap in the South of France.

Norman Rosemont, the American producer, brought me a project for a television remake of *A Tale of Two Cities*. I telephoned Leo and said I wanted to come and see him in Munich about it. He said it was OK with him and, when I arrived there, he and I and seven of his top people attended a working lunch. I offered to sell them the rights to *A Tale of Two Cities* for $1.5 million for the German-speaking territories and for France. Leo didn't say a word during the meeting, but everybody kept saying it wasn't for them, and that it was more suitable for France. When we finished, Leo asked me to look at one of his operatic films. I thought this might be boring but diplomatically agreed, whereupon we went into a screening room and I saw a wonderful opera, beautifully photographed on location. It was so enthralling, I sat right through it to the end, having intended to stay no more than an hour or so.

Leo then said he'd like me to join him, and the seven people I'd lunched with a couple of hours earlier, for dinner that evening at 8.00 p.m.

I arrived a few minutes early and all the other guests were there, except for Leo. He arrived at about two minutes past eight, and we went straight to our table. 'Before we sit down, Lew,' he said, 'I want you to know you have the deal for *A Tale of Two Cities*.' I returned to London the next morning, and a few days later I received his cheque for $1.5 million. Everyone who works for him is loyal and devoted to him, and I value his friendship immensely.

*   *   *

On 5 May 1983 I went to the Cannes Film Festival with Jerry and, as usual, stayed at the Hotel du Cap.

Jerry decided he would give a party for me on Saturday, 14 May. I thought it would be a small dinner party, and Jerry suggested I invite Kathie (who seldom accompanied me to the South of France when I was on business) to join us.

On Monday, 9 May, I received a telephone call from Gary

Pudney of ABC TV inviting me to a party in Los Angeles on 11 May to celebrate the thirtieth anniversary of the American Broadcasting Company with all their affiliate stations. What a wonderful surprise it would be for Leonard Goldenson, he said, if I turned up as well. Elton Rule also felt it would really make Leonard's day, as my association with him had lasted over ABC's entire thirty-year period.

I decided I would go, and told Jerry, who thought it a great idea just as long as I was back for his dinner party on the Saturday. I assured him I'd be back by Thursday.

I caught the early morning plane to Paris, took Concorde to New York, then made a conventional flight to Los Angeles. Gary Pudney of ABC met me at the airport and drove me directly to the Century Plaza Hotel, where I arrived at about 4.30 p.m. I went straight to my suite, quickly changed into black tie and, knowing that there was a small reception prior to the dinner at 5.30 p.m., calmly sauntered into the reception just after it had begun. It was all worth the effort for Leonard Goldenson was really moved to think I'd come all the way from the South of France just to be at his anniversary dinner. At 7.00 p.m. we left the reception and went down to dinner in the Century Plaza ballroom. There were about two thousand people present and I sat at the head of the table next to Leonard.

After dinner, there was a superbly staged show given by many of the principal stars who had appeared for ABC over the years, then Elton Rule went on stage and made a speech. He thanked me for travelling all that distance just to be with them on such an important occasion and invited me up to make a speech. This I did, with, of course, my Montecristo cigar in my hand.

The host of the show was Dick Clark, who also conducted the orchestra. As I finished my speech and was ready to leave the stage, Clark came up to me and said, 'I've always wanted you to dance the charleston on my show. Will you please do so for us tonight.' I told him that I never danced without my music. He raised his baton, and the orchestra started to play a charleston. I went straight into my routine, which brought the house down as usual.

After dinner there was a special reception in another room for the VIPs. I went up and joined them and finally got to bed at

2.00 a.m. Next morning I was up by 7.00 a.m., but, as my plane wasn't due to leave until two that afternoon, I thought I'd go over to the ABC offices which are almost next door to the Century Plaza Hotel. I had a meeting with the President and several other members of the company, in the course of which one of them said, 'Is there anything we can do for you?' 'Yes,' I said. 'I want you to buy *Champions* for television.' He asked me how much I wanted, and we fixed a deal. That's what I call killing time with profit!

I caught my plane to Heathrow, where Kathie was waiting for me, and we flew to Nice together. That night we went out for dinner and, despite the fact that I'd travelled thousands of miles, switched time zones and lost out on my usual quota of sleep, I wasn't in the least bit tired.

Saturday night duly arrived, and what I had expected to be a small dinner party turned out to be a huge formal gathering with approximately 250 people, all in black tie. I was particularly delighted because MGM were having their own party that night and Kirk Kerkorian, who is the principal owner of MGM, chose to come to Jerry's instead!

Jerry, who had hired a large Brazilian orchestra for the night, went on stage and said how delighted he was that I'd joined him and Norman Lear. I made a speech in response, remarking that although I was just over seventy-five years of age I felt like a thirty-five-year-old. I then quoted one of Jerry's favourite sayings: 'You get up every morning, you put up your fists, you come out fighting and you fight to win!' Then Jerry and I gave a performance: we both danced, sometimes together and sometimes separately. He had also arranged a fireworks display, which was spectacular, the perfect ending to a perfect day.

*   *   *

I had made promises to attend three premières of *Champions* and I kept them all.

The first première was in Israel in August 1984. It was my first visit to Israel, and during my three-day stay there I had to pack in as much as possible. I went to Jerusalem where I was the guest of Mayor Teddy Kollek and was taken around the old city and shown just a few of the fascinating sights this extraordinary place has to offer. I was also honoured with an invitation by the President of the State of Israel, Mr Chaim Herzog, to have tea with him.

My second promise was to attend the opening of *Champions* in Sydney. So, on 28 September 1984 I set off for Australia. I thought the distributors were being very thoughtful when they asked me to arrive about five days before the première, to give me time to relax and work off the jet-lag. As it was an Australian première, they wanted me to fly on Qantas Airlines, which I did. The only drawback was that Qantas doesn't allow cigar smoking. I disembarked at Sydney and the first thing I did was light a cigar. The local press made a bee-line for me and asked how I'd enjoyed flying Qantas. 'I'm never going to fly Qantas again,' I said. 'They wouldn't allow me to smoke my cigar!' I had arrived early in the morning and that evening there was a photograph of me in the paper with the caption: 'Lord Grade will never fly Qantas again because they wouldn't let him smoke a cigar.'

Having thought how sweet and kind the distributors were, I now discovered how mistaken I'd been! I had hardly had time to get into the hotel and change my clothes before they had me being interviewed on television, radio, newspapers and magazines. For five days I wasn't given a moment's free time except to sleep. Then came the night of the première which Mr and Mrs Kerry Packer had agreed to attend. This was something of a bonus because Kerry hated premières. It was in aid of a children's hospital and afterwards there was a party at which I went on stage to present the cheque for Australian $169,000 to the head of the hospital.

As I looked at the cheque it suddenly struck me what an odd number it was. So I said, 'I don't like odd numbers. If somebody will give me $1000 for the charity, I'll dance the charleston.'

A leading Sydney stockbroker, Rene Rivkin, agreed to donate the extra $1000 and, always true to my word, I danced the charleston.

I went on to the Melbourne première, which was again being held in aid of a children's hospital. Incidentally, Bob Champion was with me after my first two days in Australia and accompanied me to all my interviews. While in Melbourne Bob and I were asked to appear on the Bert Newton chat show –

during which Newton said to me, 'I heard you danced the charleston in Sydney.' I said, 'Yes, I did, but I got $1000 for charity.' He said, 'If we give you $1000 for the charity, will you dance the charleston for us?' I said, 'Just watch me,' and went on to dance the charleston to the amazement of the audience and, I think, the viewers!

I returned to Sydney for two days then flew back to London.

After I had danced the charleston in Sydney, the manager of Qantas came on to the stage and said, 'We know Lord Grade has said he won't fly Qantas again, but rules are rules. However,' he added, 'they can be bent.' And he presented me with a cigar eighteen inches long and two inches in diameter, saying, 'You have our permission to smoke on your way home.' Every change of crew was advised of this, and I was indeed allowed to smoke. It certainly made my trip a great deal more enjoyable! I just hope the other passengers didn't mind too much.

I must say, though, that I do always try to travel on British Airways whenever possible. What a blessing Concorde has proved to be for businessmen.

The next première of *Champions* was scheduled for Hong Kong, but I postponed it for a particular reason. They say you can't keep a secret from the press, but I have been able to do so.

On 24 December 1984, I went for my annual Christmas break to the Connaught Hotel in London. Suddenly I developed severe stomach pains, and on Christmas Day, which was my birthday, I was unable to eat any breakfast or lunch. Kathie immediately knew there was something seriously wrong and sent for the doctor. He examined me and said, 'I'm going to send for an ambulance to take you to hospital.' 'You're talking nonsense,' I said. 'I'm not going in an ambulance. I'll go in your car.' So Kathie, her sister Norah and I climbed into his car and he drove us to the Cromwell Hospital.

Meanwhile, he had arranged for a top surgeon to examine me. A problem with my gall bladder was diagnosed and, two days later, they were ready to operate on me. They injected me with something to make me sleepy and Kathie tells me that just before they were about to wheel me into the operating theatre I said, 'Don't forget to call Jerry Perenchio,' and gave her his telephone number not once, but twice. The staff nurse told me to keep quiet and try to relax.

When they operated they found I had a poisoned gall bladder and peritonitis. Then I contracted pneumonia. They told Kathie that it was touch and go. I remember recovering from the anaesthetic and the first thing I said was, 'Don't forget, I want Marcia here at 9.00 a.m. tomorrow morning.' I was ready to go to work, which, of course, was not possible. Ten days later when they took the stitches out, they found they had to operate on me again as there was still some infection.

I'm glad to say that four or five days later Marcia *did* come in at 9.00 a.m. in the morning.

I was in hospital for twenty-three days in all, and the press never knew about it. What they couldn't understand was why I had postponed my annual Christmas press lunch which I'd given for the past twenty-five years. These lunches weren't for the hard core City press but for showbusiness journalists with whom I felt completely relaxed. I had actually postponed the lunch that year because I'd been overseas just before Christmas – first to Australia, and then to Korea to try to secure the rights for the Olympic Games.

But the press didn't know this. Nor did they know about my being in hospital. And when, at my Christmas lunch in 1985, I told them about it, they were all astonished I'd managed to keep my illness such a complete secret.

When I returned home from hospital, my doctors told me I should take two months' complete rest, but two weeks later I was back at my desk at Audley Square and it was business as usual. I was also able to attend Lord Mountbatten's memorial service at Westminster Abbey on 14 February. Three weeks later I flew to Rome, and three weeks after that to New York and California.

I felt fine.

*　　　*　　　*

I had been responsible for financing a film called *The Biko Inquest*. It was based on a transcript of the notorious South African trial and starred Albert Finney as Biko's lawyer, Sydney Kentridge. We sold it to Channel Four in London and then tried to sell it in America. I gave it to Embassy Television Division but they weren't able to find a buyer. It had been turned down by both Home Box Office and Showtime – the two major American cable systems.

On 12 April I had breakfast with Neil Austrian, the Chairman of Showtime, Peter Chernin, his second in command, and Fred Schneier, head of acquisitions. I told them about *Biko* and said that although it had already been rejected by their organization, I thought they should reconsider. Not only was it a subject of vital importance, I said, but it would also confer tremendous prestige on the company. I'm glad to say they agreed to buy it.

With the help of Sir Run Run Shaw, we had been able to postpone the première of *Champions* in Hong Kong until the end of May 1985. Kathie didn't want me to travel on my own after such extensive surgery but I assured her I was perfectly fine. She insisted, however, and we made the long flight to Hong Kong together.

It was her first visit there and we had a wonderful time. Sir Run Run, as usual, was the most gracious of hosts, and apart from the press and television interviews, we had time to visit several places of interest. And, of course, Kathie did a little shopping.

The première was a huge success. Once again, at my insistence, it was in aid of a children's hospital and the Governor of Hong Kong and his wife, Sir Edward and Lady Youde, were present.

By the time I returned home to England I had completely recovered from my illness and was fighting fit again.

Showtime arranged through their publicity department for *The Biko Inquest* to be screened in the United Nations Building in New York, with representatives of the press and members of the United Nations Council present, on 22 August 1985.

Albert Finney, who passionately believed in the film and the issues it raised, was with me at the screening, and we were both overwhelmed by its reception. He had directed the stage play, then the television version, and had worked ceaselessly to make sure it turned out well, selecting leading British actors for all the supporting roles.

After the transmission, which was timed to coincide with the anniversary of Steve Biko's death on 12 September, the film received great critical acclaim. And, as I predicted, Showtime covered itself in glory.

*   *   *

A lot of people think that when you reach a certain age you should retire. I have so many friends who are over eighty and still tremendously active. One of them, W. Clement Stone, an extremely active businessman and great philanthropist, who had founded a huge insurance company, Combined Insurance of Chicago, and he is five years older than me! He has the vigour and energy that I wish I possessed – and I have plenty.

As I approach the end of this book, I want to make it clear that I have no intention of giving up my career until, at the very earliest, the year 2000. I've always maintained that I like even numbers, and 2000 seems like a good round figure to me. I intend to have a party, and have already invited many of the friends I've made over the years.

But that's a long time into the future. There's still the present to attend to. And the past.

In August 1985 Jerry Perenchio sold all the divisions of Embassy, which he and Norman Lear owned together, to the Coca-Cola Company. He then bought the Loews Group of Theatres, the most important cinema chain in the United States, and appointed me Vice-Chairman of the group.

It's strange how the wheels of fate work. While Jerry was still at university he decided he wanted a career in the entertainment industry. So he tried to find a position with the newly formed Lew and Leslie Grade company which we'd just opened in Los Angeles. Elkan Kaufman interviewed him, but we had no additional office space at the time and couldn't really afford to take him on. I had never known this until Jerry told me about it recently. Jerry is now not only a close friend of Kathie and mine, but we have developed such a warm relationship – both privately and professionally – that we consider him as part of our family. And I know he feels the same.

On 1 October 1985, I once again formed my own company – The Grade Company.

I am presently in the process of producing a series of TV films based on Barbara Cartland's popular novels, and am also co-producer, with Martin Starger, on Andrew Lloyd-Webber's hit musical *Starlight Express* on Broadway. In 1970 I was offered the opportunity of producing Andrew Lloyd-Webber and Tim

299

Rice's musical *Jesus Christ Superstar*, but turned it down believing it would have no commercial appeal whatsoever. Seventeen years later I have been given a second chance to mount the Lloyd-Webber bandwagon – and am happy to say that I'm enjoying the ride enormously!

Indeed, for most of the time, my life has been an exhilarating ride. Of course, there have been a few bumps here and there – but nothing I've not been able to cope with. To paraphrase a song written by John Lennon and Paul McCartney, I got by with a little help from my friends. And when it comes to friendship, I have, indeed, been blessed. Call it a knack, or a gift, or what you will – but throughout my eighty years on this planet I have made more good friends than I can calculate. Indeed, on the rare occasions I have a sleepless night, it is not sheep I count, but friends!

*   *   *

Throughout this book I have been writing about all the different events which have formed the highlights of my life, and how I have been constantly looking for the ultimate highlight. Now I know that I actually discovered that ultimate highlight forty-five years ago when I married Kathie. Sparkling and good-humoured, generous and caring, also romantic and down to earth, at twenty-one on our wedding day Kathie was all those things, and she hasn't changed to this day.

When I joined the army, Kathie bought me a gold bracelet with my army identification number on it – 1123014. I wear it to this day and never take it off my wrist, just as she, herself, is never out of my thoughts. Without her love, help, encouragement and support at all times, my life would not only have been meaningless, but there also wouldn't have been much to dance about.

It is thanks to her entirely that I'm still dancing . . . .

INDEX